Praise for *The Pure Heart of Yoga*

"Dr. Butera's hard work and clarity about the subject is felt by us all. Yoga asanas are ultimately leading to expansion of consciousness. The psychophysical practice of yoga is the main focus."

—Dr. Jayadeva and Hansaji Yogendra,
directors of The Yoga Institute, Mumbai, India

"The first phase of the emergence of yoga in the West has been the recognition of the tremendous benefits of the yoga asanas. The second phase is the deeper understanding of the yoga postures within their authentic context. Robert Butera's book is an important presentation of the deeper meaning of the postures that allows us to experience their full potential for balance and transformation."

—Joseph Le Page, founder of Integrative Yoga therapy,
www.iytherapy.com

"*The Pure Heart of Yoga* offers an illuminating exploration of the psychological and spiritual dimensions of the yoga asanas. It is an important contribution to weaving the asanas into The 8-Fold fabric of hatha yoga."

—Charles Eisenstein, author of *Yoga of Eating*

"I highly recommend this book to all yoga students who wish to practice yoga beyond asanas. Dr. Butera has filled a void in the world of yoga texts by writing a book that will help you take your yoga to a deeper level both on and off of the mat every day of your life."

—Dr. James Dougherty,
veterinarian and yoga teacher

"Dr. Butera's book is essential reading for yoga teachers and students seeking to embrace the yogic lifestyle and deepen their understanding of yoga practice and philosophy. This modern yoga text promotes a broader and deeper understanding of the physical, emotional, and spiritual health that yoga offers the sincere student. As a teacher and counselor, this is the book I have been waiting for!"

—Caroline M. Thomas, yoga teacher

"Dr. Butera brings his unique understanding, experience, and perspective to the otherwise often misunderstood or completely overlooked depth of the yoga asana . . . Beginning students can consider themselves fortunate to begin their journey with this book, and advanced students will find their practice of these teachings nothing short of life transforming."

—Julie Rost, yoga teacher, trainer, and director of

YogaLife Institute N. H., Exeter, New Hampshire

"*The Pure Heart of Yoga* will bring increased depth to your yoga practice. It is an excellent book: thoughtful, reflective, deep, and accessible. With its emphasis on the psychological, behavioral, and spiritual aspects of yoga, this book is a welcome addition to the many physically oriented yoga books available today."

—Eleanor Criswell, Ed.D., author of *How Yoga Works*

the
pure heart
of
yoga

❀

To Write to the Author

If you wish to contact the author or would like more information about this book, please write to the author in care of Llewellyn Worldwide and we will forward your request. Both the author and publisher appreciate hearing from you and learning of your enjoyment of this book and how it has helped you. Llewellyn Worldwide cannot guarantee that every letter written to the author can be answered, but all will be forwarded. Please write to:

Robert Butera, Ph.D.
c/o Llewellyn Worldwide
2143 Wooddale Drive, Dept. 978-0-7387-1487-5
Woodbury, MN 55125-2989, U.S.A.
Please enclose a self-addressed stamped envelope for reply,
or $1.00 to cover costs. If outside U.S.A., enclose
international postal reply coupon.

Many of Llewellyn's authors have websites with additional information and resources. For more information, please visit our website at

www.llewellyn.com

the

pure heart

of

yoga

Ten Essential Steps for
Personal Transformation

Robert Butera, Ph.D.

Llewellyn Publications
Woodbury, Minnesota

First Edition
Second Printing, 2009

Cover design by Ellen Dahl
Cover image © Tetra images / PunchStock
Illustration on page 131 by Llewellyn art department
Interior photos by Jeff Gurrier and Karen Batchelder
Editing by Nicole Edman

Llewellyn is a registered trademark of Llewellyn Worldwide, Ltd.

Library of Congress Cataloging-in-Publication Data
Butera, Robert, 1964–
  The pure heart of yoga : ten essential steps for personal
transformation / Robert Butera.
      p. cm.
  Includes bibliographical references.
  ISBN 978-0-7387-1487-5
  1. Hatha yoga—Therapeutic use. 2. Transcendental Meditation.
I. Title.
  RM727.Y64B88 2009
  613.7'046—dc22
                        2009016501

Llewellyn Publications
A Division of Llewellyn Worldwide, Ltd.
2143 Wooddale Drive, Dept. 978-0-7387-1487-5
Woodbury, MN 55125-2989, U.S.A.
www.llewellyn.com

Printed in the United States of America

Contents

Part III: Self-Exploration and Psychology

Part IV: Practice and Poses

Acknowledgments

This book is dedicated to the members of The Yoga Institute of Santa Cruz East, Mumbai, India; its leaders Shri and Smt. Yogendraji; and Dr. Jayadeva, Hansaji Yogendra, and Patanjali Yogendra, who teach yoga as a total approach to life.

Much gratitude is offered here to the community members and teachers from the YogaLife Institute who assisted in the foundational research and editing of this book: Julie Rost, Kristen Butera, Linda Lyng, Shirley Weaver, Steve Sonnefield, Mythri Menon, Caroline Thomas Barnhart, Carol Elia, Jim Dougherty, and Angela Nevius. Jeff Gurrier and Karen Batchelder took the beautiful yoga pose photos that are included in this book. And a big thank you to my literary agents, Michael Ebeling and Kristina Holmes, for their passion and dedication to this book. Their consistent support and guidance throughout the publishing process has been invaluable and is most appreciated. To Carrie Obry and Nicole Edman of Llewellyn Publications who transformed this work into the appealing, readable, and accessible book.

Finally, to the many members of our yoga programs, who over the years, in weekly classes and teacher-training sessions, shared personal insights that informed our understanding of the complete experience of yoga poses.

Preface

Yoga is a transformational process. This simple fact is something that has become more and more evident to me during the twenty-plus years that I have been teaching yoga. While people practice yoga for many reasons, everyone comes to realize its benefits of self-improvement and healing. Over the years, I have seen people join yoga programs to lose weight, improve their study skills, reduce stress, heal injuries, strengthen their body and mind, find compassion, feel better . . . and the list goes on. We all face challenges in life and struggle to transcend them. Yoga is a great way of doing just that.

Yoga is far more than just a physical activity. It is a lifestyle that merges esoteric philosophy with the practical realities of daily living. As a philosophy of holistic wellness, yoga leads to profound personal and spiritual growth. As you come to understand yoga as a way of life, practicing yoga both "on the mat" and in your daily life becomes an immensely powerful tool. *The Pure Heart of Yoga* offers a step-by-step, integrated mind-body-spirit approach to experiencing the true transformational power of yoga poses. This book gives you the tools you will need to chart a course of personal transformation. All that you need is an open mind and heart, a desire to learn the depth and breadth of yoga, and a sincere willingness to commit to your transformation.

The desire to deepen your yoga practice doesn't come with any other requirements. Students of every level can use the principles outlined in this book. I have been teaching students these principles in beginner, intermediate, and advanced yoga classes for twenty years. I find that most students come to yoga class assuming that they need to either possess or learn how to maintain an extreme, gymnastic-like flexibility, only to discover that their mind was the bigger hurdle. It is at the mental level that feelings of worry, dread, fear, and agitation are generated, feelings that naturally prevent us from being calm, peaceful, and self-assured. Yoga goes straight to those feelings and helps alleviate them. Perhaps one of the greatest benefits of yoga is that it puts the brain to rest.

Remembering my own path, I can see now that as a beginning yoga student, I was seeking deep inner peace, even if I was not able to pinpoint my specific goal at that time. Yoga and meditation studies were not as popular in those days, and I had no idea how to even begin looking for a teacher. As a college student traveling an alternative route to adulthood, it was raw motivation that led me to meet a host of wonderful and sometimes exotic teachers. After studying yoga and meditation intensively in Japan and Taiwan, I discovered The Yoga Institute of Mumbai, India (formerly known as Bombay), where I enrolled in the Institute's six-month teacher-training program. There I received one-on-one training from Dr. Jayadeva Yogendra, the son of the Institute's founder and one of India's great yoga teachers. During my stay at the Institute, I was introduced to the core principles of this book and I have been working since then to understand and deepen these principles in my own practice and in the lives of all my students.

I went on to earn a Ph.D. in Yoga Philosophy at the California Institute for Integral Studies, a holistic interdisciplinary university founded by Dr. Haridus Chaudhuri. It was here that I continued investigating the psychological aspects of yoga with some of the brightest yoga scholars guiding me. At this institute, I was fortunate to receive an education that explored yoga as a philosophy and way of life, as opposed to many yoga programs in the United States that concentrate primarily on the physical practice of yoga poses. Since then, I have founded the YogaLife Institute in Pennsylvania, where we hold classes for students of every age, ability, and level and also teach students how to become yoga instructors themselves. As the leader of this group, I am always inspired to see so many students motivated to learn the subtle aspects of yoga, which not only tones their bodies but also truly honors the spiritual and psychological forces at work in their lives. I am honored to work with these people, many of whom are just like you, and to be making my own contribution to the world of yoga with *The Pure Heart of Yoga*, which represents ten years of writing and more than twenty years of research.

The information in this book exists in Sanskrit texts on yoga, submerged in esoteric language that makes it challenging to understand. *The Pure Heart of Yoga* presents this ancient yoga knowledge in an easy, accessible way. You may find that you've never heard of some of the principles we're about to learn. This is true for many yoga teachers and students throughout the Western world. Over the years, I have had students come to me after practicing yoga for ten and sometimes twenty years who have never experienced the true depths of a holistic yoga practice. You may find that this book is a door to an entirely new understanding of yoga.

The Pure Heart of Yoga is an experiential book that gives you the tools and structure you need to direct your own journey of discovery. The beauty of it is that how you grow and what you learn is your own decision to make. Throughout the book, I aim to lead you to a new perspective and give you useful exercises, but never to lay out any of the answers. In this way, you don't need to fit into any prefabricated box nor do you have to buy into one particular result. You will find the yoga practice that is best for you.

Regardless of your experience, this book will introduce you to the beauty of yoga and transform your yoga practice. If you are a beginning student, you are fortunate to have found this book early in your journey. As an intermediate or advanced student, you may have never learned the steps explored in this book. That's okay! By including them in your practice now, you will understand yoga in a new way. If you're wondering if the book fits the type of yoga you're practicing, you'll be pleased to know that it does. *The Pure Heart of Yoga* affirms all forms of yoga practice as positive, meaning that you can practice the principles of this book and enrich your practice regardless of what style of yoga you are currently doing.

Even after my nearly twenty-five years of performing the same poses, my yoga practice continues to be invigorated by using the steps you're about to learn. These steps focus on spiritual and emotional growth rather than just physical mastery of yoga poses. When yoga addresses all three aspects of our nature—body, mind, and spirit—it becomes an entirely holistic and fulfilling experience. In all regards, it becomes illuminating, transformational, and I might add, fun. It requires patience and effort, and it may take years of practice to integrate every principle. Enjoy the journey of yoga and allow it to settle into the depths of your soul. Search for a teacher and practice together with patience, curiosity, and enthusiasm. Ask intuitive questions. Follow your heart and use the tools that are relevant to your life. We can all bring the essence of yoga into our lives, cultivating a balanced state of mind that transforms ourselves and the world around us.

Introduction

Many things in life transcend our ability to express them. Poetry, art, and music were created to give expression to the spiritual, mystical, and elusive forces that make the world go round. While practicing yoga poses, the idea of "connecting to the infinite" is just one of those things. It is a concept in which time and space have no relativity, and words often fail to describe its true meaning. When we connect to the infinite, we achieve a state of absolute completeness, an experience that yoga masters have described for centuries in the hopes that all practitioners may someday receive the grace of its blessing. It is the experience where a harmony occurs with our emotions and thoughts and everything directly relates to the spark of consciousness that exists within each of us and throughout the cosmos. Connecting to the infinite is a state of continued inner peace regardless of external circumstances, a feeling of complete and total love.

One of the nice things about yoga is that it contains no religious dogma and allows for anyone who practices it to follow their individual spiritual beliefs. In this way, the religious person might understand his or her connection to the infinite as a process of becoming one with God, while an atheist might call it transcending the human ego. Yoga can be adapted to a variety of belief systems while remaining equally effective and transformative. One of the reasons for yoga's popularity is that it is extremely adaptable and can be practiced alongside other belief systems. In the end, yoga provides a path to quieting the mind so that we all can feel the innate stillness and joy of being alive. Swami Aranya, the great yogic scholar and practitioner, describes the idea of connecting to the infinite (*ananta-samapatti*) in the following way: "My body has become like a void dissolving itself in infinite space and I am like the wide expanse of the sky."

One of the foundational texts on yoga is *The Yoga Sutras* written around the second century BCE by the great Indian sage Patanjali. *The Yoga Sutras* provides a theoretical and philosophical basis for yoga as well as clarifies many important esoteric concepts. It is a highly influential book on yoga philosophy and practice, and as you feel inspired, I encourage you to read for yourself. Like Swami Aranya, *The Yoga Sutras* also describes the experience and purpose of yoga, especially the poses, in terms of the infinite: "By relaxation of effort and meditation on the infinite, postures (*asanas*) are perfected." The goal of a pose is no different from the goal of spiritual life: to put you in touch with the larger universe or reality.

You may have already had an experience of connecting to the infinite, as there are many paths to it, most of which are spontaneous. It may have happened one day when you were walking in the woods, swimming in the ocean, or witnessing the growth of a child. It could have happened in a church, in a cave, or at the top of a mountain. It could even have happened while you were sitting in your favorite chair next to a roaring fire. There is no predicting when or how grace falls upon us; it comes in a flash and then disappears again. This book offers you the tools to proactively work toward that place of connection in your life, rather than waiting for it to spontaneously happen.

Honor the Process of Discovery:
The Middle Path

The lessons in this book will empower you to discover your true Self through yoga poses. It is my goal to give you new perspectives and enough information for personal reflection in the process to keep you interested for many years to come. In modern yoga, there seems to be an overemphasis on external form. If you do this pose precisely, get into the position, and breathe, then you're doing everything just fine. If you aren't flexible enough, use some props and you can get it close to perfect. With minimal teaching on the psychological and spiritual aspects of yoga, students may struggle with the *meaning* of yoga—which develops and deepens if they are able to commit to it—and are instead left on their own to possibly discover higher states of consciousness along the way. This makes learning yoga more difficult, time consuming, and ultimately less effective.

The Pure Heart of Yoga follows a middle path that offers direction and guidance as to both the physical and emotional aspects of yoga practice, but no definitive answers as to how you "should" go about finding emotional and spiritual freedom. I highlight yoga practices that can help you connect with universal consciousness, but your personal effort and exploration are fundamental to the process. In guiding you through the subtle aspects of yoga while also nurturing your freedom to choose the path that is right for you, this book sets you on a journey that is at once full of the joy of discovery and a profound personal transformational experience. *The Pure Heart of Yoga* honors both the correct physical form of a yoga pose and the attentiveness to an accompanying internal state of mind.

Determine Your Level of Experience

Everyone can benefit from yoga. The universality of yoga poses allows practitioners to adapt it to their specific experience and fitness level, allowing the practice to progress through an entire lifetime. Most people think that you have to be extremely flexible to do yoga, yet very few students come to yoga able to touch their toes. It's not the level of flexibility that determines a person's level in yoga. It's his or her capacity for patience, dedication, and concentration. After a certain point, the body's development reaches a maximum level, but transformation of the mind continues. Over time, yoga relates to the mind far more than it does to the body. To know how to best use this material, which is intended for everyone, you will need to honestly assess your level of experience with intentional yoga.

Beginner: Starts with the first yoga class. The beginner is learning how to develop proper intention and how one's attitude relates to physical movement. This stage focuses on the basics of proper physical alignment and how to coordinate breathing with movement. While all yoga practitioners are concentrating on these aspects of a yoga practice, the beginner is learning how to integrate intention, attitude, physical alignment, and breath for the first time.

Intermediate: Intermediate students begin to integrate the lessons learned from yoga poses into their daily life and probably also dabble with yoga poses at home, habitually becoming aware of their breathing on a daily basis. The positive effects of yoga start to influence their intention and attitude in daily affairs and they work to maintain a state of relaxation and equanimity throughout their day. Intermediate students continue to refine their experience of yoga poses, deeply discovering their subtle aspects, as highlighted in Part II of this book.

Advanced: Advanced students have started to master the techniques and practices described in this book while developing new levels of internal sensitivity. They practice and refine all of the foundational practices in this book and work with Steps Eight through Ten at a slow and steady pace with the goal of discovering their true Self. They are living their yoga in every aspect of their life while maintaining enthusiasm in their daily practice. And, of course, truly advanced students realize that in many ways, they will always be beginners.

Yoga Instructor: Yoga teachers can be at the level of intermediate to advanced practitioners, depending on the level of their learning and teaching experience. Regarding this book, I suggest yoga teachers review the beginner-level material in order to communicate most effectively with beginner students. Teachers must recognize the vastness of yoga and how much there is to learn. Yoga teachers remain committed (and inspired) throughout their lifetime to understanding new aspects of themselves and discovering new depths of yoga every day.

Every student and practitioner is different, and timing varies as to how long it takes a beginner to become an intermediate and an intermediate to become advanced. Assessing your level is important for your own growth and expectations, but people at any level can benefit from the steps outlined here. Try not to get caught up with the labels, instead working to create a program that allows you to have a disciplined and consistent practice. Bring an open beginner's mind to each yoga pose session and let the learning continue to unfold.

The Ten Step Approach to Mastering Yoga Poses

The foundation of *The Pure Heart of Yoga* is based on the following ten steps that I have experienced and fine-tuned throughout my career in yoga:

ONE   Intention (*Samkalpa*)

TWO   Attitude (*Bhava*)

THREE   Posture (*Asana*)

FOUR   Breathing (*Pranayama*)

FIVE   Archetypes (*Purvaja*)

SIX   Energy Centers (*Chakras*)

Treat this material as a gateway to experiencing the richness that yoga has to offer rather than as a strict, methodological program. Working through the steps is not a timed, set program; you will move back and forth, depending on your own personal challenges and goals. While the steps do build upon each other, don't get caught up in "checking off" the steps to get to the "finish." Even experienced yogis at times come back to the beginning steps in their yoga practice. The steps are a template that will grow with you over time as certain steps become more relevant at different times in your life than others. Be careful not to be in a rush to experience all the benefits these ten steps have to offer. Enjoy the process and honor your patience, and in doing so, you will notice shifts in your practice in the months and years to come.

Go to www.pureheartofyoga.com right now to download your free copy of the workbook so you can begin the transformation while you read the book.

Part I: Foundational Practices

Steps One through Four explore the aspects of Intention, Attitude, Posture, and Breathing. These four steps form the foundation of yoga practice and should be integrated into every yoga pose session.

Step One: Intention. Setting an intention to practice yoga immediately connects your mind and body to the practice in one seamless unit. From beginners to advanced students, having a meaningful purpose for practicing yoga is very important. Intention keeps you rooted in your yoga practice through time.

Step Two: Attitude. As you probably already know, yoga relates to your life before the first pose is formed. Closely aligned with your intention for doing yoga, an awareness of your attitude helps you connect with the nonphysical essence of yoga pose practice. The ideas in Step Two will improve your yoga pose experience and can be applied to daily life.

Step Three: Posture. This step clearly explains the physical alignment of yoga poses. I recommend attending a structured yoga class when possible to have an experienced yoga teacher further assist you with physical alignment.

Step Four: Breathing. Learning how to breathe very deeply is one of the primary benefits of yoga practice. The instant stress-reducing benefits of deep breathing satisfy those who like to experience immediate progress and also have many other powerful effects on the mind, body, and spirit.

Part II: Inner Yoga

At different times in my yoga teaching career, as well as in my own personal practice, I have felt bored. I love yoga, yet after a few years, even I started to daydream. Recently, this kind of boredom has been termed "yoga burnout." Part II of this book reveals many perspectives that will keep your yoga pose practice fresh and full of new personal discoveries for many years to come.

Step Five: Archetypes. This step connects yoga poses to nature and explains the story of each yoga pose by examining where it comes from. You can develop a deeper perspective on yoga by discovering the qualities that are inherent in the creative history of the pose.

Step Six: Energy Centers. This section explores the mind-body connection of the chakra system (energy centers). Step Six offers clear language and straightforward definitions to explain the holistic experience of yoga poses. While the information is simple, it is a vital component in learning how to deepen your awareness of the relationship between your body and mind.

Step Seven: Concentration. There are many distractions related to our five senses, mainly sight and sound. We explore these distractions and concentrate on select body points while in poses and notice how concentration affects your experience of the poses.

Step Eight: Energy Seals and Physical Locks. This section delves into the power of symbolic energy seals (*mudras*) and physical locks (*bandhas*) on the body to deepen your awareness of the body's energy. This step will help you understand the subtle energy bodies and how to consciously understand the flow of energy throughout your body.

Part III: Self-Exploration and Psychology

Steps Nine and Ten, concerning psychological blocks (*klesas*) and emotional transformation (*bhavana*), are placed near the end of the book but are suited for all levels of students. The power and simplicity of yoga psychology is summarized in these two chapters. Practice these concepts in your daily life, and you will learn ways to transform stress and more easily manage your daily life.

Part IV: Practices and Poses

Part IV begins with a general discussion of the logistics of yoga practice. While this section shows you how to integrate the information covered in the ten steps, you may wish to review this section first, especially if you are at the beginning of your yoga path.

As you read the ten steps in this book, you will see that I have also included a list of suggested yoga poses that correspond to the lessons learned in that step. All of these poses are described and illustrated in the catalog of twenty-three poses at the end of the book. As I mentioned before, this book is intended to be a gateway that allows you to understand and experience the greater riches that the full repertoire of poses has to offer. In other words, as you experience the relationship between these ten steps and twenty-three poses, you will begin to be able to apply everything you have learned in this book to every yoga class and pose that you encounter.

The complete study of yoga includes theory and practice. This book communicates the theory in simple ways that allow for immediate practice. The program begins by asking you to devise a personal intention and the ends with poses for you to practice. To make the theory understandable, reflection exercises are provided at the ends of several chapters. Throughout this book, I use three case studies to assist you with applying the theories we discuss in each step of the book. These stories serve as practical reminders of how to apply the information to better understand your own life. As you read, try to see how the yoga principles I outline relate to the real-life examples. The people I describe are Mary, a mother of two; Steve, a businessman; and Laura, a young professional. Each step highlights a case study with the three characters integrating the exercises and ideas into their yoga practice. These case studies are used throughout the text to show how theory can relate to practice. I also offer personal stories and tips from my studies in India and from twenty years of teaching and training yoga instructors. Scattered throughout the chapters, you will find "Connecting to the Poses" features, offering tips and ideas for studying and practicing yoga poses. Each chapter concludes with a "Connecting to the Infinite" section, recapping the current step for personal transformation and looking forward to the next steps.

At times in the text, meeting with an instructor is recommended, as learning yoga on your own can be a daunting task. If you don't have a yoga teacher nearby, feel free to contact us with your questions at www .pureheartofyoga.com.

As you are practicing, remember that each individual performs yoga poses differently, as every one of us has a different body with varying abilities and limitations. Experiment with personal variations and allow the experience of the pose to intuitively come from within yourself, rather than becoming preoccupied with forming a prescribed shape with your body. Also, there are many different yoga traditions and each of one of them has a series of poses that may not be included in this book. If you come from one of these traditions, remember that the ten steps discussed in this book are universal and can be applied to any yoga pose. Cultivate an open mind and sense of curiosity in experiencing yoga and you will greatly benefit from all that it has to offer.

PART I

Foundational Practices
Steps 1–4

Intention

Samkalpa

*Personalizing your intention
empowers your life.*

All of us would like our lives to be free from suffering, whether it be physical, emotional, or spiritual in nature. Yoga, much like other Eastern practices, doesn't distinguish between the different sources of pain. Suffering may stem from a spinal injury or the emotional anguish of a loved one passing, but it all manifests in the body and the mind in similar ways. Whatever you might be struggling with, yoga is a path to freedom. Sincerely ask yourself why you opened this book and write it down, as we will explore these reasons in more depth throughout this chapter to refine your personal intention for developing a yoga practice. As you begin to transform your perspective, you will accept that you do not need to be a new or different person—the goal is to better understand yourself. As you read the chapter, write down your thoughts and insights. We'll conclude with an exercise to help you refine your original intention as a profound statement of personal truth.

Life's Peak Moments

Can you remember the most special day of your life? Was it your wedding day, where there were months or years of preparation, a meaningful ceremony, and a joyous celebration with family and friends? Was it a special vacation or trip that you thought about for years? Was your favorite day an accomplishment, like a school graduation or completion of a tremendous project? Perhaps it was the experience of true love. Can you remember a profound spiritual experience that might have occurred when someone helped you out of a troubling time, or perhaps an experience in nature where you felt a connection to a higher reality? These "peak experiences" in life grip the consciousness and demand to be taken seriously.

There is always a driving motivation in the pivotal times of life. The experience of a wedding is based on love. Even in situations where people get divorced, they still entered into the marriage from a place of love. Achievements of various kinds are usually based on a desire to serve others, like going to school to become a doctor or teacher, or just to become a better person. Each and every peak experience is the result of a powerful intention. It is unfortunate that for many of us those special days are fleeting and can be counted on the fingers of one hand.

In terms of doing yoga, you might remember the first class you took. You might remember a special retreat, where you had a very good experience. If you're a yoga teacher, you certainly remember the training courses and the first few classes you taught. However, once you've practiced yoga for six months, it starts to lose its allure, similar to becoming comfortable in a marriage—the enthusiasm around the wedding vows sometimes fades into everyday routine.

I have noticed that the people who are able to transform their original reason for beginning yoga into an intention to make it a spiritual practice realize the greatest benefits. Treating something as spiritual practice means renewing deep-seated intentions every day. Connecting to something larger than yourself while doing yoga poses will impact your entire life, including your physical health. When performing yoga poses, a married person might think, "Today is another day to consider how to better love my spouse." Or the individual might say, "Today is another day for me to renew my commitment to a healthy lifestyle," or "Today I'm going to think of my job in terms of its larger purpose in life. I'm going to feel inspired at work, even if I feel my job is somewhat mundane." Most importantly, everyone can think, "I'm going to renew my commitment to spiritual growth."

The *Gunas*

To better understand intention, we need to consider the three basic qualities of nature, or *gunas*, from yoga philosophy. These three gunas refer to basic ways of being in the world, and you can use them to develop a clear-headed intention and commitment to your daily activities, not just yoga.

The gunas originate from Samkyha, one of the six schools of classical Indian philosophy. In Samkyha philosophy, the gunas are three "tendencies": *rajas, tamas,* and *sattva.*

In simple terms, *rajas* refers to activity, *tamas* to inactivity, and *sattva* to

---

The Qualities of the Material World *(The Gunas)*
Activity *(Rajas)*
Inactivity *(Tamas)*
Purity *(Sattva)*

---

purity or equilibrium. You can probably identify with all three states of being, whether you are feeling energetic and obsessive (*rajasic*), dull and depressed (*tamasic*), or calm, clear, and focused (*sattvic*). Yoga seeks to magnify the pure *sattvic* state of being because it best facilitates the path of self-realization. In physical practice, this means cultivating an intention that matches the lucidity and luminosity of consciousness itself.

In the examples that follow, notice how each individual's intentions are explained in terms of active, inactive, and pure. As you read these stories, think about your personal intention for reading this book and studying yoga.

Mary *is a 36-year-old woman who has come to class in order to lose weight. She has just given birth to her second child, feels unattractive, and is afraid that her husband will lose interest in her.*

The unconscious intention of her active state is attachment and egoism. If dominated by an active (*rajasic*) state, Mary turns her fear into action. She eats low-fat foods, experiments with fad diets, and tries expensive products to help her look younger and more attractive. She spends extra money to make herself as pretty as she can. She works really hard to impress her spouse in a more external way, attached to his approval. Mary desires to look like the young women she sees in magazines, and she compares herself to others in yoga class, struggling to make her body look like theirs. She fails to understand the deeper aspects of yoga. Mary's underlying belief that she is not good enough and her extreme and obsessive actions actually push her husband away.

The driving forces of her inactive state are disorder and fear. When in an inactive (*tamasic*) state, Mary has a fatalistic attitude, a sense of lethargy, and a fear that her husband will never really love her completely. In order to run away from these feelings, she secretly eats a lot of food that she knows isn't good for her but brings her comfort. Not mindful of eating three meals a day, she becomes flustered and disorganized and feels like she does not have enough time to exercise and eat well. She practices yoga in spurts, but her fear eventually grips her and she drops out. Her husband, with understandable cause, starts to be unsatisfied with their relationship.

The motivation of her pure state is self-care and love. From a pure (*sattvic*) perspective, Mary realizes that what attracts someone to us is not our external appearance, but our inner vitality. She knows that being attractive comes from being happy with who she is. Mary recognizes that by taking care of herself and doing things that are creative and fun, she will be a balanced woman, mother, and wife. She starts to see that the love that she and her husband have for one another far outweighs the shallow attraction he may have to other women. In her yoga classes, she is inspired by lectures as well as her own growing sense of self. She begins to eat healthier food to feed her soul, and her weight starts to normalize. She starts to glow and her husband notices this internal beauty. Her experience and self-confidence make her beautiful. They both realize that beauty is not skin deep, but of the soul.

Steve is a 40-year-old businessman who comes to yoga because his lower back hurts. He wants to gain flexibility and learn to cope better with stress.

The unconscious intention of his active state is competition and egoism. If Steve is more active, he works hard in order to gain external approval. He wants to have a lot of money and esteem, a fancy car, and designer clothes. He has a strong drive to succeed. Steve sacrifices his own self-care in order to work excessively and have more power. Even in his yoga practice, he seeks personal gain, focuses on physical fitness and flexibility only, and wants yoga to fix the pain in his low back. He dives into yoga and goes to class every day for two months. As he tries to compete with the other students, his practice remains external and he eventually pushes too hard. He injures himself and stops doing yoga altogether.

The driving force behind his inactive state is depression and laziness. In an inactive state, Steve feels beaten down by his job. His life has somehow disintegrated to the point where he has to have this job to support his family. He's lost his creative edge, feels slightly depressed, and has started to take some medication his doctor thought would help him get through this particular time. He's not completely inactive, in that he has some hope, because something in his gut says this is not the right course of action and he won't always feel like this. He looks to yoga to be a miracle cure and figures he'll try it for a while. When he doesn't see results instantly, he decides it is too much effort and quits.

The motivation of his pure state is self-care and illumination. In a pure state, Steve recognizes that he doesn't have a lot of skill in dealing with stress. He has read that deep breathing and relaxation can alleviate stress and anxiety. His doctor recommends yoga and Steve goes out of his way to research it, learning from various friends and family about their experiences. He arrives at yoga class with an open mind, knowing that he'll need to do the work, but hopeful that yoga will guide him. He realizes that he's been creating his own stress by putting pressure on himself to be something he doesn't have to be. Steve discovers what is most important to him and takes some of the pressure off his work life, making him more successful and at ease. He begins to notice that pain returns to his lower back when he is under stress, but that with some deep breathing and stretching, he can manage it and gain a new perspective on the situation.

Laura *is a young woman in her mid-twenties who comes to yoga for spiritual growth. She's in good shape and looks great, but is starting to feel a little stress at her job. She is beginning to think about settling down and taking life more seriously, but a lot of her peers continue to be concerned with superficial things, like going out and drinking alcohol at parties. She has noticed how people who don't care about themselves become unhappy later in their thirties.*

The unconscious intention of her active state is egoism and attachment. With an active intention, Laura gravitates toward a fitness type of yoga because she is worried about putting on a few extra pounds. She is not that concerned with the deeper meaning of yoga, but wants to look good. She attends short-term, trendy yoga events so that she can say she studied with famous yoga teachers, even though she didn't learn much about herself during the abbreviated studies. (A balanced approach would be to attend these seminars to learn more about the yoga world, but not to have them be a core spiritual practice.) Laura gets really fit, and if she's super dedicated, she becomes a yoga teacher of this style, where they do poses like an exercise workout in the name of yoga. She's probably learned to be calmer, but everyone thinks she is more spiritual than she actually is.

The driving force behind her inactive state is helplessness and dullness. With inactive intentions, Laura continues to live in the way her friends live, even though it doesn't feel right for her anymore. She signs up for yoga because her friend is doing it. When her friend changes to another exercise fad, she follows suit. She doesn't notice the difference between yoga done for exercise and yoga done with a deeper spiritual purpose. Laura is stuck in her own thoughts, worried about what people think of her and unable to see what's going on around her.

The motivation behind her pure state is spiritual growth and clarity. In a pure state, Laura discovers how important it is to have a positive attitude toward life. She realizes that her perceptions are creating a lot of her stress. She begins to read spiritual books and considers going to therapy to figure out who she really is. She attends yoga classes and practices at home, as well. Laura notices that she feels much better on days she practices yoga at home. She integrates yoga philosophy into her life and eventually signs up for a yoga teacher-training program in order to further her understanding of yoga. She decides to stop drinking alcohol because she wants to cultivate more clarity and understanding. She feels lighter and clearer as she makes small changes like this in daily life, and her deeper soul starts to radiate out.

These examples of Mary, Steve, and Laura offer a greater understanding of the different intentions people bring to yoga, as well as the results of such intentions.

How Misdirected Intention Leads to Suffering

As discussed earlier in the chapter, there is almost always an intention behind every action that we take in life. Intentions can either be beneficial or damaging to our well-being. This is certainly true in yoga. Think for a moment about what might happen to a student whose intention in doing a yoga pose is to look good and impress others. The student is inclined to push beyond his physical limitations and eventually injures himself. In contrast, a student whose intention is to

Types of Intention

Rajasic: Active, Excited, Hyper, Obsessive, Competitive, Fast-paced, Clinging, Attached, Infatuated, Ego-boosting

Tamasic: Inactive, Depressed, Dull, Fearful, Confused, Lethargic, Helpless, Lazy, Self-doubting, Disorganized

Sattvic: Balanced, Clear, Pure, Calm, Peaceful, Content, Illuminating

appreciate his body will likely be finely attuned to his capabilities and will have a deeper physical, emotional, and spiritual experience in his yoga practice. Let's further explore the three types of intention to get a sense of how they affect your life.

Active intentions are those that serve to boost the ego: What can I do and how can I work harder to look better, be more fit, and improve my external self so that other people like or respect me more? This intention is mirrored by many of the cultural values that society reflects from childhood to adulthood: study more; compete in work/school; make more money; be stronger, faster, more physically attractive; and stay busy at all times! A capitalist society promotes speed, profit, power, progress, stress, and materialism. The idea of continually seeking out "more and better" is like a cat chasing its tail, never finding the happiness that gets put off to "someday." This type of attitude in a yoga practice continues the fast pace, with no chance to rest or feel, and prohibits the slow-paced awareness required for self-understanding and healing.

Inactive intentions stemming from fear and confusion cause a person to practice yoga simply because a doctor or friend said to. Laziness leads to an intention of wanting instant results without putting forth the effort required to really change habits and perceptions. Many people start yoga and quit early in the process because they are not ready for the big changes and challenges associated with personal growth.

Freedom from suffering (physical, psychological, and spiritual) happens with the cultivation of **pure intention**—bright, calm, clear, immaculate, illuminating, and balanced—and learning how to practice these states of mind, body, and spirit. The intention for yoga poses becomes a virtue like "compassion" or "courage," changing with each day, depending on what is relevant for living well. A new perspective helps us to deal with stress and transform attitudes toward daily interactions. We discover the true source of pain, learn how to take responsibility, and become who we want to be. In this space, a yoga practice offers a fuller sense of self-awareness and facilitates the greatest healing.

Cultivating Pure Intention

Pure intention is fundamental to life, not just yoga. As you learn to cultivate pure intention in yoga poses, you'll start to do the same in your daily actions. Many of us live disconnected from our intention for doing things, whether in work, relationships, or some other area of life. How can we embody our most inspired self if we aren't clear on the reasons behind our actions?

In learning to cultivate a pure intention in yoga practice, let's once again consider *The Yoga Sutras*, one of the most revered Indian texts on yoga philosophy and practice. *The Sutras* offer The 8-Fold Path of Yoga, which provides the structural framework for yoga practice. The 8-Fold Path leads to physical, psychological, and spiritual health and is a key foundation to our studies in this book.

For our present purposes, we're going to explore the first two aspects of The 8-Fold Path, the restraints *(yamas)* and observances *(niyamas)*. They outline ethical principles to help us live an orderly and harmonious life and give direction on how to practice pure intention.

The 8-Fold Path of Yoga

1. Restraint of Negative Behavior (*Yama*)
2. Observance of Positive Behavior (*Niyama*)
3. Yoga Postures (*Asana*)
4. Breathing and Energy (*Pranayama*)
5. Sensory Mastery (*Pratyahara*)
6. Concentration (*Dharana*)
7. Meditation (*Dhyana*)
8. Perfect Concentration (*Samadhi*)

RESTRAINTS (*Yamas*)

The restraints *(yamas)* are the first step in The 8-Fold Path, and they describe behaviors to avoid in thought, word, and deed. As you read, keep in mind that the restraints are stated in their more positive sense (for example, the principle of non-violence urges students to not be violent, and truthfulness to not lie), but they are advocating against negative behavior. Use the following information to identify the principle that relates to your life. Do not attempt to practice all the restraints at the same time, just select one or two that are relevant to your intention.

The first of these is **non-violence**. Non-violence is an umbrella concept that weaves its way through all the other restraints. We practice non-violence when we refrain from causing distress or harm to other people and to ourselves. In yoga poses, we practice non-violence when we avoid pushing too hard and refrain from being self-critical.

Restraints (*Yamas*)
Non-violence (*Ahimsa*)
Truthfulness (*Satya*)
Non-stealing (*Asteya*)
Moderation (*Bramacharya*)
Non-attachment (*Aparigraha*)

Mary's Non-violence: In Mary's situation, her deep-seated belief that she is unattractive reflects low self-esteem and negative self-talk. She constantly compares herself to others in yoga class, and this harmful behavior feeds her low opinion of herself. If Mary can recognize her area of suffering, she can begin to cultivate the opposite in her yoga practice. What would be the opposite of Mary's self-violence? She would practice yoga with an attitude of self-love, compassion, peace, love, or acceptance.

The second restraint, **truthfulness,** is that which is pure, honest, and good, and promotes the welfare of all living beings. Truthfulness is free from illusion, judgment, fear, or hatred.

Laura's Truthfulness: Let us remember Laura, and how she knows in her gut that her lifestyle is no longer what she wants, but in an inactive state, remains a follower of her friends without honoring her truth. In practicing truthfulness and honoring her true needs, Laura might stop going out with the same friends, but would need to remember the common thread of non-violence in the effort to communicate this to them. She would be mindful of not carelessly hurting their feelings in her desire to express the truth. In a yoga practice, she might cultivate the intention of truth, wisdom, self-respect, courage, or honesty, and notice how those virtues affect the way she breathes, moves, thinks, and feels in a yoga pose.

The third restraint, **non-stealing**, has to do with refraining from taking or desiring something that belongs to someone else, particularly without their permission.

Mary's Non-stealing: Mary covets the physical beauty of other women in yoga class, while stealing from herself the opportunity for her own inner beauty to shine. Stealing is subscribing to a "poverty mentality." *The Yoga Sutras* instruct us to avoid this behavior and abundance will flow through like a current of water. In yoga practice, Mary might identify this tendency and practice the opposite intention of contentment, inner beauty, peace, faith, trust, or abundance.

Moderation, the fourth restraint, is the act of limiting sense pleasures in order to maximize the amount of energy that can be channeled to actions to benefit others and promote self-realization.

Laura's Moderation: Laura notices that her friends' careless consumption of alcohol and other pleasure-seeking activities don't actually make them happy but rather seem to lead to a lot of distraction and suffering. She realizes that in moderating pleasure-based activities, she enjoys a renewed sense of energy and self-understanding. In yoga practice, she might cultivate the intention of balance, non-attachment, focus, or awareness.

The final restraint, **non-attachment**, refers to greedlessness or voluntary simplicity, acquiring only that which is really essential for life.

Steve's Non-attachment: Steve realizes that he is trying to be someone he is not in order to impress others and win recognition. Once he lets go of those old beliefs and greed, he reduces a lot of stress in his life. He no longer works excessively to pay for the expensive clothing he thought he needed in order to look good. He begins to have more focus and energy for self-understanding. He realizes that practicing non-attachment to material things brings him lasting joy and a sense of liberation.

Observances (Niyamas)

The observances (*niyamas*) are the second step of The 8-Fold Path and, with the restraints *(yamas),* form the foundation of spiritual practice. The observances are positive behaviors, so rather than practicing the opposite as with the restraints, the observances are guidelines for practicing positive intention.

The five observances are governed by the first: **purity**. On a physical level, you practice purity through healthy food choices, adequate water intake, regular exercise, relaxation, proper hygiene, etc. The cultivation of purity in the mind comes through positive thinking, including healthy choices about what we mentally consume, like the television shows we watch, the music we listen to, and the company we keep. Spiritually, we engage in purity through yoga practice, or through prayer, meditation, inspirational readings, and community activities.

Observances (*Niyamas*)
Purity (*Saucha*)
Contentment (*Santosha*)
Discipline (*Tapas*)
Study of self/Introspection
(*Svadhyaya*)
Surrender to an Infinite Reality
(*Ishvara Pranidhana*)

To purify the body in yoga practice, focus on the breath. A complete exhalation eliminates toxins, carbon dioxide, and stale air from the lungs, while inhalation oxygenates the blood throughout the body. Deep breathing promotes relaxation and releases tension. The energetic channels (chakras) are also balanced and cleansed. Purifying yoga practices increase body awareness, resulting in a natural desire to take better care of yourself. With practice, the mind focuses easily and is not distracted by desires or sensory input.

Contentment is the art of appreciating what we have and desiring no more than what is necessary for maintaining our life. It is neither a state of like nor dislike, but simply being and delighting in oneself to radiate inner harmony and love. Contentment is choosing to see the positive in life, others, and oneself. In yoga practice, we can appreciate the body and mind as it is. Balancing poses make us newly grateful for having two legs and feet. Moving the hands reminds us of our appreciation for all they touch, do, create, hold, and heal. Awareness of the breath brings gratitude for the gift of life. Integrate the attitude of contentment into every yoga pose and notice how it affects the experience of the pose.

Discipline, in yogic philosophy, means "to generate light or heat." This refers to the psychic energy generated by the voluntary practice of various disciplines that purify the body and mind and generate spiritual radiance. Motivation to go to yoga class or commit to home practice finds its original power from discipline. Notice that some poses require more discipline than others. Sun Salutations are a classic example of poses that "raise heat" or encourage a sense of discipline, as are the warrior poses.

The underlying theme of the observances, purity, may be misunderstood as soft and easy. As a result, people may see discipline as being in conflict with the overall goal of purity because of the intensity of discipline. In other words, if we are being harsh and critical in order to maintain discipline, are we practicing purity? When discipline is understood as power or effort, then it becomes the driving force of purifying actions. It is common that childhood experiences bring a penal view of discipline. As adults, it is possible to recognize discipline as a virtue. *The Yoga Sutras* 2:43 states, "with discipline, impurities are eliminated and perfection gained." This ultimately coalesces into the development of the subtle senses of intuition, grace, unity, and harmony in the body and in life itself.

Study of self or introspection means self-observation and inquiry without judgment. This behavior provides an opportunity to become aware of the various affects of thoughts and behavior. For example, in practicing introspection, we might notice that eating refined sugar has an energizing effect, followed by a lethargic effect, leaving us feeling cloudy-headed and sleepy. Sometimes, self-study helps us to distinguish between perceptions and reality—we may feel depressed or irritated, but can recognize such an emotion as separate from who we are. In this way, we can respond with a wise understanding from the true Self. Meditation and reflection upon sacred texts offers a chance to learn from others who have gone before us and experienced many of the same life lessons. To read such sources directly offers a chance to connect to the energy and inspiration of those who were divinely inspired. It is sometimes said that when we practice yoga poses, we are practicing with all others who are practicing in that moment, as well as throughout history. In such a way, within each pose, we connect with an ancient wisdom and spiritual energy that increases self-awareness and direct experience with a Higher Reality.

With the final observance, **surrender to an infinite reality**, letting go is a key action. When we accept that our limited human minds are ultimately not in control of reality, we surrender our ego to a higher principle. Whether we believe it to be the Universe, Higher Self, Nature, God, Goddess, Krishna, Allah, Buddha, or Jesus, this higher principle is a very personal choice. In yoga poses, "letting go" can be practiced while exhaling in poses that release tension. Here we can cultivate faith by learning that the world does not rest on our shoulders or even revolve around us. Going deep into a yoga pose does not come through effort, but through surrender.

Cultivating the Corresponding Opposite Feeling

We now have the tools for recognizing when we are engaging in thoughts and behaviors that do not facilitate healing and growth. To avoid becoming overwhelmed, choose one simple theme to practice. It can be helpful to remember that countering deep-seated tendencies toward negative thinking requires regular and diligent practice. The subconscious mind operates according to suggestions that have been programmed from early childhood, even when they are harmful and cause suffering. These subconscious thought patterns come from parents, friends, teachers, mass media, and other cultural symbols and values. Patanjali, author of *The Yoga Sutras*, recommends not indulging or rationalizing such negative influences, but rather, cultivating the opposite.

On the other hand, it is worth noting that sometimes it may be necessary to feel a negative emotion. In surrendering to the emotion, you allow a deeper level of understanding to surface. (If this does not occur in time, consult with a counselor.) By sublimating the emotion into a greater good, ask, "What am I supposed to learn from this situation?" A wise woman once said, "Anger is like the force which pushes the tulips from the ground in the springtime." What is anger trying to tell you to change? How might depression help you take better care of yourself? Perhaps it is telling you to remove yourself from a particular situation. When that is not possible, you can use the opportunity to practice equanimity and non-attachment to negative reactions. An emotion can be acknowledged without giving it control. It's not that yogis don't have emotions, but that they understand their emotions very well. Becoming aware of our emotions affects how we respond to circumstances in life.

Steps for Setting Your Intention

Think of two or three personal goals. Let's say you'd like to improve your health, relationships, and spirituality. Investigate the deeper purpose for the intention in these particular areas. For health, perhaps you think happiness equals losing a little weight, a very common health concern. Be very careful to recognize that a specific physical goal is not the most effective intention. Start to ask yourself why. "Why do I want to lose a few pounds?" The first answer, if you look to the qualities of reality, might be an inactive response based on fear: "I want to lose weight because people will like me more." Or, "I'm afraid of having a heart attack."

In their essence, these desires are not bad, they just need to be connected to a deeper intention. There's nothing wrong with wanting to look good or be healthy. **The problem is when the desire becomes the intention**. Ask yourself *why* you want to look good. Let's suppose that your deeper desire is to improve your love life. The spiritual aspect of this desire is love. Follow the intention of love and your yoga practice becomes centered on the giving and receiving of love.

With the example of wanting to lose weight in order to be healthier, again ask yourself why. Perhaps you want to live longer and be there when your children grow older. The reason for losing weight is now a virtue: to help others. The intention of your yoga practice is to become a strong and healthy person in order to serve other people.

All that is required to be successful in setting a deep intention is a little time. Ask why until a virtue is reached. Some common examples of virtues would be love, compassion, peace, joy, service, balance, faith, trust, hope, acceptance, forgiveness, patience, and devotion. Intentions are not limited to these virtues, but these are good examples.

Throughout this book, it is recommended that you study at a yoga studio or community center near you. If you have questions about intention, discuss it with a yoga teacher, trusted counselor, religious leader, or friend.

Steps for identifying intention:

1. Choose an area of your life in which you'd like to set an intention, such as health, relationships, work, family, or spirituality.

2. Within your chosen area of life, create a goal that is important to you. You may immediately identify the goal or it could take more time to figure out exactly what you want it to be. Once you've figured it out, write down your goal in clear terms. Try to be as specific as possible (e.g., I want to lose twenty pounds, or I want to volunteer at a women's shelter). You might have many goals at first, but narrow it down to one to start.

3. Now ask yourself why you want to achieve this goal. Take this answer and ask yourself, once again, why? The first reason you identify will be at a surface level. The second reason will likely be broader and more spiritual. You can repeat this process several times if you wish.

4. If the intention is based on fear or ego, try to go deeper to identify the pure or balanced version of desire. For example, if the reason you initially identify for losing twenty pounds is so that people find you attractive, search within yourself to find a pure intention for losing the weight (yet be mindful that the intention still feels sincere). You might realize that a more meaningful goal would be improving your health. This pure intention would have all sorts of effects, such as feeling stronger and more energetic, which might in turn open up new opportunities in your work and personal relationships. Now that you've identified the positive intention of your goal, write it down clearly.

5. When you next practice yoga poses, focus on that intention. Afterward, note any interesting insights or thoughts about the experience in your journal.

6. Finally, write down your intention in bold letters on a bookmark, and use it to keep your place in this book.

As you progress, everything you learn should help you integrate the essence of your intention. The intention may evolve as you study yoga. After a period of time, you will notice that one intention remains consistent for each season or even years.

While I suggest using your original intention for a period of time, know that you can always change your intention. If you're feeling weak one day, you might adjust your intention to having courage to practice yoga. Or if you're filled with a deep sense of gratitude, you might hold the intention of offering gratitude to the world through each yoga pose. The most important thing to keep in mind in using intention in your practice is that it is heartfelt and sincere. If your intention doesn't fit your mood, there's no point in setting that intention, because it's not going to serve your practice.

Many students arrive at their intention with great precision but wonder how to apply this intention to yoga poses. Or, the yoga teacher says to "choose an intention for this class" but doesn't say how to apply this intention. I offer you the image of a chalice, a holy cup. Name this chalice after your present intention. Let the lessons and experiences of your yoga session fill the cup. Let insights related to your intention fill the cup; let the deep feeling of peace fill your cup. Let the inexplicable mystery of spiritual connection fill your cup. Think of your intention as a focus for receiving and enriching your perception of the experience.

Connecting to the Infinite

Now that you have a greater understanding of the power and importance of intention in yoga poses, you will practice yoga in a totally new way. You'll find that you have greater control over the physical poses through the cultivation of pure (sattvic) intention, and your mind and spirit will become integrated in the process as never before. The restraints provide specific examples of harmful behavior, and by practicing the opposite (your list from Exercise 3 on page 31), we can put a positive virtue in its place. The observances, on the other hand, highlight healthy behaviors to use as a focal point for physical practice.

It goes without saying that the guidelines for cultivating positive intention also apply to how we live our life. Whether or not we recognize them, the underlying intention in all activities and thoughts determines the result. Seen in this way, daily life is like a yoga pose. And, vice versa, yoga poses embody life in that moment. Rather than avoiding the deepest and perhaps most difficult parts of life, we tune in and listen to the callings. Our spirit's healing potential is allowed to come through and change what needs to be changed. Practicing yoga means continually working toward a pure approach of awareness and acceptance. There is no perfection, just the ever-evolving journey. For this reason, finding like-minded friends and a yoga community is very helpful. We look to the yogic wisdom collected by the masters and practitioners over thousands of years and discover we are not alone and never have been.

Exercises

1. After you read the case studies on intentions, in a sentence or two, write down why you are practicing yoga. Even if the reasons seem selfish, be honest and write them down. The more honest you are, the more relevant and revealing your exploration will be. Some common reasons might be, "I heard yoga will help me get the body I always wanted," "I need to get rid of my stress," or "I want to be enlightened."

2. Now that you have discovered the possible qualities of an intention, how does yours compare to those from the case studies? Take a look at your list of reasons for practicing yoga from Exercise 1 and write down any flaws you see. Perhaps you wanted to fit in with your friends, or maybe you wanted to get in shape. Continue to be honest with yourself, even if you know the "right answers."

   Reflect on how these reasons help or hurt you. Consider each reason individually and ask yourself if it's beneficial for your body, mind, and spirit. You will very likely find that some of the reasons are preventing you from achieving health and vitality. Use the restraints and observances to redirect your intention for doing yoga, deepening your practice and pointing you toward a more fulfilling life.

3. Look at your list of reasons for doing yoga and identify those that are not aligned with pure intention.

   Next, take these misaligned reasons and ask yourself what the source of suffering is behind those reasons. For example, if your reason for practicing yoga is that you want to get a date, your source of suffering might be loneliness. Perhaps you've become desperate, anxious, or impatient in your desire to find a partner. Write down the pain that is motivating you to do yoga. Even if you have several improperly aligned reasons for doing yoga, they usually boil down to one or two core sources of suffering. For example, inferiority and a lack of self-confidence, or a feeling of emptiness and not "having enough."

Now, consider the restraints in relation to your suffering. Which one relates to it the most? In the examples above, inferiority and a lack of self-confidence would relate to the principle of non-violence, and the feeling of not having enough would relate to non-attachment.

Brainstorm positive virtues that represent the opposite of your pain. Write down this virtue; it will be closely related to your intention. Be very subjective with your choice of positive virtue. One person who feels low self-esteem may elect to focus on confidence, while another person will find acceptance powerful. Think deeply about the topic and discover a personal response.

4. In considering the five observances, which one inspires you the most? Perhaps the principle of contentment encourages you to trust that your yoga practice is exactly where it needs to be, even if you can't contort your body like other students in the class. Or maybe discipline resonates with a need to establish a home yoga practice in addition to going to class. Choose one of the five observances as your intention for practicing yoga, or alternatively, any positive concept that motivates you on a deep level. Take it out for a test drive to see if it resonates in the depths of your soul.

Attitude

Bhava

*Creating harmony of mind, body, and spirit
through attitude.*

It is said that a Native American shaman can tell everything about a person by looking at their footprint. The traditional Chinese doctor feels the pulse and examines skin tone, eyes, and tongue to determine the physical and mental health of a patient. The yogi observes breathing patterns and posture to understand a person's state of mind. These are simplifications but are examples of how healing traditions take a mind-body-spirit approach to wellness. As in other (typically Eastern) practices, yoga teaches that the condition of the mind is reflected in the body and vice versa.

The state of the mind in yoga pose practice is known as "posture," "attitude," or "conscious mental pose." Whether a student is feeling depressed, joyful, upset, or enthusiastic, an experienced yoga teacher will be able to see it in the alignment and physical expression of the yoga pose. And while a student's posture in a pose reflects his or her emotional, psychological, and spiritual condition, yoga can actually transform these aspects. (Note that while posture is reflected in physical position, the idea of posture here includes more than just sitting up straight.) In other words, attitude is something that you have naturally throughout your day (positive or negative), and it's also something that you can consciously cultivate through yoga pose practice. Yoga poses are a way of purifying your attitude as well as physical body. Many yoga students notice a subtle or obvious energetic shift after practicing yoga, often described as a balanced state of mind, a heightened feeling of physical or emotional well-being, or just a general uplifted feeling toward life.

CASE STUDY Mary the Mother

Everyday posture reflects attitude toward life.

Let's consider Mary's posture, the woman we introduced in Step One, who is 36 years old and has come to class to lose weight. She has just given birth to her second child and feels unattractive. Mary has been carrying a baby on her right hip for the last four years, while holding groceries and other things in her left arm. She feels tightness in her shoulders, confounded by sleep deprivation, lack of time to exercise, and forgetfulness concerning her eating habits. Mary used to be an energetic woman who exercised regularly, ate three balanced meals, and was very attractive. As a result of her current lifestyle, she has gained thirty pounds, causing her body to curve forward, her back to ache, and her belly to soften.

All this can be seen from Mary's posture. Previously, her looks and robust health fueled her self-esteem. With less vitality, she feels beaten down, and the initial glow of motherhood has passed into the difficult years of chasing children. Her self-esteem was never strong in the first place, as it was reliant on external approval. She feels overwhelmed and has allowed her fears of being unattractive to make motherhood an unappealing chore. If Mary learns to understand herself more clearly, she can realign her posture as a form of self-esteem that comes from within. She will start to feel proud to be a mother and reclaim her self-respect.

As Mary takes control of her attitude toward life, her posture automatically straightens without her even trying to align her back and shoulders. She doesn't look weak or feel quite as heavy in her body because she's straightened up. As her self-respect grows, she isn't as fearful that her husband is going to leave her. Most profoundly, she becomes more attractive by respecting and loving herself, regardless of her weight.

Alignment of Yoga Poses Is Influenced More by Attitude than by Physical Effort

The teaching of proper alignment in modern yoga is largely dominated by a physical approach based on anatomy and physiology (we will cover physical alignment in Step Three). Yet in its truest nature, yoga is a psychosomatic (body-mind) practice. This means that the mental and spiritual components are as important to yoga as the physical ones. If we are to fully appreciate the benefits of yoga, we must go beyond the anatomy and physiology of a yoga pose to explore the mental and spiritual aspects of yoga. Remarkably, our physical practice is transformed when we approach yoga holistically. This helps to explain why practicing yoga is such a different experience from one day to the next. While a pose may come easily on certain days, on others you may find it quite challenging. The attitude of a student is so important to proper physical alignment of a pose that I believe it's actually more relevant than physiology.

CASE STUDY **Laura the Professional**

Attitude before practicing yoga influences the experience.

When Laura enters a yoga class, laughing with her friends on a Saturday morning, she practices yoga in a very free-flowing, relaxed way. On the other hand, when Laura joins a class after a stressful day at work, rushing to change into yoga clothes and missing the opening breathing exercises, it is a very different experience. No matter what suggestions the teacher makes about her physical alignment, she's tense in every pose for the first fifteen or twenty minutes of class. No amount of anatomical instructions can change Laura's attitude and that attitude is manifested in her physical posture.

Imagine, instead, that as Laura hurries into class from work, feeling pressured from the rat race, the teacher gives a short talk about nonviolence. This gives her a chance to adjust her attitude. It doesn't take her long to balance her emotions and choose a more positive stance. As a result, Laura is able to concentrate in her poses and leaves class feeling invigorated.

Yoga classes that include a brief discussion of yoga philosophy at the beginning of class inspire students to adopt a positive attitude prior to practicing poses (one of the many reasons yoga philosophy needs to be taught in class). Fewer instructions on alignment are required, providing the students with a quieter experience and thus the opportunity to cultivate inner observation and wisdom. Students who come into a yoga pose in a relaxed, open-minded manner will often grasp the proper alignment just by observing and mirroring the teacher and be able to experience the attitude of the pose from within.

States of Mind
(*The Bhavas*)

Classical yoga theory divides attitude into four major themes, each reflecting a positive feeling, state, or mood: duty *(dharma)*, knowledge *(jnana)*, non-attachment *(viaragya)*, and mastery *(ishvara aisvarya)*. Every yoga pose helps us to develop one of these four major attitudes. It may be helpful to think of attitude as simply your state of mind, known in Sanskrit as the *bhavas*. As you cultivate the attitude inherent in each pose, you will begin to integrate your body, mind, and spirit, leading to greater health and well-being. The following section explains these ancient categories of attitudes from yoga philosophy. We'll consider the philosophy initially and then later in the chapter, we'll explore how to cultivate these attitudes through yoga poses.

Duty (*Dharma*)

The first attitude is **duty**, which has to do with our priorities and roles in life, including responsibilities to self, family and friends, work, society, and all of humanity. Neglecting our duty leads to conflicts and problems in daily life. Some typical examples would be over-working, having poor eating habits, not resting sufficiently, not exercising enough, or emotionally neglecting our families. Duty includes such concepts as routine, discipline, self-direction and responsibility, inner control, and desirable character.

Duty (*Dharma*)
Responsibility
Routine
Discipline
Self-direction
Self-control
Moderation
Commitment
Concentration
Character

When we integrate the attitude of duty in our lives, we are able to restrain from impulses, regulate desires, accept internal authority, and achieve internal mastery. Duty is a means through which we can achieve self-realization (i.e., the true Self, which we will discuss in greater detail later in this book). We acknowledge the importance of discipline and moderation in helping us carry out routine and our commitment to others. Through practicing yoga poses that have duty as their central attitude, we develop a conditioned and still mind, as opposed to being lethargic and unfocused. Ultimately, the path of duty saves us from pain and suffering.

The attitude of duty corresponds to meditative yoga poses. The original purpose of all yoga poses was to be seated comfortably in meditation. Pose *(asana)* literally means "seat." *The Yoga Sutras* (2:46) tell us that yoga poses should be "comfortable and steady." While all yoga poses have a meditative quality to them, some poses are defined specifically by their meditative nature. Balancing poses such as Tree Pose are also good for cultivating duty. Following is a list of the meditative and balancing poses, good for cultivating the attitude of duty:

❄

CONNECTING TO THE POSES

Balance	*Meditative*
TREE POSE, PAGE 256	EASY POSE, PAGE 298
DANCER POSE, PAGE 258	HALF LOTUS POSE,
BOAT POSE, PAGE 260	PAGE 298

KNOWLEDGE (*Jnana*)

The second attitude, **knowledge**, begins with self-awareness and includes the physical, emotional, and spiritual realms. Central to the concept of knowledge is a deep realization that we can find everything we need within ourselves. The external world *(maya)* pulls at our attention, keeping us busy looking for purpose and meaning, but usually leaves us confused and frustrated. By practicing the attitude of knowledge, we can stay grounded within ourselves regardless of our circumstances.

Knowledge (*Jnana*)
Awareness
Wisdom
Understanding
Self-inquiry
Consciousness
Balance

Knowledge is acquired through concentration, coordination, sense training, breath awareness and control, and balance. This attitude corresponds to poses involving upward and sideward stretches, extremities, and breath control *(pranayama)*. Through these poses, we develop body consciousness, starting with awareness of the muscles, breath, and then internal organs. More advanced students may begin to feel shifting energy in their energy centers (chakras), or particular emotional and spiritual qualities of each pose. The following poses can be practiced to cultivate the attitude of knowledge:

✳

CONNECTING TO THE POSES

Upward	Sideward	Extremities	Balance
PALM TREE POSE, PAGE 262	TRIANGLE POSE, PAGE 276	BUTTERFLY POSE, PAGE 284	TREE POSE, PAGE 256
		PIGEON POSE, PAGE 286	DANCER POSE, PAGE 258
			BOAT POSE, PAGE 260

Knowledge refers to the wisdom of the body. Rather than just following a yoga teacher's instructions, be sensitive to your own experience in the poses and aware of tension in your body. This simple awareness sends a signal to the nervous system and tells it to let go of old tension patterns. If you pay attention to your body and do what feels right for you, your body will respond and heal itself. With this level of awareness, you will be able to detect imbalance or dis-ease in the body before it escalates into something worse. During the first six months to a year of practicing, new yoga students often comment on how their health has improved.

Benefits of Body Awareness for Beginners

- A sore throat can be a reminder to drink more water, get more rest, reduce sugar consumption, and limit other immune-suppressing actions.

- Tenderness in the low back or shoulders is a signal to evaluate and correct daily posture, or to avoid lifting heavy objects.

- Relaxation reduces sinus, back, and jaw tension, and the host of psychological problems that come with them.

- Cultivation of a positive mood decreases impulsive emotional eating and improves dietary discipline and health and normalizes weight.

- Unusual soreness in yoga poses motivates a student to see her doctor and learn that she has a disease (for example, Lyme disease). The early detection of many diseases greatly reduces the severity of symptoms and shortens recovery time.

NON-ATTACHMENT (*Viaragya*)

Non-attachment is the third attitude. Traditionally, it was the renunciation of worldly or material attachments, but people living in the world today must fulfill their duties to family. In current times, it may be most appropriate to think of non-attachment as a state of being in the world but not of the world. Non-attachment involves humility, objectivity, faith, ego reduction, acceptance, and surrender to a larger reality.

Non-attachment (*Viaragya*)
Letting go
Humility
Objectivity
Reducing ego
Acceptance
Surrender
Witness
Faith

Non-attachment confers the ability to step back and view our lives as an objective witness, seeing everything but suffering nothing. When we cultivate the attitude of non-attachment, we're able to live with our struggles but not be defined by them. Non-attachment also involves being ready for the teacher (spiritual or otherwise) to appear, and, once that happens, cultivating humility and learning to receive the guidance and light required for self-development and self-actualization. In daily life, this is the practice of learning to say we're sorry and helping those who are less fortunate than we are.

Non-attachment is the attitude through which we can see how we are related to one another. It is the practice of *karma yoga* (the yoga of action described in a sacred scripture of Hinduism known as the *Bhagavad Gita*), where working, especially the most humbling acts like washing the dishes or cleaning the toilet, become the path to serve, worship, and reduce the ego. We make contributions to others without the desire for reward, without attachment, leading to a balanced state of mind.

In yoga poses, non-attachment corresponds to letting go in relaxation poses, forward bends, and head-low postures. Twisting poses offer a chance to look from a new perspective, one we may not have seen in our everyday, forward-moving tunnel vision, while forward bends provide an opportunity for reflection. Non-attachment offers us an experience of forgetting our self. The following yoga poses are conducive to the attitude of non-attachment:

CONNECTING TO THE POSES

Relaxation	Forward	Twists	Inversions
CORPSE POSE, PAGE 296	WHEEL POSE, PAGE 264	PARTIAL SEATED TWIST, PAGE 280	SHOULDER STAND, PAGE 292
	SEATED FORWARD BEND, PAGE 266		PLOUGH, PAGE 294
	CHILD'S POSE, PAGE 268	SUPINE TWIST, PAGE 282	

Practicing non-attachment frees us to live with robust vigor by living in the present moment rather than being attached to a desired outcome. This can be mistaken as being aloof, uncaring, distant, or not invested in life. Quite the opposite, non-attachment allows us to live a richer and deeper life because we're not consumed with worry about how the future will play out. Through cultivating non-attachment in yoga practice, you'll find that you can focus on the immediacy of the present task. The pressure of accomplishment is removed, so you're able to concentrate on what you're doing, which actually improves the outcome. As a result, you may enjoy new and unexpected results that create more harmony in your life. This is true for experiences both "on" and "off the mat."

MASTERY (*Ishvara Aisvarya*)

The final attitude, **mastery**, refers to a stepping forward or achievement. When we truly understand the first three bhavas of duty, knowledge, and non-attachment, we arrive at mastery with a humble feeling of achievement, satisfaction, and knowledge. This adds a subtle confidence to the personality, as opposed to being superficial and showing off to others. This path is easiest to cultivate through experiences of self-reliance, perseverance, and faith.

Mastery (*Ishvara Aisvarya*)
Stepping forward
Achievement
Confidence
Self-reliance
Fortitude
Power
Strength
Self-esteem
Perseverance

Mastery makes us stronger in mind, body, and spirit, helping us to rise above our human nature and protect us from undesirable impulses. The practice requires willpower and the cultivation of positive thoughts and actions, resulting in self-efficacy, positive body image, competency, and high self-esteem.

To cultivate the willpower necessary for mastery, I suggest practicing poses for attaining strength, steadiness, relaxation, and higher awareness. These might include backward bending poses as well as the backward bending aspects of Sun and Moon Salutations included in Part IV. The following poses correspond with mastery:

CONNECTING TO THE POSES

Backward	*Inversions*	*Extremities*
COBRA, PAGE 272	DOWNWARD DOG, PAGE 290	WARRIOR I, PAGE 288
BOW POSE, PAGE 274		(WARRIOR II AND III ALSO)

You realize the power that mastery confers when you align with the higher Self. Mastery involves the ability to view life from a larger perspective, beyond the small vision of limited ego perception. Rather than imposing our will onto something, we let go and trust in the divine order of the universe. In simpler terms, this is what we mean when we say "go with the flow." This is the intention of Sun Salutations, to salute the sun and all of nature by flowing through a series of poses with a sense of surrender, gratitude, and reverence for life. It is like paddling a canoe in a lake with gentle currents. By understanding the currents, we can paddle in such a way that the current carries the boat. When we work against the current, we make little to no headway, sometimes moving backward instead of forward. The quiet time during yoga pose practice can be used to align the body and mind in such a way that the currents of life are revealed. Then we can better navigate our relationships, work, and health. Practicing a yoga pose literally opens us to the flow inside our own bodies. By understanding the microcosm of our minds and hearts, we become more connected with the macrocosm that surrounds us.

Do you remember how you felt after taking your first steps? Most of us don't, but if you have ever seen a baby take the first few steps of its life, you may have noticed that it expresses a sense of mastery. And rightly so, as it's quite an accomplishment! Think of the number of muscles involved in walking and the coordination between those muscles to make it possible. To further our abilities in yoga, it's important to acknowledge our achievements just as a baby delights in walking. As you practice yoga, feel uplifted by the mastery you have over your body. As you do, you'll find yourself less inclined to compare yourself to other students and much more satisfied with your own practice.

How to Integrate Intention and Attitude

Let's now consider intention in light of our discussion on attitude. Attitude is our state of being at any given time, yet it's an intrinsic quality found in each yoga pose that can be used for self-development. We may go into a yoga class grumpy and tired, yet through consciously practicing the attitude within each pose, we can come out of class feeling energetic, peaceful, and content. In order to transform our physical, emotional, and spiritual well-being, we must create an appropriate intention and then practice poses that focus on the specific attitude we are seeking to cultivate. Intention lights the path to follow and attitude gives us tools for setting the journey in motion.

Let's take a look at a few examples:

CASE STUDY **Steve**

Steve recognizes that his stress response is causing him lower back pain, and he wants to transform his reactions to stressful situations. Steve's balanced intention is self-care and illumination. He focuses on poses that have duty as their primary attitude to help him develop a routine of taking care of himself. Steve asks his family to help him have fifteen to thirty minutes of quiet time every day to practice self-reflection and meditation. By cultivating a meditation practice, Steve achieves clarity about personal goals and direction, including a desire to become more focused on his responsibilities as a father. His spiritual discipline also affects his work life, causing him to feel more focused, productive, and at ease.

CASE STUDY **Laura**

Laura recognizes that she has spent most of her life seeking the approval of others to the detriment of her own self-exploration and development. Though she's in her mid-twenties, she still doesn't have a real sense of who she is and what she wants in life. She identifies her balanced intention as spiritual growth and clarity. Laura decides to focus on yoga poses that share the attitude of knowledge to expand her self-awareness and inner wisdom. While in upward stretching poses, she identifies with her desire to "reach for the highest" within herself. While practicing poses that focus on the extremities of the body, she becomes aware of muscles that she didn't even realize she had, giving her a greater understanding of how her body functions. As she observes the massaging of her internal organs in the sideward stretch, a desire grows within her to nurture and feed her body with nutritious foods. Through balance poses, she practices the art of balancing her own needs with those of her friends and family. Laura's life takes on new meaning as she connects with her intention and develops a rich sense of self.

CASE STUDY **Mary**

Mary recognizes that caring for herself will help her become more confident, and she identifies her intention as self-care and love. She explores poses that have non-attachment as their inherent attitude so that she may release old thought patterns, including feelings of fear and low self-esteem. Mary practices forward bending poses to surrender fears and old habits, and to cultivate faith. Twisting poses provide a different view of life and give her a sense of self-assurance. In relaxation poses, Mary connects with the perspective of being a witness to her own life, helping her to see that regardless of life's ups and downs, everything will work out as it should.

From these examples, can you identify the type of bhava, or attitude, that best suits your intention? If you need to, reread the descriptions of each attitude and take some time to contemplate which is most appropriate for you. If you're still not sure, that's okay—we'll come back to this later in the chapter. We'll now take a closer look at each pose category and the attitude that they emphasize, and give you further direction on integrating the awareness of attitude in your yoga practice.

Practicing Attitude in Yoga Poses

When we practice yoga poses mindful of their inherent qualities of duty, knowledge, non-attachment, and mastery, we integrate our body, mind, and spirit. This integration, or lack thereof, affects overall well-being. As we've now realized, yoga poses can be practiced in order to cultivate the various feelings, states, or moods, and to bring an overall balance and harmony into being. The following is a quick reference list for the qualities each pose category provides:

Qualities Outline for Practice

Pose category	Attitude	Bhava
Balance	Knowledge	Knowledge
Upward	Striving	Knowledge
Forward	Surrender	Non-attachment
Backward	Vigor	Mastery, Knowledge, Duty
Sideward	Flexibility	Knowledge
Twist	Openness	Non-attachment
Extremities	Self-reliance	Mastery, Knowledge
Inversion	Inward	Mastery, Non-attachment
Relaxation	Non-attachment	Non-attachment
Meditative	One-pointed	Duty
Salutations	Devotion	Elements of each

Note that each specific yoga pose has its unique expression of an attitude. There are no absolute rules or regulations for the attitude of a pose. For example, if the famous Tree Pose represents rootedness to you, then you may receive an attitude of groundedness. It is equally correct to feel the heart in the Tree Pose and feel a sense of love as the attitude as you extend your arms like the branches of a tree. The key point is to be aware of the relationship of your attitude while in poses as well as the inherent attitude of that pose.

Let's figure out which set of poses best suits your chosen intention. Keep in mind that just as your intention will change over time, the attitude that you work with will also shift according to your needs. Remain aware of your subtle changes and allow your yoga practice to address your specific needs. Otherwise, yoga practice may grow stale and boring, but more important, you won't be achieving optimal health in mind, body, and spirit. This is not to say that you will need to change yoga routines on a weekly basis. However, re-evaluating your intention and attitude each season would be appropriate. You may also consider going on a yoga retreat once or twice a year for further reflection.

Before we move on to the exercises, here's one final note about intention and attitude: While the intention serves as your guiding light throughout your practice, don't complicate your yoga practice by trying to force the simultaneous expression of your intention and attitude. Focus on the attitude you're exploring and as it feels natural to do so, simply reflect on how the attitude (your daily approach to yoga poses) relates to your intention (your ultimate goal for doing yoga). For example, if you practice relaxation poses, then relax. Don't superimpose your intention for inner peace onto relaxation. Simply notice how relaxation relates to inner peace. You'll learn more from the poses by not overcomplicating your practice and being receptive to learning what the wisdom in each pose offers.

Connecting to the Infinite

Body posture expresses attitude and attitude governs posture. This step bridges daily life and yoga poses as attitude accompanies every action. Attitude of yoga poses is a key place to recognize your perspective on yoga. With attention focused on attitude, the mind-body benefits of yoga poses are immediately recognized. Your physical alignment is positively impacted by understanding proper attitude. To further delve into alignment or how to perform yoga poses, continue on to Step Three.

Exercises

For this exercise, use the pure intention you chose in Step One.

1. As you think about your intention, consider again the reasons why you chose that intention. Examine your intention in terms of the four bhavas:

   a. How does duty expand your understanding of your intention?

   b. How does knowledge expand your understanding of your intention?

   c. How does non-attachment expand your understanding of your intention?

   d. How does mastery expand your understanding of your intention?

   Which of the attitudes can give you the tools for living out your intention? It may help to review your notes from the exercises in Step One as well as the descriptions of the attitudes in Step Two. Choose the attitude that feels like the best fit for your intention. You can always change your mind, so don't worry too much about it being the "right" choice.

2. Focus on poses from this attitude category while including other poses for a well-rounded practice. If you've chosen the attitude of non-attachment, focus on relaxation poses, twists, and inversions. You'll still practice other ones, like strength and balancing poses, to round out your practice. It's a matter of emphasis on your time and effort.

   As you practice yoga poses, focus on the attitude of each pose and contemplate how this relates to your intention. Practice each pose in a steady and comfortable manner, pay attention to your breath, and let go of tension you are holding in your body. The goal is to center the mind on a spiritual intention and be receptive to the positive feeling of the attitude of the pose. The effort is in being effortless. Allow your thoughts to organize by letting go, similar to the effect of a restful vacation.

STEP THREE

Posture

Asana

*The body is an essential part
of spiritual experience.*

L et's go do some yoga!" Steve says to Mary.

"Okay, Steve, let me grab my yoga mat," says Mary. "That would be fun!"

Most people will not find anything peculiar about the scenario above. In the West, yoga has come to be equated with yoga poses or yoga pose exercise class. However, the poses are just one aspect of yoga. The word *yoga* means "union of the lower self to the higher Self," or as we described in the introduction to this book, a holistic way of living and healing, aimed at uniting the mind, body, and spirit. It is my great hope that through this book and your own experiences, you'll come to understand the role that physical poses have within the larger holistic system of yoga. Then the conversation above might sound more like:

"Hey, Mary, let's go do some yoga poses today," says Steve. "Would you like to catch a yoga class with me?"

OR

"Let's go do some yoga!" Steve says to Mary.

"What type of yoga practice are you talking about?" responds Mary. They might decide to meditate, eat healthy food, discuss ways they can minimize stress in their lives, study scriptures, or go for a long walk. All of these activities are part of yoga because they integrate our body, mind, and spirit, leading to inner peace and ultimately, to connection to the infinite.

Physical Yoga and The 8-Fold Path

An appropriate place to begin our discussion about yoga poses is The 8-Fold Path from *The Yoga Sutras*, which provides the structural framework for creating physical, psychological, and spiritual health. The ultimate goal of The 8-Fold Path is to achieve a state of trans-consciousness, known as *samadhi*. Its etymology derives from *sam* ("together" or "integrated"), *a* ("toward"), and *dha* ("to get," "to hold"). Samadhi is a state of complete integration or wholeness. The highest possible state of consciousness, samadhi is existence beyond thought.

We discussed the first two steps of The 8-Fold Path in Step One, known as the restraints (*yamas*) and observances (*niyamas*), which are concerned with outward behavior. The restraints limit destructive behaviors under the cardinal theme of non-violence, while the observances cultivate positive behaviors and outlooks under the theme of purity.

The third step in The 8-Fold Path is physical yoga pose (*asana*) practice. The term *asana* originally meant the surface upon which the yogi sat or the foundation for the seated posture. Through the centuries, the meaning of this word changed and it is now synonymous with the physical poses. Yoga poses were created thousands of years ago by early Indian mystics and were derived from observing aspects of nature, including animals, natural elements, and man-made structures. Many pose names reflect this etymology such as Lion, Fish, and Cobra. Throughout the ages, the number of poses has been distilled from several hundred to eighty-four commonly practiced poses.

Yoga poses teach us how to focus and control our mind. This is a wonderful skill to develop and absolutely essential for connecting to the infinite (samadhi). However, if your life isn't healthy and balanced, no amount of yoga poses will free you from suffering. Some people have extravagant lifestyles that require them to work fifty- or sixty-hour work weeks, racing from responsibility to responsibility. At best, they do a half-hour of yoga poses to release the stress of the day. While this is a step in the right direction, they're robbing themselves of yoga's true benefits if they don't cultivate balance in the other areas of their lives. This ties into the Step One discussion about using yoga poses like a pill—it just doesn't work. In order to experience yoga's mind-body-spirit benefits, we must shift our focus from yoga poses as a magic pill to yoga poses as a tool in a wider system of holistic health wisdom and knowledge.

Yoga as a Comprehensive Physical Exercise

To expand our perspective of yoga, let's talk about the word *exercise*. In the English language, exercise is understood as a physical activity and yoga is often practiced as a form of exercise. In India, the birthplace of yoga, people view themselves through a holistic lens. In other words, they don't associate exercise with being just a physical activity. Yoga exercise includes yoga poses, but it is also expected that a yoga teacher understands other branches of yoga such as meditation, nutrition, ethical living, and study of spiritual texts. These two very different definitions of exercise reflect distinct cultural ways of perceiving human nature.

In the West, exercise is often a mindless escape evidenced by the image of zoning out at the health club. Athletes are sometimes viewed as unintelligent by the intellectual world. However, the mind-body connection is clearly evident in highly skilled athletes. For example, the physical prowess of an Olympic athlete in the height of competition reveals a mind that has been highly developed through years of practice and concentration. By the sheer requirement of the goal, the athlete learns how to harness every ounce of power. This focus and determination enables them to use the mind and body in unison for the ultimate stages of physical achievement.

As athletes approach a zone of higher consciousness within their sport, it could be said that they are approaching the goal of yoga in uniting their mental, physical, and spiritual layers into a harmonious whole. They enter a state of effortlessness where the mind, body, and spirit are in the present moment and the whole becomes greater than the sum of its parts. Athletes will lose track of time as this type of meditative mindset develops. In the book *Zen in the Art of Archery*, the Japanese Zen practice of archery holds that when all aspects are in unison, the arrow shoots itself (Herrigel and Suzuki). Many athletes report that while they have to be disciplined and practice hard, in the end they achieve greatness because of their ability to get out of their own way. There is a certain surrender required to ease into mastery.

A Yoga posture is to be steady and comfortable.
Yoga Sutras 2:46

Mastering yoga poses requires the same unison of mind, body, and spirit. While many yoga students develop great physical strength and flexibility, yoga's true accomplishment has little to do with physical ability in the poses. A student in a yoga class might be extremely flexible, but if his mind is distracted, thinking of a to-do list or competing with the person next to him, he is not truly practicing yoga. On the other hand, a focused 75-year-old woman smiling in her modified form of the Tree Pose is mastering a whole different level of a yoga pose.

From the relaxation of tension, and connection to the infinite, we experience supreme consciousness.
Yoga Sutras 2:47

Yoga does not exclude students who are inflexible or physically limited due to injury, disability, or age. Though you may experience some initial physical discomfort when you begin doing yoga poses, with consistent practice you can achieve deep relaxation and effortlessness. Correctly practiced, yoga poses help our bodies achieve a feeling of non-existence, becoming like the wide expanse of heaven and earth merged into one.

As we learn to surrender our ego, we are empowered to change the way we live. The psychological shifts in perception that occur when we are mindful in a yoga pose can change our view of the situations in life that cause us stress or suffering. With practice, both in yoga poses and in life, the external world begins to have less power over us and the internal world is more at peace.

Physical Benefits of Yoga Poses

While yoga's goal is not only physical, it does confer distinct, powerful benefits to the body. The sense of ease, peace, and well-being from practicing yoga poses results from a harmonization, revitalization, and balancing of all the systems of the body, most notably the nervous system, the musculoskeletal system, the lymphatic system, and the healthy circulation of blood, oxygen, and bio-energy. While we will discuss these benefits separately, realize that they are only achieved through a holistic, balanced approach to yoga. You must manage your stress level, get sufficient rest, and consistently eat nutritious whole foods. As you read about the specific benefits of yoga poses, try to avoid looking for one solution to a physical condition. Instead, remember that the key is to do a little bit of everything. Expect the benefits of yoga poses to develop as your overall lifestyle improves—you may continue to discover new benefits from your yoga poses years into the practice.

ENHANCED FUNCTION OF THE NERVOUS SYSTEM

We'll begin our discussion of yoga's physical benefits with the nervous system, as it controls all the other functions in the human body. The nervous system includes the brain, spinal cord, and nerves. Nerve cells, or neurons, make it possible for multiple parts of your system to communicate with one another through the brain and spinal cord. The spinal cord, located in the vertebral column down the center of the back, acts as a conduit for all the messages from the nerves to reach the brain and vice versa. If the spinal column is healthy, internal organs function not only properly but with optimum efficiency.

When the spinal column is compressed, misaligned, or impacted in some other way, challenges in the nervous system can occur. A primary reason for this is impingement on what is known as the vertebral foramen. The foramen are openings in the sides of the vertebra through which nerves extend from the spinal column to various internal and external locations in the body, including the organs. When impinged upon, messages from the spinal column to the rest of the body are disrupted, causing various physical ailments.

One of yoga's great benefits is the strengthening of the trunk or core muscles (back and stomach), enhancing the integrity of the spinal column. By developing a stronger core, overall body and organ function improves, nerve pain like sciatica is often relieved, and vertebral alignment is corrected, usually alleviating back pain. You can achieve a healthy spinal column by practicing non-fatiguing poses that control, purify, and coordinate the nervous system.

Enhanced Function of the Musculoskeletal System

The musculoskeletal system refers to the muscles, tendons, ligaments, bones, joints, and associated tissues that move the body and maintain its form. These structures help you to balance your body, twist, bend, turn upside down, rest, move, and breathe. When your musculoskeletal system is strong and flexible, your body is able to perform at its best. Yoga asanas limber the body's tissues in a way that builds strength from the inside out, a metaphor for the overall effect of yoga practice but also an essential factor in preventing injury.

The nervous system and musculoskeletal system are intimately related, with the former playing a pivotal role in causing muscles to relax or tighten up, either permitting or limiting stretching. The length of muscles fibers is increased through prolonged stretching and decreased as a result of inactivity. It is nerve impulses that cause muscle or tissue cells to stretch, move, contract, and relax. The more nerve impulses that are acting on the muscle, the more muscle fibers will contract and pull on the tendons. Fewer impulses result in less contraction of the muscle fibers and less tension on the tendons. If the nerve impulses are minimal, the muscle relaxes.

The coordination of nerves and the impact they have on the muscles is what allows us to move through postures, simultaneously tightening and relaxing a variety of muscle groups. In Corpse Pose, the goal is to decrease the number of impulses to the muscles in order to maintain a relaxed position. In the Tree Pose, on the other hand, there is simultaneous increase in the number of nerve impulses to the legs, and a decrease in the number of impulses to the shoulders in order for them to relax while the arms are raised overhead and clasped to complete the pose.

Yoga poses are very effective at stretching and relaxing the opposing pairs of muscles along the spine, and the poses naturally adjust the vertebrae. This stretching relieves the pressure on the spinal nerves and aids circulation (toning the capillaries and their end organs). Ultimately, improved muscle strength and flexibility leads to an increase in the size and efficiency of the controlling nerve cells in the spinal cord and brain. A complete yoga practice exercises the body in such a way that every part of the body, even the smallest ductless gland, receives the daily attention it needs in order to function properly.

ENHANCED FUNCTION OF THE DIGESTIVE SYSTEM

Yoga poses are very helpful in maintaining a healthy digestive system. Let's discuss the digestive system, what it does, how it interacts with the nervous system, and how it is affected by yoga. Simply put, the digestive system is responsible for breaking down food into nutrients that the body uses for its various functions, turning nutrients into energy for those functions, and eliminating waste that our body doesn't need. The process of digestion occurs from the moment we eat something to the moment that it is eliminated, and it involves several important stages.

Nerves signal internal organs in the same way they signal muscles. In particular, one of the motor divisions of the nervous system, known as the parasympathetic nervous system, is very important in digestive function. The opposite of the sympathetic nervous system, the parasympathetic system creates the internal conditions required for sleep, rest, and digestion. When the nervous system relaxes, the parasympathetic nervous system is able to dominate the sympathetic nervous system. The sympathetic nervous system is often characterized by the "fight or flight" response because it is through this mechanism that the body is able to react in a powerful way when faced with an extreme stressor. All the body's blood is pumped to the muscles so that we can fight and defend ourselves from imminent danger or death.

In the modern world, our bodies frequently kick in to the fight-or-flight mode even though we are not usually fighting for our lives. We perceive a variety of stressors in daily life that range from work situations to financial concerns to the care of our families and loved ones. Being in a constant state of "high alert" is not healthy—it creates toxicity and tension in the body, which over time takes a significant toll on our health.

The parasympathetic nervous system, alternately, enables us to relax, digest, sleep, and think beyond mere survival. Yoga asanas help the parasympathetic nervous system to function well. As a result, we digest our food better, assimilate nutrients in a way that the body can absorb them, and effectively eliminate toxins from the body.

As you move the body through various poses, gentle pressure is placed on the internal organs, increasing blood circulation within and through the organs. For example, in the Posterior Stretch Pose, the internal organs are compressed and massaged, enhancing their overall functioning. Another example of this principle is in the practice of the Root Lock (see Step Eight), which is the contraction of the muscles of the pelvic cavity. In this pose, the body does not appear to move; however there is an internal contraction of the pelvic floor that impacts the organs located in that area of the body. In typical exercise, such as running or biking, blood tends to be diverted away from the internal organs. Yoga does not deprive the organs of their normal blood supply, but actually increases blood flow to them. This increased supply of blood is richer in quality due to increased respiratory activity.

Enhanced Function of the Circulatory, Immune, Respiratory, Endocrine, and Cardiovascular Systems

As mentioned earlier, yoga positively impacts every function of the human body. One of the key components of yoga's benefits is that all parts of the body are enhanced simultaneously. An example of this can be seen in the circulatory, respiratory, and cardiovascular systems. Yoga gently enhances blood flow to muscles and internal organs, while deep, rhythmic breathing oxygenates the blood, coordinating metabolism and preventing fatigue. Respiration is actually a form of cardiovascular exercise when practiced in this manner, but without strain. All of the other systems of the body receive tremendous benefit from the increased oxygen in the blood.

Yoga poses that gently compress the internal organs assist in the function of the lymphatic system, an important part of immune system health. Lymph nodes remove waste matter and bacteria from your tissues, which is eliminated by a clear fluid known as lymph. Through compression in yoga poses, lymph flow is increased, improving immune function and making us less susceptible to illness.

As for the endocrine (gland) system, the study of the glands and the production of hormones is not fully established in the scientific field. I can't say that a specific yoga pose helps the thyroid gland, for example, because current research has not demonstrated this to be the case. However, many people who start practicing yoga alter their lifestyle in holistic ways and find that their bodies simply function better as a result. It may be true that an inversion pose like Shoulder Stand, where the feet are elevated above the heart, promotes extra blood flow to the brain, thereby helping the pituitary, pineal, and thyroid glands. As research continues, we'll likely discover more about yoga's benefits on the endocrine system.

Many of the comprehensive health benefits of yoga have been scientifically proven to be effective; most recently, the ability to reverse or lessen the effects of coronary artery disease. Positive effects have been seen as a result of improved nutrition and changes in diet, but are also strongly correlated with adherence to stress management techniques that rely heavily on yoga practices, including gentle stretching, breathing exercises, and meditation, along with group support, imagery, and the healthy expression of emotions.

Enhanced Mental Function and Emotional Health

As I've stated earlier, the physical practice of yoga poses is an important key to creating emotional well-being and a sharp, focused mind. The purpose of yoga poses is to release the physical blocks that interact psychosomatically through the body to the mind. As the body strengthens and relaxes, the mind becomes more balanced.

For many of us, emotional stress causes tension in the upper back, neck, and shoulders. When stress is reduced, tight muscles relax. Stress can be addressed in two ways. The first is by changing your perception of the situation that is stressing you out. A good example of this can be seen in Prayer Pose, where the mind is focused on creating harmony and balance, thereby reducing stress. In this state, the nervous system is relaxed and the frontal lobe of the brain is activated. The frontal lobe is the part of the brain that holds consciousness and the capacity for higher awareness. As a result of increased frontal lobe activity, mental concentration and memory are improved.

The second way of reducing stress is to physically relax the body. In meditative or restorative poses, the muscles relax, releasing built-up stress from the body. In this way, we can alleviate emotional stress through physical means, and at the same time alleviate the physical symptoms that the stress is causing.

Alignment in Yoga Poses

As we've just learned, there are many physical benefits of yoga poses. The poses strengthen and stretch our muscles, and tone and purify every element of the human body. In order to realize these benefits and enjoy a safe yoga practice, you must properly align your body in the poses. I can't emphasize this enough! Misalignment of the spine can affect the cervical spine (within the neck), thoracic spine (upper back), lumbar spine (lower back), pelvis, hips, and legs. You can actually do yourself more harm than good if you're not practicing correct physical alignment.

So how exactly do you go about learning physical alignment? Go to a yoga class! As I mentioned earlier, no instruction this book offers should replace the experience of learning yoga poses from a well-trained instructor. It's challenging enough to learn proper alignment from a teacher. Trying to learn yoga pose alignment from a book without real-life application will thwart your progress. Not only is learning alignment easiest in the classroom setting, everyone's body is different: an arched lumbar spine may be a misalignment in one person while it is a natural body curve in another. A good yoga teacher can notice these differences and will provide you with consistent and accurate guidance on alignment in each pose.

Typical alignment instruction in a yoga pose focuses on where or how the body is positioned, but this is only one part of alignment. True alignment begins with your intention and attitude, as discussed in Steps One and Two. If your intention is to exercise or strive to perfect a pose beyond your ability, your alignment will be skewed by pride or over-striving. If your attitude is not aligned with the yoga pose, you won't perform it correctly. This will cause stress to the nervous system as the ego forces something to happen, while the pose may not be intended to do that. In a pose, remember to use correct physical form but also to think beyond physical alignment to mental and spiritual alignment as well. Again, we're seeking to practice yoga holistically, and this requires exploring the non-physical aspects of yoga that we may not be as familiar or comfortable with.

An example is the gymnast or ballet dancer who is very flexible on the exterior and may appear to be perfectly aligned in a yoga pose. But "perfect" alignment also includes the ability to relax in a pose, breathe properly, understand the archetype or deeper meaning of the pose, have a clear spiritual intention, mentally focus, and remain open to self-discovery while in the pose. Can anyone really boast a *perfect* yoga pose? The alignment process is different every day, because *you* are different every day. Some days you may be motivated and energetic, while other days you may feel like you're running on half-empty. What it takes to be in alignment one day will not be the same the next day. When explored with this understanding, pose practice is fresh and inspired and every day is a new experience.

If you're the type of person who likes to practice very strenuous types of yoga as a way of building muscle endurance, you probably have a lot to learn about yoga as a holistic practice. But take heart, because you also have a lot to gain. There is nothing inherently wrong about vigorous types of yoga; however, they often don't adequately address the psycho-spiritual aspects of yoga. I think you'll find as you explore yoga from a holistic perspective, your experience of yoga and your life will take on a rich new dimension.

The following instructions are organized according to the general categories of yoga poses from the point of view of how these poses affect the human body. After a section on balance, we will cover the five directions in which the spine moves: upward, forward, backward, sideward, and twisting. We'll learn about poses that focus on extremities (arms and legs), and finally inversions, the poses that raise the feet above the heart, or lower the head below the heart.

Note: Every school of yoga has its own particular approach to yoga poses. Invariably, some of our instructions may challenge what you have learned in class. If we're saying something different from what your teacher has shown you, recognize that your teacher's instructions are probably also correct within the system of yoga studied. Feel free to discuss these points with your teacher and practice the version of a yoga pose that feels right for your body.

BALANCE POSES

Attitude alignment: How does posture and the ability to balance reflect your current state of body, mind, and spirit?

Postural alignment:
- Sensation of being grounded through all parts of the foot/feet
- Bend knees slightly (not visibly) so as not to hyperextend
- Slightly tuck tailbone (like you have a heavy tail)
- Release muscles around the root of the spine
- Engage belly/core muscles
- Breathe fully and freely (yogic three-part breath, see Step Four)
- Relax shoulders, arms, and hands
- Round shoulders slightly back (stick out chest/open the heart)
- Lengthen spine upward (stand tall)
- Practice against wall to feel back of head aligned with shoulder blades and tailbone
- Relax face muscles; smile gently

Common problems:
- Head forward
- Shoulders hunched
- Leaning of the spine in any direction
- Tailbone over-tucked
- Feet or hips not aligned
- Knees hyperextended

Specific benefits:
- Corrects postural misalignment before entering more complex standing postures

- Increases awareness of body, including tension patterns, weaknesses, or imbalances
- Focus on balance instantly quiets the mind
- Begins to connect the mind and body via the breath
- Builds strength in the legs and core muscles of the body

Cautions:
- Be careful of losing balance; if it is difficult for you to balance in a standing pose, use a wall or chair for assistance

CONNECTING TO THE POSES
Balance

UPWARD POSES

Attitude alignment: Reaching to the highest potential or devotion. As you are reaching, what are you doing with your mind? What is holding you back from reaching? Are you trying too hard? Do you have faith?

Postural alignment:
- Reach and lengthen arms while relaxing the shoulders
- Open the heart by bringing the shoulder blades together in the back—this helps bring upper arms closer to the ears
- Don't hold the breath, except when consciously practicing breath retention
- Coordinate movement with breath
- Balance over feet
- Importance of focus (third eye)

Common problems:
- Arms in front of body
- Head forward
- Shoulders, arms, and hands tense

Specific benefits:
- Decreases crowding of organs and compression of spine, and relieves congestion of spinal nerves
- Full body stretch strengthens the thoracic, lower abdomen, and skeletal muscles
- Strengthens ankles and calves
- Tones muscles
- Improves balance and coordination of muscle activity
- Builds limberness in shoulders
- Strengthens the nervous and endocrine systems
- Improves circulation, digestion (stretches intestines), and heart function

Cautions:
- Try not to exert too much effort
- Remember to breathe

CONNECTING TO THE POSES
Upward
PALM TREE POSE, PAGE 262

Forward Poses

Attitude alignment: Surrender, release, and letting go. What can you let go of?

Postural alignment:
- Bend forward from the hips
- Bend knees as a modification
- Come forward with a long back with neutral curvature as far as hip flexibility will allow
- Surrender (completely relax) the head, neck, face muscles, shoulders, arms, and hands

Common problems:
- Overexerting with rounded back rather than maintaining spinal alignment and modifying the pose, often due to lack of hip flexibility. The main impediments to hip flexibility are the hamstrings and thigh abductors, muscles that draw the body back in from an outstretched position. So, continual stretching of (or releasing) these muscles in poses like high or low lunge, Warrior I, or Pigeon Pose can help prepare you for forward bends.
- Holding tension in the head and neck, not fully relaxing

Specific benefits:
- Tones muscles of neck, spine, and abdominal walls
- Tones pelvic organs by compression
- Deep intra-abdominal compression stimulates proper elimination of waste from colon and relieves constipation
- Increases blood flow to and from sex organs
- Develops sacroiliac, hip, waist, and lumbar flexibility
- Stretches shoulders and back, as well as hamstring, glutei, and psoas muscles

- Stretches posterior muscles of the trunk and neck, contributes to muscle tone and venous circulation in spinal column
- Corrects curvature of the spine and faulty posture
- Increases clavicular breathing (especially advantageous for women, who have smaller lung capacity than men)

Cautions:
- Those with acute lower back pain may wish to avoid forward poses, as they may aggravate that condition
- Be careful not to overdo it to the point of strain, pain, or fatigue
- Those without good hip flexibility should be particularly cautious. I suggest using blocks to help you practice forward bends in a safe way (ask your teacher to demonstrate). Poor hip flexibility causes people to bend from the lower back, which compresses the vertebral column, stresses intervertebral disks, and strains ligaments from the sacrum to the head.

CONNECTING TO THE POSES
Forward
WHEEL POSE, PAGE 264
SEATED FORWARD BEND, PAGE 266
CHILD'S POSE, PAGE 268

BACKWARD POSES

Attitude alignment: Vigor, fortitude, courage, achievement, self-reliance, and power. How do you express your vitality?

Postural alignment:
- If standing (e.g., Wheel), do not move your pelvis (this will injure the lower back); instead, hinge from the waist up

- Open heart and tilt top of pelvis / sacrum forward (stick butt out), arching the back rather than leaning back, which would strain the lower back
- Inhale when coming into a backward bend
- Make modifications until core strength is developed

Common problems:
- On an emotional level, there may be a fear of opening up the heart, which can create fear of the pose itself
- Hyperextension of the back, which can include compression of the neck, is to be avoided, especially while using the arms in a position, such as the Upward Dog, where the strength of the arms can push the back beyond its capacity. Practice with awareness of your spine's natural curvature and be sure not to collapse the back of your neck.

Specific benefits:
- Stimulates the sympathetic nervous system
- Stretches and massages muscles of the abdomen and pelvis
- Tones and strengthens the muscles that control the spine
- Tones spinal nerves
- Improves circulation by bringing fresh blood via compression of the ovaries, stomach, pancreas, bladder, appendix, urinary tract, etc.
- Corrects postural and neuromuscular imbalances of the vertebral spine
- Enhances emotional well-being and vigor
- Increases confidence and helps you to embrace life and face fears

Cautions:
- When standing, be careful not to lose balance

- Practice backbends with caution during menstruation, pregnancy, and times of fertility
- Injury tends to occur when coming in and out of the pose, so take caution and move slowly
- Those who are more flexible may overestimate their strength and risk injury

CONNECTING TO THE POSES
Backward

Cat/Cow combination, page 270

Cobra Pose, page 272

Bow Pose, page 274

Sideward Poses

Attitude alignment: Flexibility, awareness, knowledge. Do you recognize limits while being flexible?

Postural alignment:
- If standing, keep body in the vertical plane (as though standing between two sheets of glass, or as if standing against a wall) without letting the body come forward or backward, or twisting
- Use moderation in sideward movement, bend sideward only as far as you need to in order to feel the stretch in the spine
- Muscles contract on one side and stretch on the other

Common problems:
- In order to reach farther, people shift their pelvis, or let one hip move forward or backward, changing the sideward bend into a forward or twisting pose
- Bending beyond the strength of the core muscles can cause the pelvis and hips to shift and cause further misalignment that strains the body

Specific benefits:

- Promotes elasticity of muscles

- Balances right/left postural muscles

- Strengthens abdominal and pelvic viscera

- Bends the spine in a direction that is not common in daily use

Cautions:

- Injury is more frequent if one does not have the core strength prior to trying a more advanced sideward bend (like Triangle Pose) and then pushes oneself too far

CONNECTING TO THE POSES
Sideward

Triangle Pose, page 276

Extended Side Angle, page 278

Twist Poses

Attitude alignment: Openness, insight, seeing a new perspective or approach, and untying the tangled knots of life.

Postural alignment:

- Twist from the core muscles

- Come into the twist in three parts—core, upper chest/shoulders, and the head/neck

- Maintain erect spine while twisting

- Relax forehead, jaw, and any other muscles not required of the twist pose

Common problems:

- Twisting from the shoulders, but not from the lumbar spine

- Spine hunches forward

- Neck tension can limit ability to twist fully
- Shoulders tense
- Head comes forward

Specific benefits:
- Exercises the muscles that support the spine
- Makes spinal column more flexible
- Stimulates spinal nerves
- Stretches abdominal muscles, alternately compressing and stretching them
- Enhances *pranic* (energy) flow around navel
- Nourishes digestive organs, rejuvenating tissues and alleviating digestive disorders
- Regulates secretion of adrenaline and bile
- Wrings out toxins from the body
- Relieves sinusitis, hay fever, bronchitis, constipation, colitis, menstrual disorders, UTIs, and cervical spondylitis
- Assists alignment of back and improves rounded shoulders

Cautions:
- Avoid if pregnant more than 2 or 3 months, or with peptic ulcer, hernia, or hypothyroidism
- Take great care if you have a slipped disc or sciatica
- Move slowly in and out of the twist and maintain body awareness

CONNECTING TO THE POSES
Twist

PARTIAL SEATED TWIST, PAGE 280

SUPINE TWIST, PAGE 282

Extremities Poses

Attitude alignment: Self-reliance, knowledge, awareness, wisdom, under-standing, self-inquiry, consciousness, and balance.

Postural alignment:

- Maintain upright alignment of the spine
- Move the extremities to the best of your ability

Common problems:

- Lack of mobility due to long-held tension in shoulders, calves, ankles, and/or hips
- Tendency for shoulders, spine, and head to round forward

Specific benefits:

- Awareness of our arms, hands, legs, and feet
- Through increased body awareness, you develop the ability to detect and release tension in the body

Cautions:

- Modify for weakness or injuries in shoulders, knees, or wrists (ask your yoga teacher for modification suggestions)

CONNECTING TO THE POSES
Extremities

BUTTERFLY POSE, PAGE 284

PIGEON POSE, PAGE 286

WARRIOR I, PAGE 288

Inversion Poses

Attitude alignment: Going within, seeing the world from a different perspective. Are you able to relate to yourself outside of your ego? Focus on love, surrender, wisdom, or union.

Postural alignment:
- Practice inversions in stages, beginning with gentle poses like the bridge or a simple inversion
- Modifications include supporting the back/hips with the arms and hands or practicing against a wall
- The full weight of the body in a modified inversion (Shoulder Stand) should initially be on the upper back, supported by the arms and hands. As one develops strength and balance, and moves into a full Shoulder Stand, the weight of the body moves to the shoulders and back of neck. At this point the hands can move toward the floor and support the upper back.

Common problems:
- Difficulty lifting or rolling hips off the floor
- Lack of upper body strength and balance

Specific benefits:
- Improves posture by relieving pressure in spinal nerves
- Increases circulation to spinal cord, head, and brain
- Tones internal organs due to nerve stimulation
- Improves health of the nervous system
- Benefits digestive system and the reproductive organs
- Increases deep venous circulation of the abdomen, pelvis, and organs, which is essential for health
- Tones glandular system
- Tones muscles supporting the spine
- Stimulates thyroid and parathyroid glands

- Improves eyesight, breathing, circulation, fatigue, and sexual function

Cautions:

- Avoid strain in these head-low postures

- Poses are best explored in phases—practice less strenuous variations of the poses and work your way toward the more challenging variations. For inversions, this might mean elevating the legs only and once you have become stronger in the pose, elevating the torso as well.

- Avoid turning head from side to side once in the posture and avoid excessive pressure on base of neck

- Practice beginner inversion if pregnant or menstruating

- Those with heart and lung disease, high blood pressure, prolapsed uterus, hernia, eye conditions including cataracts and glaucoma, and spine and neck problems should use caution in inverted poses

- Best on an empty stomach, after eliminating bowels

CONNECTING TO THE POSES
Inversion

DOWNWARD DOG, PAGE 290

SHOULDER STAND (FULL OR MODIFIED), PAGE 292

PLOUGH, PAGE 294

Nomenclature of Yoga Poses

The *Hatha Yoga Pradipika*, a fourteenth-century authoritative text describes yoga poses and illustrates eighty-four yoga poses, the names of which are agreed upon by most yoga schools. Each pose has numerous variations that often involve a different hand or foot position, altering the precise experience of a pose. Over the centuries, hundreds of yoga schools have developed, each of them crafting and teaching different varieties of poses and sequences. In this context, it is easy to see why there are so many types of yoga as well as variations of the poses. All of this is to say that the names attributed to poses in this book may not correspond to the names or poses from your local school. Though this text contains just twenty-three yoga poses, the knowledge that you will gain from it will work with any yoga pose from any tradition.

One of the main purposes of this book is to empower you to discover and own your personal yoga practice. With the plurality of yoga traditions offering conflicting instructions, we hope that you can listen, learn, and decide for your body. We think that all instructions are true for some people. The way to understand your yoga pose experience is to experiment with the type of practices that suit your body.

Connecting to the Infinite

The first two steps of The 8-Fold Path begin with lifestyle suggestions; the third step has to do with physical yoga poses, as discussed above. Next we will discuss Step Four, which develops postural alignment in connection with breathing, pranayama.

EXERCISES

1. List the desired time, duration, and place for your yoga practice. Remember to consider your lifestyle and be reasonable about what you can truly do.

2. List ways in which you can help yourself stay committed like practicing with a friend or joining a weekly yoga class. Perhaps you can treat yourself to a smoothie at a café after class or purchase an eco-mat with an artistic design that inspires you to practice. Think creatively about how you can stay focused on your practice. And have fun!

3. If you are a beginner student, find a local yoga class to attend. If this is not a possibility, use an instructional video to aid your practice. If you are in a class, ask your instructor to give you feedback on your physical alignment. Most teachers give feedback to their students as part of the instruction, but always speak up for individualized attention. Regardless of your level of experience, invigorate your life with the support of your local yoga community. If one doesn't exist in your area, create it yourself!

STEP FOUR

Breathing

Pranayama

The breath is a bridge to divine consciousness.

An old yoga story describes a discussion between Sight, Hearing, Smell, Taste, Touch, and Breath, about which one was most important. One of them said, "Let's see which one humans can live without!" So, Sight left, and the group realized that in fact humans could live without their sense of sight. Then Hearing left, and once again they realized Hearing was not the most important. Taste, Smell, and Touch took their turns, only to discover they were not essential for the human experience. When Breath left, however, the human being could no longer live.

Breath awareness is perhaps the most valuable tool we gain from yoga. We are not taught how to breathe properly in our culture and as a result, our breath is often restricted by habitual stress responses over time. Being aware of the breath helps us to reduce stress, sleep better, feel healthier, and be our best Self! Breathing exercises improve our physical, mental, and spiritual vitality, and when practiced properly, can also enhance the practice of yoga poses.

Understanding Bio-energy or Life Force

In yoga philosophy, it is believed that breath is the vehicle for *prana*. The root word of *prana* is *an* which means "to breathe." All cultural traditions of the world describe the breath in a spiritual manner because breath gives life, as witnessed by a baby's first breath. The Chinese concept of *chi* is often compared to prana, referring to life force or all-pervading energy of the universe. Prana can perhaps best be understood as a combination of energy and breath.

Ancient yogis studied prana in tremendous detail and discovered three major channels of energy in the body along which prana flows called *nadis*. This is first noted in the early eighteenth-century text, the *Shiva Samhita*. The nadis include the left channel (*ida*), the right channel (*pingala*), and the central channel (*sushumna*). The left channel begins at the base of the spine and exits out the left nostril when you breathe. The right channel does the same, but exits out the right nostril instead of the left. If you pay attention to your breath, you will notice that sometimes one nostril is more open, or predominant, than the other. This is called the infradian rhythm and it naturally alternates every one and a half to two hours throughout the course of the day.

Sometimes the nostrils are open equally, signifying that the central channel is open. In this state, the mind and body are in balance and the energy of the body flows freely, often between four and five in the morning. This is the common time of day chosen for meditation, as the senses tend to be less affected by the external world and the endless stream of thoughts from the unconscious mind slows considerably. The three channels wind up and intersect along the spinal column and the intersections are known as energetic power centers called *chakras* (see Step Six). The chakras highlight the connection between the breath and the subtle energies that flow throughout the entire nervous system.

We all have a pranic (energy) field that surrounds us; in scientific terms this is recognized as a measurable electromagnetic field. Yoga poses strengthen the vertebral column and the trunk of the body, improving the function of the central energetic channel. As we develop body awareness, we may begin to notice the subtle flow of energy during a yoga pose. Once we recognize the flow of energy, we can consciously direct it, helping us to achieve greater health.

The Roots of Breathing Exercises

The fourth step of The 8-Fold Path of Yoga relates to breath, specifically to regulating inhalation and exhalation. It is known as *pranayama; prana* meaning life force energy (closely related to the breath) and *yama* relating to control, restraint, or regulation. The yogis discovered that the breath is one of the few involuntary processes in the body that can also be consciously controlled. *Pranayama*, therefore, refers to the conscious control of the breath, with the intention of affecting the life force.

In the English language, the words *inhalation* and *exhalation* both come from the same derivative *hale*. It is interesting to note that *hale* is also the same root for the words *whole* and *heal*. Another word used to describe inhalation is *inspiration*. Not only does the word *inspiration* typically refer to feeling inspired, the root *spirit* is the foundation of the word *inspiration*. It is no wonder that the concepts of breath and spirit are linked in many different cultures.

The Sheaths (*Koshas*)

Yoga's philosophy of breath can be better understood by studying the *koshas,* or sheaths. As presented in the ancient Sanskrit text the *Upanishads*, the sheaths demonstrate that each level of consciousness, or layer of being, is guided by a subtler counterpart. The outermost sheath is made up of matter, or the physical body. The physical body changes significantly over time as we age. We come to realize that we are more than just physical manifestation. Within the body sheath, and slightly more subtle, is the prana, or breath. The body affects the breath and the breath can affect the body. By developing conscious breathing practices, we can influence this subtle relationship; this is the fundamental reason that we study pranayama today. When we breathe deeply into the diaphragm, the body relaxes and lets go of stress; when breathing is rapid and shallow, the body becomes tense.

Within the prana sheath, and even more subtle, are our emotional responses to external situations. When we are frightened, we gasp for breath or stop breathing altogether. The body becomes very tense. When we cry heavily, breath comes in short spurts and the body quivers. When we are content, the breath is deep and slow, and the body is relaxed. These heightened states of emotion have profound effects on breathing, in turn affecting the physical body. Even more subtle than the emotions is the intellect. This is the higher Self, the voice of wisdom that says "Yes, I'm feeling sad, but this too shall pass." When we are connected to our true Self, the breath is more likely to be peaceful regardless of emotional or external circumstances. Finally, the most subtle of all the sheaths is the bliss sheath, the state of universal consciousness through which we are connected to all beings.

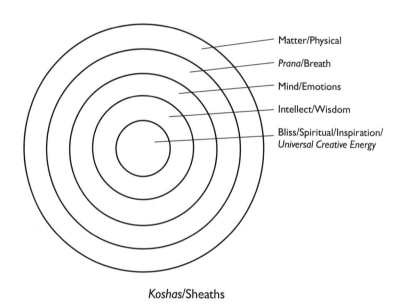

Koshas/Sheaths

Through conscious direction of the breath, we can connect the various aspects, or sheaths, of our being, from the physical plane through to universal consciousness. Conscious breath control can transform you at every level, supporting total health and vitality. By correlation, the breath is a reflection of the spiritual self, mind, emotions, and body. It is reported that ancient yogis could read the mind of a person just by observing their breath! The yogis noted people who were vital, healthy, and long-lived, only to find that those with the most vitality knew how to breathe slowly and deeply. They also noticed that animals with a slow deep breath, such as the elephant or tortoise, had long life spans. Animals with short, rapid breathing patterns such as a mouse or insect, lived relatively short lives. In yoga, there is a saying that we are given a certain number of breaths in life and in order to live to an old age we have to be sure to make each breath last as long as possible!

Benefits of Breath Control

Note: The information about pranayama is extensive and in order to truly master it, long-term, structured study with a yoga teacher is required.

In regards to physical health, modern scientists are now rediscovering truths about breathing that yoga has known for more than four centuries. Inhalation and exhalation are the mechanisms used to draw oxygen to the lungs and expel the waste product of carbon dioxide. Conscious deep breathing develops the respiratory organs and aids in the circulation of blood.

Diaphragmatic breathing (see page 84) enables more oxygen to enter the body because it reaches the lowest part of the lungs, where most of the blood vessels for absorbing the oxygen and transmitting it throughout the body are located. When we are stressed out, we primarily breathe into the upper

Breathing
↕
Increased Oxygen
↕
Increased Vitality and Function

chest, limiting oxygen metabolism. Increased oxygen metabolism helps the body metabolize food and produce energy.

Another benefit to breathing into the lower portion of the lungs is the gentle intra-abdominal compression that results from inhaling and exhaling. As the stomach expands on the inhale and contracts on the exhale, the internal organs are massaged. This massage increases blood flow in and around the organs, energizing the cells with vital oxygen. This increases the health and vitality of the digestive, reproductive, and eliminatory organs, as well as adrenal glands (which regulate hormone balance) and the lymphatic system (which cleanses the body via muscular contraction and relaxation).

The slowing down and deepening of the breath has three positive benefits: First, your lungs can only absorb a certain amount of oxygen in any given moment. The tiny air sacs of the lungs, known as alveoli, absorb oxygen like a dry sponge soaking up water—it takes a few moments to absorb everything. A slow inhale allows for maximum absorption. Second, the heart rate decreases with a slow exhale, reducing the amount of work the heart has to do. Finally, breathing slowly calms the nervous system. When the nervous system is relaxed, the digestive system functions better and sleep, relaxation, and peace of mind come more easily.

The psychological benefits of pranayama are significant. You can automatically shift your emotional response to situations by changing your breath to a slower and deeper pattern. Deep breathing can calm your mind and alleviate stress. The old adage of taking ten breaths before responding in anger is wise advice! Ultimately, the breath anchors and steadies the mind.

Breathing
↕
Relaxed Nervous System
↕
Balanced Mind

Pranayama relaxes the nervous system and enables the frontal lobe of the brain to function, thereby increasing the capacity for higher consciousness and reasoning. Typically, the sympathetic nervous system is activated in order to prepare us to fight the situation when we are under stress or in some kind of emotional imbalance. All of our blood (and therefore oxygen) is sent to the muscles in preparation for battle. If we learn to practice relaxed breathing in these situations, we can enjoy greater connection to the higher Self, our source of inner wisdom. Where the mind goes, the breath follows. And yet the opposite is true as well. Rather than be ruled by anxiety or stress, we can learn to be calm in challenging circumstances through breath regulation.

Remember that the breath is not a cure-all, but rather an essential element of the yoga lifestyle. Breathing is the most common focal point used in meditation techniques across cultures and traditions. It is a way of training the mind to become still, which must occur if we are to achieve the highest states of consciousness.

Breathing
↕
Clarity of Thought
↕
Connection to Higher Self

Focusing on the breath, however, is no easy task! It is said that the average mind can focus for about 3.5 seconds before wandering to another thought or sensation. Most people have never experienced a moment of their mind being truly still. If this includes you, that's okay! You have a lot to look forward to. It is this state of stillness or a quiet mind that invokes the words *nirvana, bliss, ecstasy, union, oneness,* and countless other explanations for the highest states of consciousness reached through yoga.

In its essence, breathing is an act of both giving and receiving. Experienced as such, the breath connects us to every other living being on the planet. As we inhale, we receive the gift of life through oxygen and prana. Without this gift we would be dead in a matter of minutes. As we exhale,

Breathing
↕
Still Mind
↕
Union with Higher Consciousness

we return the gift to the universe in the form of carbon dioxide, without which the plants on earth would die. The breath can also be viewed as a metaphor for letting go. Holding on to the breath creates suffering in a matter of twenty or thirty seconds! So the simple act of breathing, when we are tuned in to it, has a great capacity for peace and well-being.

Breathing Exercises

The breathing exercises listed here are adapted from the yoga program at The Yoga Institute of Mumbai, India, in part due to the simplicity of the exercises. The field of yoga at large offers hundreds of breathing exercises that combine elements of the exercises listed below. Like most aspects of yoga, years of study reveal subtle lessons.

Please use caution when doing breathing exercises. It is fine to be aware of normal breathing throughout the day, but avoid practicing more than thirty rounds of breathing exercises (a round equals one inhale and one exhale), two times per day. The lungs, like every other system of the body, require time to improve. Furthermore, your heart rate is accustomed to your breathing pattern, and abrupt changes can strain the heart and disrupt other systems of the body. Allow three to six months of gradual daily practice to reach a slow, easy breath. What you will probably discover is that as your emotional state of mind balances through holistic yoga practice, your breath will deepen.

As with other yoga practices, intention in breathing exercises is important. Think about the unconscious thought that is absorbed with each breath. If breathing is rushed, we absorb a disturbed intention. When breathing is consciously regulated, we align our personal intention with each breath. As you experiment with the exercises below, notice how at first your mind is busy with learning the exercise, but, once you are in a rhythm, the mind has a tendency to wander. At this stage, it will help your concentration significantly if you align the breath with the inspiring personal intention that you chose during Step One.

Natural Breath Observation

Many people have little experience with observing their breath, so exploring it can be a profound experience. Begin by closing your eyes and simply observe your breath flow in and out of your nose. Nostril breathing (with the mouth relaxed and closed) is recommended because the nose filters and warms the air before it reaches the lungs. Breathing through the nasal passages also tones and balances the mucous membranes. Breathing through the mouth can irritate the throat. If you're unable to breathe in through the nose, inhale through the mouth and out through the nose only, if possible.

> At a breath of two seconds in and two seconds out, we breathe about 21,600 breaths per day. How many of these breaths are we aware of?

Breathing Observation Points

- What does it feel like to observe your breath?
- Can you feel the physical sensation of the breath in and out of the nose?
- Is the temperature warm or cool?
- Is the breath slow or rapid?
- Is it smooth or bumpy?
- Is your breath restricted and, if so, where?
- Which part of your body moves when you breathe? This will show you which part of the lungs you are using.
- Do you hold your breath after inhalation or pause after exhalation?
- Does the force of the breath stay consistent, or is it stronger at the beginning of the cycle?
- Is your breath longer on inhalation or exhalation, or is it even?

For the next few days, pay attention to your breathing for five minutes a day, becoming more familiar and intimate with your natural breath. This will help you develop awareness of your breathing patterns and begin using the breath as a tool for developing physical, mental, and spiritual well-being.

DIAPHRAGMATIC BREATHING

Breathing into the stomach can seem like an unnatural thing to do when you are accustomed to breathing into the upper chest. When babies breathe, their stomachs rise and fall with their breath—this is the original state of breathing we are all born with. Restrictions in breathing develop over time, usually due to stress. The technique of **diaphragmatic breathing** is a practice of re-learning the natural breath. It may feel difficult at first. *Please remember not to force this breath, but allow it.* It is very important to learn how to practice breathing in a slow, deep, relaxed fashion before approaching the different breathing techniques.

Diaphragmatic breathing is new for most adults and requires both relaxation as well as the development of some of the lesser-used abdominal muscles. Many people hold tension in the belly without even realizing it. This may have to do with the habit of sucking in the stomach to look thin. And it can also involve repressed emotions that get stored in the muscles and energetic system. Letting go of the stomach muscles might mean losing emotional control. Be aware while practicing pranayama (and yoga poses, as they also involve breathing regulation) that emotional release can occur as the muscles in the stomach relax. For this reason, it's suggested to practice pranayama in a safe, undisturbed environment.

It is easiest to practice diaphragmatic breathing while lying on your back on the floor, knees bent, arms relaxed at your side, eyes closed. Place one hand on your stomach and one hand on your upper chest. Keep the hand on the chest still, while you notice the hand on your stomach rise and fall. Breathe into the stomach, allowing the muscles to relax and expand as you inhale. With the exhale, pull the stomach back toward the spine, creating a concave feeling, or a feeling of sucking in or compressing the stomach. You might imagine pulling the navel in and up under your rib cage. Feel the stomach fill with air again and then release. Using the image of a balloon inflating and deflating can be very helpful. This should be a very comfortable exercise. If the floor is not comfortable, you can also practice sitting in a chair or crossed legged on the floor. When in a seated position, sitting with a straight spine is best. If your spine rounds, sit on a blanket or pillow to tilt your pelvis forward, which will naturally straighten your spine.

Though you're concentrating on breathing into the stomach, you are not actually breathing into the stomach, but into the lower lungs. At this point, it's helpful to know a bit about the relationship between the lungs and the diaphragm. The diaphragm is a large umbrella-shaped muscle between your abdomen and rib cage that assists the lungs in breathing. As you inhale, the diaphragm is pushed down and the lungs fill with air, causing the abdominal organs to push downward and the abdomen to bulge forward. As you exhale, the abdominal wall contracts and pushes the abdominal organs upward against a relaxed diaphragm, compressing and emptying the lungs.

Just starting out, I recommend ten rounds diaphragmatic breathing as beginners practice. For the first couple of rounds, simply count the length of your inhalation and exhalation. Then gently slow your breath down. Try to make the count even for both (for example, five seconds on the inhale and five seconds on the exhale). Start with a count of three to five seconds and work your way up one second per week to five to ten seconds and beyond as it is comfortable.

Three-Part Yogic Breath
(Diaphragmatic → Thoracic → Clavicular)

After mastering the diaphragmatic breath, you can move on to the **three-part yogic breath**. In three-part breathing, three portions of the lungs are involved in respiration—the lower, middle, and upper lungs. The lower lungs are utilized in diaphragmatic breathing, as explained above.

While lying on the floor (alternate positions would be sitting or standing and leaning slightly forward), place your hands on the rib cage and try to feel your ribs, as well as the muscles between your ribs. These muscles are called intercostal muscles, and they have the ability to expand with inhalation. When flexible, these muscles play a role in natural, effortless breathing. Most of us do not use these muscles on a daily basis, and often we're not even able to distinguish them. As a result, it may take some practice to isolate these muscles. Don't worry if you can't detect movement at first; with time you will be able to isolate breathing into the rib cage.

Breathe into your lower lungs, watching your belly rise. Allow the breath to rise up and expand the rib cage laterally, thereby engaging the middle portion of the lungs. Be careful that you don't start breathing into the top part of the lungs, which lifts the rib cage. As soon as the rib cage begins to lift, it is impossible to expand laterally. As you exhale, use the same muscles to pull the rib cage in, pushing air out of the lungs, until the ribs press in slightly. This requires more contraction than when you are just resting. Many people think that emptying their lungs is bringing the rib cage into a position similar to when you're reclining in the chair. To exhale fully, you'll have to squeeze the ribs in.

After you have experienced breathing into your ribs, you can move on to the final part of the three-part yogic breath. Allow the breath to rise up and fill the upper portion of the lungs. Return your hands to their original position, one on the stomach and one on the upper chest. It can be helpful to take a deep inhale and then just when you think you've inhaled completely, inhale a little bit more. You may feel a deep expansion in the upper lungs and a lift in the upper clavicle area. This type of breathing is usually only felt in very rigorous exercise. Once you have completely inhaled, release the breath and contract the upper chest, rib cage, and stomach, respectively. An image of exhaling would be one of wringing or squeezing water out of a washcloth. The complete three-part breath cycle begins on the inhale in the stomach, rises up to expand the rib cage, rises up to fill the upper lungs, and then releases in reverse order. Try practicing ten rounds right now and notice how you feel afterward.

When performing a yoga pose, try to breathe like this, as you'll get more benefits by doing so. When you are just beginning, inhale for six seconds and exhale for six seconds. Gradually increase one second per week until you reach fifteen seconds in and fifteen seconds out. If you find that you need more time to adjust, increase your breath by one second every two weeks; proceeding gradually and at your own pace is most important.

Some individuals will be able to increase their breathing pattern to 15–25 seconds in and 15–25 seconds out. At this point, you should feel completely comfortable breathing into each part of the lungs. You are able to articulate the breath into each section of the lungs and have good control over the length of the breath. Inhalation and exhalation are of the same duration and the breath harmonizes in an easy, consistent flow through the three areas of the lungs. When this mastery is achieved, three-part lung breathing is known as **equal breathing.**

Motivational Example

A college gymnast was completing her thesis on stretching as a physical education major. She could do a full split and contort her body similar to an advanced yogi. However, her breath was restricted to the upper chest or clavicle region. Her face was tense as she pushed her body into an advanced pose. At this moment, I asked her to observe her breathing, instructing her to exhale completely and then inhale from the diaphragm first, intercostal muscles second, and upper chest last. She recognized two things immediately. First, she relaxed and smiled. As she relaxed, the discomfort from stretching was released. The flexible gymnast discovered that she was quite inflexible in her intercostal muscles, which move the rib cage laterally. Needless to say, her final thesis included a discussion on the benefits of breathing!

Breath Retention

Breath retention involves holding your breath after inhaling. To work on breath retention, inhale to the count of four, retain the breath for eight, and exhale for four. It's that simple! When you practice, do ten rounds and again, notice how you feel afterward. If four seconds is too short or long of an exhale/inhale count, adjust to what is comfortable for you.

Breath retention helps improve lung capacity and heart health. It forces open every unused air-cell in the lungs and stimulates the sluggish ones to healthy action. Respiration is improved through increased exchange of oxygen and carbon dioxide, reducing strain on the circulatory system. The yogis believe this practice facilitates increased health, longevity, and concentration.

Breath Suspension

The opposite of breath retention, breath suspension, involves holding the breath after exhaling. To practice, sit in a comfortable position. Count your natural inhale, then exhale at the same count, and finally suspend your breath for twice the count. Using the earlier example, inhale for four, exhale for four, and hold for eight with the lungs empty. While your breath is suspended, draw the abdomen in toward the spine. Do ten rounds. Breath suspension is best practiced in the morning prior to breakfast.

This breathing exercise is extremely useful for a weak stomach or sluggish colon. It is contraindicated for those with serious heart conditions, women who are pregnant, and children under the age of twelve.

VICTORIOUS BREATH

This breathing technique involves closing the mouth and drawing the breath in and out through the nose, creating a slight constriction in the throat. This partial closure of the glottis creates a sound that can be described in many ways—a soft snoring sound; the sound you would make to fog up and clean your glasses; the sound Darth Vader makes; the sound of the ocean; or the sound of "sa" on the inhale and "ha" on the exhale. Whatever description resonates with you, breathing is slow and deep and the sound created is even and continuous. During inhalation, you contract the abdominal muscles slightly and during exhalation, you hold the diaphragm in for a few seconds until all the air is expunged.

This breathing exercise can enhance ventilation of the lungs, calm the nerves, create vitality, reduce phlegm, and improve conditions of the throat.

ALTERNATE NOSTRIL BREATHING

Alternate nostril breathing balances the energy channels on the left and right sides of the spine. In this exercise, the fingers are used to alternately close off the nostrils to allow the inhalation/exhalation to happen on either side. Start in a comfortable seated position and bring the right hand close to the face. Bend the middle and pointer finger down toward the palm so that you can use the ring finger and thumb to close off the right and left nostrils. Inhale deeply. Close off the right nostril with your thumb and exhale from the left nostril. Take a full inhale into the left nostril and close it off with the ring finger as you lift the thumb from the right nostril and exhale from it. Repeat to inhale into the right nostril, close it off, and exhale through the left.

As you become comfortable, inhale for a count of five, hold the breath in for a count of ten, and exhale for a count of five. When you're just starting out, do five rounds on each side (ten rounds total); you can add more rounds with more experience.

Breathing in Yoga Poses

When practicing yoga poses, it is important to coordinate movement with breath. By breathing quietly and with intent during practice, we can slow the heartbeat, reduce blood pressure, and increase oxygen absorption in the body. In addition to these physical effects, breath focus during yoga practice enhances awareness of our internal environment. As we move through the poses, the focus on breath anchors the mind in the present moment and makes us more aware of how we are feeling emotionally and spiritually. Coordinating breath with movement synchronizes the body and brings about a sense of harmony.

It is very common for yoga students to hold their breath while in a pose, particularly when learning. When you're focused on physically performing the pose or are feeling discomfort, it can be challenging to concentrate on your breath. Don't be hard on yourself, but make an effort to breathe fully and smoothly as you move through the poses. As the bridge between mind and body, observing the breath in a pose will bring you into the present moment and help you achieve mind-body-spirit union. Breath awareness makes the poses much easier to practice.

Over time, the rhythm of your breath in yoga poses will make more sense. For example, when bending forward, the stomach contracts as you exhale. If you try to inhale deeply as you bend forward, you'll find it difficult, as both the stomach and lungs are compressed. Bending forward actually facilitates a full and complete exhale, which is also generally true in twist poses. As you twist, your lung capacity is restricted and it is easier to exhale. The exhalation enhances the twist and helps us release a bit more into the stretch.

Breath in Yoga Poses
Forward: Exhale
Twist: Exhale
Upward: Inhale
Backward: Inhale
Sideward: Both

On the other hand, when practicing an upward stretch like Palm Tree, inhaling actually helps your body to reach upward. As you breathe into the lungs, your body will feel lighter, almost like a balloon, and you'll rise upward with ease. Similarly in backward bending stretches, the opening achieved in the chest enables the lungs to expand maximally. In a pose such as Cobra, where we lie on the stomach and lift the upper spine using the lower back muscles, inhaling helps us to rise up. Exhalation is a natural response to coming out of the pose, as the compression and emptying of the lungs lowers us to the floor. As your practice develops, you'll find a natural breathing rhythm as you move in and out of the poses. Experiment and observe how the inhale and exhale enhance a particular movement within a pose.

In sideward bending stretches like Angle Pose, you can either inhale or exhale when coming into the pose; there are positive effects with either. When bending sideward to the right, the right lung is compressed, so it might feel more natural to exhale. However, in this same stretch to the right, the left lung is free to expand, so inhaling might feel comfortable as well. In general, exhaling as you come into the stretch may have the most benefit as it puts you in the frame of mind of releasing or letting go. In many ways, exhalation always offers us this benefit of encouraging the process of relaxing, and therefore going deeper, into a pose.

Most yoga classes cover the basics of breathing in the poses. However, if you're interested in more advanced breathing techniques, you'll want to work one-on-one with a yoga teacher trained in pranayama. In the previous example about the extremely flexible gymnast who had never performed breathing exercises, she is really no different from a beginner in yoga poses. Until she learns how to open her lungs, I would not recommend that she try any advanced breathing techniques. Instead, I'd encourage her to focus on smooth, rhythmic breathing and the effect that breathing has on her body, mind, and spirit as she moves through the poses. After she is comfortable with "the basics," it's appropriate for her to move on to more advanced styles of breathing under the supervision of a yoga teacher.

As you progress in yoga, you'll find it easier to deal with stressful situations, in no small part due to mastering breathing techniques. A good example of this is Mary, describing a typical day at home with her two children. She just heard the clock chime noon and has yet to get out of her pajamas. As she watches her infant and three-year-old throw toys and food all over the house, Mary's shoulders meet her ears and her face grows tense. She realizes that this is all part of motherhood, but does it have to feel so out of control?

Later, during the kids' midday nap, Mary takes a deep breath and reflects on her morning. She tries to breathe in, but her chest feels tight and her breath is ragged. Remembering yoga's teachings about breath as a reflection of state of mind, Mary exhales and inhales a deeper breath. After a few more breaths, her shoulders start to relax and a smile spreads across her face. In that moment, Mary realizes that for the next few years, the house is going to be this way, and she'll struggle less if she just stops resisting the situation. Even more poignant, she's reminded of how important her role as a mother is.

Mary's discoveries have meaning to those who feel stress and/or blockages in the body (that includes almost everyone!). The first thing to consider as you explore breathing is to simply notice what's going on in your body and mind. We're so accustomed to overlooking stress that it takes conscious awareness to become attuned to it. Breath sensitivity helps us to acknowledge that we are feeling stress—a great first step to get ourselves back in physical, mental, and spiritual harmony. The second step is to breathe into the areas of stress and tension until they release. You'll notice that if you concentrate on relaxing tense areas of the body through breathing, that you're able to "convince" the muscles to release. The third step is to become aware of the origins of your tension. As we come to understand the issues that are creating stress in our lives, we begin to notice tension when it first begins. By simply paying attention to the breath in daily life, it's possible to eliminate stress before it becomes lodged in the body.

Steve's story demonstrates just how transformative breathing exercises can be. Each afternoon at work, Steve typically reaches for a cup of coffee and a sweet snack as a pick-me-up to get through the day. Since Steve started doing yoga, he's been paying more attention to how different foods affect his energy. After his coffee break, he experiences an initial lift in energy, followed by a frenetic feeling later in the day, only to be completely drained just two hours later.

After noticing this pattern, Steve decides to bring in herbal tea and a piece of fruit to replace his usual sugar and caffeine snack. He feels good about taking control over a habit that causes him daily stress. With this positive attitude, he unconsciously starts taking deeper breaths and he realizes how shallowly he's been breathing all day long. Steve makes a commitment to consciously breathe throughout the day, starting with three minutes of deep breathing every two hours.

The increased sensitivity that Steve is developing through yoga has profound physical and emotional effects. Beyond the physical benefits of taking deeper, slower breaths, Steve is noticing his behavioral choices throughout the day. He's realizing how his emotions drive him to reach for junk food and is learning to work through his emotions, making him not only thinner but at greater peace with himself. He stops overeating at lunch or reacting emotionally to every new situation. Instead, he takes a deep breath, has faith in himself and his co-workers, and takes care of problems as they arise. There have even been days where Steve has felt no stress in a workplace filled with problems and chaos.

Steve exemplifies the single most valuable benefit from a beginner's yoga class: Learning how to be aware of emotional states. The breath, as the foundation of yoga pose practice, is a valuable tool in developing emotional sensitivity and remaining stable, calm, and positive in every situation.

Connecting to the Infinite

Breathing exercises, or pranayama, are instrumental in practicing yoga and experiencing a healthy life. Through conscious awareness and control of the breath, you have the means to transform yourself physically, mentally, and spiritually. Breathing connects your physical body to the more subtle layers of your being, right to the core of your highest consciousness. It is an extremely powerful method for accessing your true spiritual nature—the wisdom that pervades all living things at every moment in time. Pranayama can be studied and practiced for many years, and still not be mastered. Take your time, enjoy the process, and commit to feeling good!

Exercises

1. Are you able to breathe into the three areas of your lungs: diaphragm (belly), intercostals (lateral expansion of rib cage), and clavicle (upper chest area)? If not, where do you feel constricted? Can you try to relax these areas? Is your breath erratic, or slow and steady? Try to relax your body and breathe with as much ease as possible. If your breath feels constricted, erratic, or shallow, try breathing in another position. If you're sitting with a straight back and feeling uncomfortable, try standing up or lying down in order to adjust your breathing pattern. Then, return to the seated position. If this continues to be difficult, consult a yoga teacher or a health professional.

2. Do you remember to pay attention to your breathing in every yoga pose? Usually, when you're struggling the most in a pose, you're not fully breathing. Try to remember this as you practice and consistently ask yourself, "Am I breathing?" Come into and out of the pose on the inhale and exhale, depending on what is appropriate. Most importantly, breathe slowly and be aware of how you're feeling as you practice the poses.

3. Do you maintain awareness of breathing throughout the day? What do you notice about your breathing patterns? Experiment with the breathing exercises described in this chapter. Is there one that feels particularly relaxing? Zero in on one or two exercises that you practice off and on through your day. For example, you may find that breath retention helps you unwind through increased oxygen absorption.

4. Once the breathing exercise becomes easy and comfortable to practice, remember to apply your personal intention from Step One. What do you notice as a result of applying intention to the breath?

PART II

Inner Yoga
Steps 5–8

Archetypes

Purvaja

*Experience the cosmic nature of reality
through archetypes.*

Think for a moment about the following expressions: "strong as an ox," "sleek as a fox," "graceful as a swan," "pure as a dove," and "quiet as a mouse." Aren't they interesting? We use idioms like these quite often in the English language but rarely do we consider their underlying meaning or origin. These expressions reflect deep-seated archetypes, the focus of the next section and an intriguing aspect of yoga philosophy and practice.

Traditional Definitions of an Archetype

An archetype is an original model or type after which other similar things are patterned. In Sanskrit, the language in which yoga was codified, archetype is known as *purvaja*. *Purvaja* means "ahead of all others or firstborn." An archetype may be derived from, but not limited to, the following: elements found in nature, mythological stories, spiritual symbols, aspects of character, geometrical patterns and shapes, and certain words.

Archetypes East and West

The concept of archetypes varies between Eastern and Western philosophies. You may be familiar with Carl Jung's work in the early twentieth century, in which he said that the unconscious made its expression in symbolic forms. In Jungian psychology, an inherited pattern of thought, or symbolic imagery, is derived from the past collective experience, or "collective unconscious," and these symbols are present in the individual consciousness. Jung derived specific archetypes from the mystical symbols of many cultures and traditions as expressed in fairy tales, legends, and myths. Jungian archetypes may be patterns based purely on nature or complex human emotions, such as Hero, Mystic, or Princess.

Jung's work has significantly impacted a number of other disciplines in the Western world, yet it's not the focus of our study on archetypes in yoga philosophy. A good place to start our discussion of yoga pose archetypes can be found in the cosmological story described in the ancient yogic text, the *Upanishads*. To create the universe, a unified energetic field (*Brahman*) gave birth to Nature (*Prakriti*) and Consciousness (*Purusha*). This story, incidentally, is reflected in many traditions around the world. Nature and Consciousness represent the original archetypes from which all others developed: Feminine and Masculine, Mother and Father, and Material and Spirit. When yogis speak of archetypes, what they are ultimately talking about is the deepest part of human nature— who and what we are when connected to the most intimate level of our psyche. The archetypes reflect the state of wholeness and universal consciousness that pervades every particle in all existence. As you're probably already becoming aware of, there are many levels of understanding we must go through before coming to the complete awareness of the ultimate archetypal creative forces.

Through embodying the archetypes in yoga poses, it is possible to discover the deepest layers of our existence. Archetypes offer a way of accessing universal consciousness (samadhi), much like breathing and the other aspects of yoga that we're exploring in this book. For some, particularly artists and visually oriented people, understanding archetypes will come naturally and easily. For others, it may take time to realize their value and be able to integrate them into their yoga pose practice. Either way, the value of archetypes in advancing our yoga practice is significant.

Archetypes in Yoga Poses

In Indian culture each aspect of nature, whether it be an animal, plant, element, or societal role, is perceived to have a unique quality or archetype. The lion is fearless and represents courage. The willow tree, bending and swaying with the wind, represents flexibility; its wood is used for weaving baskets for this very reason. The ancient yogis observed each of these unique qualities and sought to personally integrate them through yoga poses. In other words, they modeled the poses after an aspect of nature that represented a particular archetype with the purpose of embracing those qualities within their own character. **Tree Pose** is modeled after the tree, which represents strength and balance, for example. From the perspective of archetypes, the purpose of practicing Tree Pose is to maintain a balance between the mind, body, and spirit, and to develop the strength to be present regardless of external circumstances.

Sounds simple enough, right? While it's fairly easy to understand the archetypes on an intellectual level, integrating them into our practice is another matter! It takes disciplined practice with the archetypes to experience the transformative power they can have on our lives. Archetypes take time to understand because of their mystical origins, as well as their subjective nature. While there are generally agreed upon archetypes that the yogis identified for each pose (we'll discuss these a bit later in the chapter), the archetypes that students relate to in each pose vary. Who's to say whether a cat should represent independence, curiosity, or fearlessness? These are all valid archetypes. Part of developing a rich yoga practice is discovering what you need and applying what resonates with you in that moment.

Using the example of the cat, let's consider how archetypes may be applied in yoga pose practice. Many people associate curiosity with the cat. Cats like to explore the world around them: they climb up trees, chase shiny objects, and find all sorts of nooks and crannies to get into. Now, I can already see that some of you may be wondering if exploring the archetype of the cat will involve tree climbing, and while I don't want to disappoint, I can assure you that it does not. Archetypes are taken figuratively rather than literally! Curiosity in **Cat Pose** can be explored very slowly with attention to the subtle adjustments of the spine, the extension and contraction of the small back muscles and all of the micro-movements that take the pose to another level.

While curiosity is certainly an appropriate archetype of the cat, you might prefer to focus on another quality, perhaps agility. That's great! Exploring archetypes is a very personal process and as you develop experience with integrating them in your practice, you'll find a balance between the more traditional archetypes and those that you personally relate to. There's an ongoing discussion in the yoga community as to whether it is possible to have a completely objective view of an archetype. Because archetypes are influenced by cultural heritage, religious influences, language, tradition, topography, and history, your personal interpretation of archetypes may vary from those provided in this or any book.

However, in studying archetypes, some students will continue to relate to the same archetype in a variety of poses (e.g., mountains represents strength, as does a lion and a tree). This fact may illuminate a personal issue (e.g., developing strength), or indicate a need to be open to a wider range of archetypes and attitudes in order to inform the body-mind. The mountain, lion, and tree archetypes, though sharing certain qualities, also have inherently unique attributes.

As a second example, the **Peacock Pose**, whether done in the modified or traditional form, embodies an archetype of overcoming fear. The peacock uses its brilliantly colored feathers to scare away a would-be attacker. Those of us who have faced adversity in our lives and have learned how to overcome these threats will connect to the Peacock Pose with ease. As an example, Jeane was a theatrical performer as a child and had to overcome a fear of public speaking at an early age. Having an audience helped her to overcome stage fright. She learned how to flash a smile, project her voice, and walk with confidence on the stage. From her childhood experiences, she was able to teach people and speak in almost any public situation without fear. Her story is one version of mastery of the wisdom of the peacock.

However, not all of us have performed in front of hundreds of people in the school play. Many adults are extremely shy or lack self-confidence, and this affects many different aspects of their lives. For this group of people, which I'm going to estimate constitutes at least half this book's readers, mastering the Peacock Pose is essential. Peacock Pose, or one of its derivatives like Cobra Pose, helps us to concentrate on a feeling of power in the heart and cultivate a sense of courage. As we develop these qualities in our yoga pose practice, they naturally radiate out into our lives. After all, what we're essentially doing with these archetypes is integrating them into our character. If we cultivate courage in yoga poses, we're more able to cultivate courage "off the mat," as well.

It bears repeating that archetypes are highly subjective and not absolute fact. Be inspired to discover and define your own archetypes. While I will offer suggestions, they are not absolute truths. Furthermore, the suggestions are in no way comprehensive! There is so much to be said on archetypes that many volumes could be written on the subject. And the real purpose of this chapter is not to provide every possible aspect of the archetypes, but to help you discover their power.

Archetypes and Personal Growth

Each of us has an attraction, or sometimes an aversion, to certain archetypal patterns, which can be a powerful call to a greater understanding of our emotional and spiritual patterns. Consider the ego, which often protects us from pain that we do not wish to feel. This protection may actually be a good thing at the time, perhaps allowing us to functionally survive trauma, but it leaves us with scar tissue in the form of mental and physical blockages that manifest as repetitive behaviors. While our lives may sometimes seem like a collection of unrelated incidents, viewing experiences from an archetypal or symbolic viewpoint can help us to bring cohesion and purpose as we work through certain repeated patterns and ego defenses.

CASE STUDY **Mary's Self-Image**

Having gained weight during her second pregnancy, Mary was comparing herself to a certain animal that may seem derogatory—the pig. Mary understood that it was essential to be honest about this negative association, and while in a confidential setting, she confessed that she was feeling this way. She held the image so strongly in her mind that when she talked about it, it brought tears to her eyes. Many of us can relate to negative feelings associated with weight gain. If Mary feels like a pig at the subconscious or conscious level, she will tend to behave like one, eating whatever is in front of her without any thought or concern for her own true needs. Therefore, the archetype of the pig was not serving her. If Mary just had an illness where she lost a lot of weight, the archetype of the pig might be the perfect approach. The "pig" archetype is not bad, but Mary's view of it is.

In Step One, Mary's intention was identified as self-love and self-care. Her reflections on attitude led her to practice non-attachment from her old ideas. In the process of Mary devising a positive archetype, she needed to adopt an image to replace the pig. Mary first thought of the lioness, a protective and fierce mother, but the lioness also has the quality of being somewhat aloof. Mary realized that perhaps the lioness is a little too detached for her present needs, which require self-love and a strong community. Then she thought of the cobra, which is also a very strong archetype. Is strength what she really needs? Mary realized that strength was not her issue.

Finally, Mary decided on the third image that came to mind, the goddess, who is represented in the Moon Salutation series. Since becoming a mother, Mary often felt overwhelmed caring for her young children and had lost touch with her body. Focusing on the goddess helped her create a positive feminine image in her psyche. The goddess is caring, wise, and beautiful, but not necessarily skinny. Relying on that image allowed her to accept herself and find the inspiration to eat right and take better care of her health. In her yoga practice, Mary continued to hold the attitude of non-attachment and the image of the goddess, and she observed how the archetype of each yoga pose fed her needs.

Mastering the Archetype Regardless of Physical Capability

Mary's process of cultivating the image of a goddess occurs in her mind, even though the archetype is explored in a physical pose. **The Goddess Pose**, which turns the arms and feet out and includes a squat that challenges the groin area to open, is a challenging pose for many. Most students can only open their feet partially, and they squat shallowly due to flexibility and strength limitations. An Indian dancer could lower herself into the goddess pose and be capable of maintaining perfect form for minutes at a time. However, both the inflexible housewife and the flexible dancer can master this pose if their minds connect to the goddess archetype in the heart. Likewise, if the dancer is distracted due to unrelated thoughts, her form is correct but she is not complete in the yoga pose.

Yoga Pose Archetypes

YOGA POSES FROM ANIMALS

Every animal has a sacred gift for humans to learn. Animal poses can help us to connect with powerful aspects of the soul that we often repress in our busy lives. Before coming into an animal pose, it can be helpful to imagine what it feels like to be that animal. Try to envision where the animal lives, how its body moves, how it eats, and how it plays.

Cobra

The cobra moves with its belly on the ground but must reach up to see clearly, much as we are often kept busy with worldly pursuits and have to make an effort to reach for higher goals. It takes faith and courage to rise above the material world and peer into the unknown spiritual world. Once the upper body is poised above the ground in **Cobra Pose**, we must accept whatever it is we see from this new vista. The lower back is consciously relaxed while the eyes remain focused on heaven.

The cobra's ferocious nature cannot be ignored. It comes up suddenly and with deadly force, much like the workings of nature or the trappings of the world. The cobra's gift is in its ability to shed its skin. It is this shedding of skin that allows the cobra to continually transform and renew itself.

The very nature of life involves frequent shift and change. How do you feel about change and transformation? How do you feel about death? Many people are afraid to die, yet this fear prevents us from fully living. The archetype of the cobra inspires us to see the possibilities inherent in every situation, accept whatever challenges we may be facing, and embrace all stages of life.

Lion

The male lion is often seen as the most masculine animal and is closely associated with the sun. Power, courage, protection, and stewardship are just some of the aspects of the lion as the Father Protector. The lion shoulders much responsibility and this is as much a burden as it is a blessing. One interesting aspect of the lion is that it only protects kin and will destroy all males that are not of their bloodline. As an ethnic or racial metaphor, the lion gives us reason to stop and think about how we treat others that seem different or strange. Do you judge other people? How do you judge yourself?

The roar of the lion offers the power to declare battle with obstacles in your path to spiritual freedom. But power must be wielded with a deep sense of integrity and responsibility. When in **Lion Pose**, ask yourself, What is your relationship with power? Do you support others in their endeavors or do you condescend to those that you perceive as beneath you? In terms of asserting yourself, do you speak up when you feel compelled to do so? Or, do you refrain from letting your voice speak to who you really are or ask for what you really want?

Cow Face

The cow is the sustainer, comforter, nurturer, and a symbol of the Mother. The cow represents Mother Earth, which gives this pose a very grounded quality. From the cow, we obtain milk to feed ourselves. Symbolically, we extract the milk of liberation.

Use **Cow Pose** to reflect on your ability to give and to receive sustenance in its many forms (food, water, love, emotional support, spiritual support). Do you feel comfortable receiving support from others? How do you feel when you give of yourself to support others? Are you able to give yourself what you need or do you starve yourself of self-love and nourishment?

Pigeon

The country pigeon is known for puffing up its chest in pride. While they're not often recognized for this, pigeons have a unique ability to find their home from a distant location. Homing pigeons symbolize assurance and confidence in challenging situations. They represent a feeling of safety and security that allows a positive sense of pride about who we really are.

Are you a proud person and if so, in what ways? Is your pride justified by accomplishments or overcoming challenging circumstances? Is your pride ego-related? For some of us, pride is a mask that hides feelings of incompetence, low self-esteem, or unworthiness. Are you at home with yourself? Tapping into the joy of your power and talent through the **Pigeon Pose** can help you develop confidence and assurance.

Butterfly/Cobbler's Pose

A symbol of transformation, the butterfly inspires awe among children and adults alike as it morphs from an ordinary caterpillar into a vibrant winged creature. Unlike most animals, the butterfly literally transforms its physical form! This is a very apt metaphor for many of us that need to change old ways in favor of a healthier and happier reality. Before transformation can take place, we must shelter ourselves from negative influences inside a spiritual cocoon. This may mean refraining from food, drink, thoughts, or activities that aren't in alignment with our well-being or simply engaging in the higher company of fellow seekers who also wish to take flight. It might involve releasing thoughts of fear, doubt, and worry to welcome the possibility of a better way of life.

The **Butterfly Pose** opens the groin area, the seat of the sacral chakra (see Step Six) and the repository of creative, transformational energy. The stunning markings of a butterfly are among the most imaginative demonstrations of natural beauty. What would you create in the world if money and material wealth weren't issues? Who would you become, where would you live, and what relationships would you enjoy if you pursued your deepest dreams?

Fish

The fish resides in water and embodies marine qualities, including fluidity. When in Fish Pose you may experience a floating feeling, as if the body is buoyant. Being able to float through life empowers us to be like water and adapt to many different situations.

Fish Pose gives you the opportunity to reflect on your ability to go with the flow, as well as encounter aspects of yourself that are rigid and resist change. If you observe fish in the wild, they seem almost as fluid as the water that houses them. Are you able to flow with the energies that surround you or do you tend to fight against the current? Exposing and opening the heart in Fish Pose, do you feel vulnerable or have faith in the general goodness of creation?

Eagle

The eagle's superior vision relates to the third eye chakra (see Step Six). The gift of clear sight relates directly to the concentration we develop in yoga. Clear vision exists when the mind is focused and calm. When we practice balancing poses like **Eagle Pose**, concentration is aided by fixing the eyes on one point.

The challenge of the Eagle Pose is twisting while balancing on one leg. This can be extremely difficult at first, but gradually we become more flexible and stronger. As we settle into the pose, our purpose becomes clearer. The third eye chakra (the seat of sight and intuition) opens, improving vision. Just as the eagle can spot a mouse from thousands of feet away, Eagle Pose helps us to see what is important in life. Unfolding from the pose, our metaphorical wings spread, conveying a sense of lightness and a freedom from hindrances.

What hinders your insight? What blocks your vision? What disturbs your balance?

Dog

Downward Dog mimics a dog as it wakes and stretches. This keystone pose of the Sun Salutation series contains a few important lessons from the animal kingdom, like how to relax, stretch, and feel joy in the body! Dogs are endearingly faithful, expressed through their bright eyes, energetic demeanor, and incessant tail wagging. They love being part of "the pack," getting exercise, and being out in nature.

Downward Dog asks us to express our faith while enjoying the journey of our yoga practice. Are you enjoying your yoga practice? Are you able to have fun and remain relaxed even while putting physical effort into your poses? While yoga is practiced individually, we can find sustenance in community. How are you a part of the yoga community?

Yoga Poses from Nature

Through observing the natural environment, we see our own reflection. The sky contains the planets and stars; the earth and sea alone contain a diversity of existence that continues to evolve and amaze us. New discoveries of plants, insects, and animals happen every day! Observing even one small part of the natural world can give us insight into how we are connected to every living thing through universal consciousness. Poets of all cultures highlight deep truths by observing the flow of water, the energy of the sun, and the power of a mountain.

CASE STUDY Laura's Self-Image

Laura, in her reflections in Steps One and Two, chose an intention of spiritual growth and clarity, and the attitude of knowledge in order to further her practice of self-awareness and inner wisdom. As she learned the information in this step, Laura was very quick to understand her archetype. She's somewhat artistic, and as a child she always drew flowers. Looking back, she realized that she always wanted everyone to be happy, and drawing flowers was her way of expressing a need for approval. As a result, she would often do what other people wanted and then convince herself that she really enjoyed fulfilling other people's wishes.

Laura's flowers symbolized her desire to reach toward the sun. While aspiring to high ideals is a great ethic, there are other qualities of the flower that don't serve Laura. For one, flowers are transient, coming and going with the seasons. After a lifetime of catering to other people's needs, Laura's archetype needs to reflect stability, strength, and endurance. Laura found inspiration in the mountain because it reaches up to the sky yet remains strong in its rootedness to the earth. The mountain endures all types of weather through time. With this archetype in mind, Laura is able to be herself regardless of what other people think, and draws on the qualities of strength and endurance as she moves through her yoga pose practice.

Mountain

Mountains appear to be such peaceful and permanent structures that it is easy to forget the violent volcanic explosions and powerful movement of continental plates that formed them. While the mountain is a dynamic part of nature, it is also the most stable structure as well. The mountain archetype suggests vitality, stillness, durability, and stability.

The base of **Seated Mountain Pose** is the lotus position or a crossed-legged position, which encourages the mind to become still. Once we have quieted physical and mental needs, we can begin our ascent to higher states of consciousness. At first however, the mind may feel like a tumultuous volcano. In the face of the ever-changing reality, the mountain maintains unwavering stability. Seated Mountain Pose is incredibly helpful for people navigating challenges and changes in life. Consider the relationship between your mind and the stress around you—are you able to remain cool and calm in difficult situations? As you practice Seated Mountain Pose, try to connect with the part of you that remains unaffected by external influences. As you move through your life, see if you can access this deep layer of your being for support and clarity.

Tree

An archetypal cousin of the mountain, the majestic tree roots deeply into the ground as its branches extend toward the sky. Trees are strong but flexible, and typically quite resilient. A tree cooperates with and sustains other natural forms such as birds, mammals, and insects. Trees breathe life-giving oxygen into the world and all the life forms them as they exchanges carbon dioxide for oxygen. Insects and vines may destroy a tree, yet it keeps on giving, breaking down into nutrients to sustain other life forms. Because of its many beneficial qualities, a tree may be viewed as the ultimate example of selflessness.

Reflect on your balance with others. How do you cooperate with your family, friends, and society in general? How do you feel when the winds of change blow through your life? What ways do you give to and receive from others? How do you support others?

Sun

The **Sun Salutation** encompasses a range of poses, but they all reflect the intensity of the sun, which is the epitome of fire. While fire can destroy, it also purifies and is the precursor to renewal. As the sustainer of all life on earth, the sun is the focus of many world traditions and religions.

While performing the Sun Salutation, it is difficult to think of anything but the flow of the poses; we are forced to remain in the moment. We build heat and purify our system as we seek en*light*enment, for what is higher consciousness but allowing ourselves to be filled with light?

Fire quickly transforms all it touches. How do you feel about changes that you can't control? What are your goals for personal transformation? How do you express the fire of your ideas and passions?

Moon

The moon is often associated with feminine energy. As the powerful counterpart to the sun, the moon is highly intuitive and receptive. As it goes through its monthly phases, the moon affects life here on earth, evidenced by the tides. The sun and moon are of central importance to *Hatha* yoga, its name being derived from the sun (*Ha*) and moon (*Tha*). Yoga helps us to harmonize their opposing energies so that we can live a balanced life. The moon reflects the sun, illuminating the night sky and those parts of our psyche that we try to hide under the cover of darkness. As the moon affects water here on earth, it also influences the emotions (the feminine) that may be subjugated in the name of logic (the masculine).

Do you identify with your emotions? Do you change like the tides? Are you able to understand your emotions? Do you feel comfortable exploring them? As you lean to one side or the other in **Moon Pose** or **Half Moon Pose**, are you avoiding feeling an emotion you think of as "negative"? What would it take to develop a greater sense of awareness about seemingly negative emotions? Often, negative emotions provide the opportunity to look deeper within an issue and explore mysterious aspects of our own emotional and spiritual landscape. As you practice Moon Pose, let yourself receive and be open to the experience.

Lotus

With its home in the mud, the lotus flower is a metaphor for the human condition; we are stuck in the vicissitudes of life while we strive toward purity and contentment.

The **Lotus Pose** makes a triangle of the lower body as the base of the spine and the two knees form the three points. The symbolism of the pose involves a balanced approach to physical needs and spiritual pursuits. As we learn to be comfortable in this pose, we discover how to thrive amidst our struggles in life. When practicing Lotus Pose, cultivate a sense of ease and relaxation, even if the pose is challenging.

The *Hatha Yoga Pradipika*, the original Sanskrit book on yoga poses, notes that Lotus Pose is difficult to achieve. For some, this pose may never be physically possible, yet all can practice the archetype of this pose while sitting cross-legged on the floor in preparation for meditation.

On a more esoteric level, the lotus also represents the many natures of both divine and human existence. What stage of life are you in? Do you identify with society's paradigms about what you should be doing relative to your age (getting married or retiring, for example), or are you creating your own vision for your life? What is your body teaching you about your spirit and emotions?

Stick

The stick or staff represents the power to transform and heal on any level. The caduceus, a type of staff surrounded by intertwining serpents, is a familiar symbol in the medical world. In Roman mythology, Mercury received a caduceus from the god of music with which he could control the living or dead and turn anything into gold.

In **Stick Pose** we stretch our body to its horizontal limits, enabling the spine to decompress and to allow healing fluids to come in between the vertebrae. We reach in both directions, simultaneously lengthening and opening.

As you reach with your arms, legs, and spine, can you connect to the highest and reach beyond your ego? Can you relax, even in the effort of this pose? Can you tap into your own healing power?

YOGA POSES FROM TOOLS

Modern human society would not be where it is today if certain tools had not been invented. When we think of the ubiquitous use of the plough and the wheel, it is no wonder that tools have become archetypes in their own right.

Plough

The plough is used to clear a field so that earth can be cultivated and her plentiful bounty reaped. It may seem like improvidence to ask for more than what is already provided for us in the forests, plains, and seas, and there is certainly a kind of violence involved in furrowing the soil. As we plough, we turn over the dirt, uproot unproductive plants, and reveal creatures that are normally not seen or thought about. To plant the seeds that will result in new life, we must first furrow out the unnecessary impediments we harbor below the surface of our being.

In **Plough Pose**, our breathing is quite constricted. This can cause some people to feel claustrophobic or anxious. Plough Pose mirrors how we handle various mental and physical restrictions and helps us to uncover perceived limitations and push boundaries. Through the pose we empower ourselves and plant the seeds that soon turn into new growth. Enhancing the breath enables us to see that we have power even in the most limiting situations.

Are you able to find comfort and strength in the midst of strain? Do you have faith that tilling new areas of life will bring forth fruitful results? What seeds are you planting with your yoga practice?

Bow

The bow is used to aim an arrow with the purpose of killing an animal for food or bringing down the opposition in a time of war. We may aim the bow to hone our skills for when they are truly needed or simply for the pleasure of the sport. In our body, the spine represents the bow. As we move our spine in a backbend position, we must treat the body like a bow, challenging it and learning to use it effectively, but always within its limits.

In **Bow Pose** you may tense yourself like a bow that is ready to shoot. What is it that you are aiming at? Are your goals well defined and purposeful? It takes strength and skill to aim the bow properly. Are you ready to bring your entire being into reaching your target? Is the target worth the effort?

Wheel

The wheel is arguably the most useful tool ever created. It revolutionized societies, allowing people to quickly and effortlessly transport objects from one place to another. In modern times, the wheel still plays a very important role in transportation. But where is it that we are headed and how far have we really come? The wheel is the number zero and the circle. It shares zero's symbolic link to the eternal: all emanates from and returns to the universe in an endless circle.

As we move through our lives, we may not be aware of eternity, only the material world as we go through our cycles of birth, life, death, and rebirth. In **Wheel Pose**, we have the opportunity to connect with a deep, unchanging aspect of our nature, allowing us to step outside of our own personal problems and into a collective reality. While the outermost edges of the wheel move through many different landscapes, the hub of the wheel is always constant, stable, and unaffected by the activities on the edge. The great lesson that the wheel provides is to observe our life without reacting to it, to be witness to our emotions rather than subjected to them.

Do you feel as if you have any control over your destiny or do you feel like life keeps throwing you unwanted curveballs? In what ways do you contribute to your problems? Do you see patterns in your life repeating like the wheels of nature spinning?

Boat

The boat carries us from one place to another, down a small creek or across a vast ocean. Just as the ancients were adrift in the water with only their ship and the stars to guide them to solid land, we are also adrift in the emotions and events that carry us through our lives. In **Boat Pose**, we look forward, opening to whatever "waves" come our way with courage and faith that the journey will bring what is needed. The vessel of yoga helps us cross the river of struggle to a place of inner peace.

What directions are the currents flowing in your life? Are you drifting or are you rowing with intention? Do you use spiritual practices to help steer your mind through the currents of life? Are you going with the flow of life or are you creating struggle? If you feel like life is a constant challenge and presents obstacles that seem to be outside of your control, take a look at your responses to them. In every situation, we make choices that determine the direction our life takes and influence the kind of person we become. As we direct our thoughts and actions positively and productively, life naturally improves.

CASE STUDY **Steve's Self-Image**

Steve enjoys doing yoga poses for their physical benefits. To his surprise, deep breathing has helped create tranquility in his mind, causing him to manage his daily life with more grace. Through his yoga practice, Steve realized that he is yearning to discover a rich life purpose, something that his work environment just isn't providing. It seems to Steve that the day-to-day grind never seems to end. As soon as he completes one task, another task immediately surfaces. He feels as though he is walking in a circle like an ox in a mill, incessantly grinding grain into flour. There seems to be no end in sight to his mundane work, nor any sustaining purpose to it.

Steve recognizes that he feels trapped just like an ox harnessed to a yoke. Continuing to identify with the sensation of being trapped is never going to help Steve realize the life purpose that he so deeply desires. He changes his perception, envisioning an endless flow of water that symbolizes his life. Life flows like a stream, constantly changing through the seasons. Steve realizes that life never stays the same and that he has the power to change his circumstances.

As Steve considers the archetypes, he remembers the boat; how the wind fills its sails as it glides over endless water. Steve works at cultivating the boat, an image of freedom to glide and flow with the breeze. Steve is inspired to reevaluate his career and discover what he's truly passionate about. He travels internationally, takes a sculpture class, and buys several cookbooks that he and his wife use to make dinner together each week.

Yoga Poses from Structures

Throughout human history, we have built structures like the windmill to harness natural energies for our own use. As yoga poses also harness and direct natural energy, it is no surprise to see that a few poses are named after structures. Every part of nature from a cave to a building to the human body is a structure.

Triangle

In the ancient world, the triangle had special meaning. Almost every culture has some affinity to the pyramid or triangle in their traditions. The triangle has a base on the ground consisting of two points and third point extending to the sky.

The concept of three is fundamental to the triangle and represents archetypal qualities upon which all others are based. These qualities are balancing energies whose movements predicate every action of every object from the creation of the solar system to a person getting out of bed in the morning. In the Tao, we know these energies as *Wu, Wei,* and *Yin/Yang.* In Christianity they are the *Father, Son,* and *Holy Spirit.* In Hinduism they are *Brahma, Vishnu,* and *Shiva* and their consorts *Saraswati, Lakshmi,* and *Kali.* In Ayurveda, an ancient Indian system of holistic medicine, the three primary body types are Air, Fire, and Earth.

Does each aspect of your life feel in balance? When in the **Triangle Pose**, do you lean in one direction over another? Can you find strength in balance? As you strive for balance in your life, it may be helpful to think of it as an intention rather than a destination. Because of life's constantly changing nature, what we need to stay balanced varies through time. Consider those areas of your life that are pulling you in different directions, think about what adjustments you can make to bring yourself back to center, and take action. Even minor changes can make a significant impact.

Windmill

The windmill is a passive machine that relies on the forces of nature in order to operate. Flowing with the wind, the windmill provides energy for human use. As we open our hearts in **Windmill Pose**, we can imagine ourselves receiving, transforming, and spreading love. Love is not only an emotion, but a powerful way of being in the world. Once your heart opens, you're able to receive love as you bow forward, bringing love from the upper to the lower or earthly realms. We use love energy to open the back of the heart chakra as we twist to one side (see Step Six on chakras), and in our daily lives, we allow ourselves to feel supported and nurtured.

Can you open your heart to the power of nature? Are you able to receive and give love to yourself and others? Are you learning to cultivate energy and direct it in ways that enrich your life and the lives of those around you?

Angle

From a base of stable hips, the upper body stretches to the side for a pure side bend. In this pose, we can feel both the flexibility of the spine as well as its limitations. The qualities of **Angle Pose** are complementary: through observing the boundaries of your capabilities, you create freedom in the pose. Angles are very helpful in strengthening and cleansing the physical body. However, this is only achieved by being mindful of your capabilities. You don't want to lean over so far that you strain the body, but you need to challenge yourself in order to receive benefit. Finding that precise balance of striving and relaxing is the goal of Angle Pose.

When in a side bend, consider whether you accept the limitations of your body. Do you overstretch and create added tension in your system? In what ways are you pushing beyond your means in life, perhaps financially or in your relationships? Do you overdo areas of your life?

Candle

The straight candle inspires **Shoulder Stand Pose**, which gives us a new perspective on those burdens that we feel are ours to shoulder. By literally turning our world upside down, we have to use different muscles to support the body. The weight borne by our spine shifts and there is compression in the opposite direction. Not only are we upending our physical body but our psychic (energy) body as well.

As you practice Shoulder Stand Pose, you may notice a constriction in the throat that can cause a trapped and/or suffocated feeling. Once you surrender to the pose, the throat can relax and you'll become refreshed and mentally focused. You may also experience a release of emotional baggage through the pose; these are responsibilities and burdens that you may feel you're forced to shoulder alone. By releasing the need to assert our will and surrendering to a larger reality, our perceived burdens are lightened and we can fulfill our duties with a sense of service and ease.

What is weighing you down in life? Perhaps you're caring for an ill person, or maybe you're holding on to past regrets. How does your perception of reality contribute to the feeling of heavy burdens and responsibilities from which you cannot escape? What shift in perception is needed to help you experience freedom and joy?

Yoga Poses from the Human Experience

Traditionally, cultures around the world had rites of passage and ceremonies to honor important stages in life, including birth, childhood, adolescence, adulthood, marriage, parenthood, retirement, and finally, death. Some of these transitions are still celebrated today, but their symbolic importance is often overlooked in modern societies. Through yoga pose practice, we can discover the quintessential essence of these important junctures in the human experience.

Child's Pose

While seemingly simple, **Child's Pose** is a powerful archetype that has relevance through every stage of life. Working through the shadow side of the child archetype frees us to reclaim our power as adults. For example, a person who identifies with the "wounded child" archetype may blame childhood trauma for anything negative that happens in adult life. Learning to forgive is the lesson of the wounded child.

Child's Pose, also known as Womb Pose, is a forward bend that brings all parts of the body into close contact, much like a fetal position. As infants in the womb, we are seamlessly connected to our mother and to our environment. When we are born into the world, we struggle to maintain this state of connectedness. And as we grow older, we often lose touch with our original vitality and exuberance. However, we continue to carry aspects of our child selves throughout our lives. Taking care of the child within us through Child's Pose can heal old wounds and reveal the simple joys of discovery and play.

If you watch young children breathe, you'll notice that they inhale deeply into their belly. As we discussed in Step Four on pranayama, breathing reflects a person's emotional and physical well-being. In Child's Pose, notice if your breathing is ragged and uneven, or smooth and full. Are you able to look at life through the eyes of a child? Do you allow yourself to feel vulnerable in your relationships? Do you feel connected to something greater than yourself?

Warrior I

Warrior I is an ideal pose to cultivate strength and confidence in times of conflict. In this position, the heart is turned open and boldly faces the enemy. The warrior, also known as the hero, faces great challenges, with the goal of bringing back wisdom that protects the tribe. Similarly, we may need to challenge ourselves to see the spiritual lessons we have the opportunity to learn in difficult circumstances. **Warrior I** helps us to conquer our emotions so that we can achieve higher consciousness.

In Warrior I, do you tend to look up (away from what is approaching) or face forward? Are you able to breathe fully or are you restricted in any way? When confronted with challenging situations, do you look to internal or external resources for the solution?

Warrior II

The balance and strength for **Warrior II** comes from the navel center. It takes a sense of personal power to remain steadfast in the face of opposition, and the spiritual path presents opposition/opportunity at every turn. Warrior II helps us realize new abilities through our efforts and reveals spiritual strength that we can tap into when needed. This pose can resolve conflicts through right action.

In order to restore alignment, can you be brave enough to feel your imbalances? Can you relax into the pose, re-establish balance and be comfortable in knowing that perfection may never be attained? Are you able to strive in life and remain unattached to the results of your efforts?

Dancer Pose

Within every pose, there is an ongoing process of balancing the body, mind, and spirit. This is definitely true in **Dancer Pose**. In this extreme backbend, some students may never be able to connect their foot with their hand or reach their arms all the way over their head. Yet in this very struggle, there is a great opportunity to witness the dance between journey and destination. In whatever capacity we perform this pose, focusing on the process of achieving balance offers us a way of living the experience, rather than living for the outcome. By focusing on the archetype of the dancer, we can tune in to the beating of our own heart, feel the rhythm of our body, and connect with the joy of creative expression. Without this archetypal attitude, a flexible student may physically reach mastery of the pose but not experience the inner dance that brings joy to the heart. In the dance of life, do you feel free to express yourself? Do you have the joy of the dancer in your life?

Standing Prayer Pose

There are many different ways to pray and yoga poses are prayers in their own right. **Standing Prayer Pose** connects the hands to the heart, and actions with loving intentions. In connecting to our heart's desire, we come home to our true Self.

Standing Prayer is the easiest balancing pose because both feet remain flat on the ground. However, the body's natural tendency to sway makes it nearly impossible to remain perfectly steady, particularly with the eyes closed. This imperfection reminds us that regardless of our prayers, reality is outside of our control.

Can you pray just for the sake of praying? Are you able to show devotion to positive pursuits even when the results are not as you would wish? Can you find inner peace while your life is swaying to and fro?

Half Spinal Twist

Named after the famed tenth-century yogi Matsyendra, who may have been the first *Hatha* yoga teacher, **Partial Seated Twist** (*Ardha Matsyendrasana*) offers the archetype of the yogi. The twist represents purification as it tones the organs of the body, as well as seeing new perspectives. Twists are not always easy, but they are among the most beneficial poses. Matsyendra was renowned for his discipline and fortitude. Focusing on his image as you perform the twist can bring out the fire of purification that magnifies its effect on the body.

Do you have the ability to face impurities and allow those impurities to be released? Are you able to feel comfortable in a twisting position in spite of the restriction? Think about how this might relate to your life. People are often summoned to live with challenges like physical pain or the loss of a loved one. Twists can help you learn to live well despite these problems through dedication and discipline.

Standing Forward Bend

The **Standing Forward Bend** resembles bowing. In ancient times, the subjects of a kingdom would bow their heads to royalty to show respect. Bowing was also a way of protecting the king so that guards would be able to identify anyone with a raised weapon. Today, bowing remains a sign of reverence, as well as an expression of prayer.

Most forward bends symbolize surrender and acceptance. We bend forward and accept our humanity and physicality. We elongate the spine and allow the weight of our thoughts to release with the head, neck, and shoulders. The thinking mind surrenders to the feeling heart. This pose leaves us vulnerable and exposed, but gives us the opportunity to cultivate a trusting attitude. This is the first step in surrendering the ego, accepting what we cannot change and feeling comfortable regardless of our circumstances.

When you lower into the forward bend, are you releasing your neck and shoulder muscles fully? Can you let go of your thoughts and worries, at least for a moment? Can you lay your ego to rest and feel the joy of being alive? Can you surrender your thinking mind to your feeling heart?

Corpse

In ancient times, death was experienced by the entire community in a very intimate way. When a family member passed away, the family displayed the body in a visible place for days, sometimes in front of the house. Depending on the death rites of the culture, the family and community prepared the body for burial. From a young age, children were exposed to death and understood it as an integral part of life. Death was viewed as a part of the cycle of existence, in stark contrast to our modern funeral homes where bodies are prepared by strangers and kept out of the sight of loved ones. Even in our burial rituals, there is an underlying implication that death is separate from us, though we know rationally that this is not the case.

Depending on your personal beliefs, you may think of death as the ultimate end or as another transformative step in the cycle of life, death, and rebirth. Whatever your views, most of us have powerful feelings on the inevitability of our own demise. Feelings on this subject can inform our life experience.

Corpse Pose completely relaxes physical and mental tensions. After a brief time in this pose, we may feel as though our body is much lighter, almost completely disconnected from the physical being, much as we might imagine happening upon death. Those uncomfortable with death may use the image of an animal hibernating in a deep sleep. Corpse Pose is unique in the sense that one remains conscious while detaching from worldly concerns. A restful proposition, Corpse Pose is one of the most popular yoga poses, usually practiced at the end of a yoga pose session.

As you practice the pose, concentrate on letting go of thoughts, worries, and concerns, and relax every muscle in your body including your face. How do you feel about out-of-body experiences? Is letting go of thoughts and worries difficult? Try not to be critical of yourself when you find yourself thinking in Corpse Pose. Just observe the thought and let it float away as you relax your body. Focus on your breath to bring you deeper into yourself.

Connecting to the Infinite

While often overlooked by students, archetypes are a fundamental aspect of yoga poses. In fact, the poses were modeled after archetypes. Whether it's the enthusiasm and loyalty of a dog, the strength and courage of a lion, or the joy and vulnerability of a child, archetypes offer us the opportunity to cultivate that which we lack.

After you have had some experience with the physical poses, take your time exploring the qualities of each pose. Realizing that the archetypes are fairly subjective, feel free to discover qualities that are meaningful to you. You can research the mythology, history, and biology as appropriate for any of the archetypes for inspiration. As you practice the poses, cultivate receptivity and sensitivity to intuit their hidden meaning. Above all else, know that there isn't a "right" answer when it comes to archetypes, but rather what feels right for you.

As you work with the archetypes, try to incorporate them into your intention and attitude. How are the archetypes helping you to connect with your intention and embrace your chosen attitude? Emphasize those poses that complement and advance your chosen intention and attitude. This may mean that you focus on poses that help you to see a new perspective, discover courage in challenging times, or foster self-confidence. Take your time and be aware of the effects that an archetype has on your body, mind, and spirit. While you'll continue to practice all the poses, the goal is to concentrate on those that best support your personal transformation. The process isn't to be rushed! Before moving on to the following steps, get comfortable with using the archetypes in your yoga pose practice.

Energy Centers

Chakras

*Go beyond the physical and
connect to a higher reality.*

While Western medicine has made great strides in knowledge about the physical systems of the body, Eastern medicine has a much more sophisticated understanding of the body's energetic system. The energetic system in yoga is comprised of seven major chakras, or energy centers, and the *nadis,* or energy lines, which connect to the chakras and through which energy flows throughout the body. The concept of chakras appeared in modern literature in the fourteenth century but was written about much earlier in the ancient yogic text, the *Upanishads*, 2,500 to 3,000 years ago.

The word *chakra* means "wheel (or vortex) of energy." The chakra system addresses the human being in terms of mind, body, and spirit. The heart chakra, for example, corresponds to the heart, the thalamus gland, feelings of love, the color green, the element of air, and spiritual devotion. We will study each of the seven chakras in detail in this step.

Energy Lines (Nadis)

The chakra system includes the three major energy lines (nadis) reviewed in Step Four on breathing. The yogis observed psychological and physiological correlations associated with each of these energy lines. When the body is functioning optimally, the flow of energy along the nadis is constant and unobstructed.

The moon current (*ida nadi*) spirals up the spine and exits out the left nostril. When the left nostril is open, the moon current flows freely. This energy line correlates to the parasympathetic nervous system and has a cooling and calming quality. It is associated with the right side of the brain and with quiet, spatial, and passive types of thinking. An open left nostril also signifies that salivation and hunger are minimal, indicating a need to drink water rather than eat food for better digestion, or to rest and sleep rather than be active.

The sun current (*pingala nadi*) spirals up the spine and exits out the right nostril. When the right nostril is open, the sympathetic nervous system dominates, bringing heat to the body. It reflects left-brain dominance and is responsible for active, alert, and logical types of thinking.

If you would like to check which nostril is more open at any given time, simply place the right and left index fingers beneath the respective nostrils and exhale with moderate force—you will be able to feel the exhale of the dominant nostril over the non-dominant one. Ideally, we want both nostrils to be open so that the body, mind, and spirit are in balance. Nostril dominance can be controlled through breathing exercises, including alternate nostril breathing. This breath control exercise, referred to as channel purification (*nadi shodhanam*), has the effect of balancing the sun and moon currents, and harmonizing both sides of the brain and body.

These exercises activate the third major energy line, the most powerful channel (*sushumna nadi*), which travels through the center of the spine to the crown of the head. This channel is activated when yogis experience deeper states of meditation.

Chakras Are Emotional/Spiritual Feedback Systems

A chakra, or energy center, is where the three energy lines intersect as they spiral up the spine. These energy centers have unique physical associations where subtle environmental/life/spiritual energy is absorbed and distributed to the cells, organs, and tissues. It is generally understood that there are seven major energy centers, which have some association with the nerve plexuses and endocrine glands, but more specifically with the Chinese system of acupuncture meridians.

As we discussed in Step Four, the combination of breath and energy in the body is known as life force, or prana. Our life force is affected by our choices and experiences, whether physical, emotional, or spiritual in nature. Each chakra processes and "remembers" emotional events and trauma. This appears to be an important contributing factor in explaining why some people become ill and others do not. Along with heredity, diet, exposure to environmental toxins, and bacteria and viruses, chakra energy may be the weakest link in the chain, as it is typically the first to break under emotional and spiritual stress.

When we work with the chakras, conscious or unconscious blocks in our emotional, physical, and/or spiritual development are revealed. By focusing on a particular chakra, we stimulate the energy associated with it and awaken dormant areas of the brain, allowing us to experience a higher state of consciousness. In yoga practice, therefore, it can be enlightening to practice poses that heighten awareness of specific chakra areas. Later in the chapter, you'll find specific information on yoga poses and their effect on each chakra.

As you focus on the chakras, you will very likely find some sort of block, perhaps a "broken heart." While it takes courage to move through emotional or spiritual challenges, it may be comforting to know that working with the chakras is highly effective in transforming the underlying problem. When we are faced with an issue like a broken heart, it makes sense to emphasize poses that highlight the chakra associated with that issue—in this case, the heart chakra. In this way, the dominant chakra of each pose serves to enlighten understanding of the particular chakra we are focusing on.

Chakras as a Holistic System

Chakra theory is a holistic paradigm that includes fields like psychology, physiology, astrology, and energy anatomy (how prana moves through the body). It also considers naturalistic elements such as color and sound. Chakra theory examines the interaction between the whole and the part, and can also be called holistic awareness. The system encompasses every level of human nature from the intangible spirit to the tangible atom and everything in between.

The following paragraphs offer brief summaries of the seven chakras. Each overview begins with a descriptive energetic anatomy that defines the related paradigms followed by the physical location. Sense, sound, food, color, and elemental properties are also briefly outlined. A functional description in terms of what a balanced and unbalanced chakra may feel like is also included. Helpful breathing, meditations, and affirmations are suggested. At the end of the chakra summaries, you'll find personal reflection questions and a brief case study. After the seven chakra summaries, we'll explore using chakra awareness in yoga poses.

Chakras (Energy Centers)

First Chakra: Root (*Muladhara*)

Energetic Anatomy: Rootedness and connection to earth. The basic qualities of human nature, including biological family and early social environment. Group thought forms, authority figures, and tribal instincts. Primal energy. The past and present. Elimination of physical and emotional waste—that which no longer serves the greater good.

Physical Location: Located at the base of the spine. Also associated with the legs, knees, feet, ankles, toes, large intestine, elimination system, lower back, anus, colon, prostate gland, skeleton, teeth, nails, blood, and bone marrow.

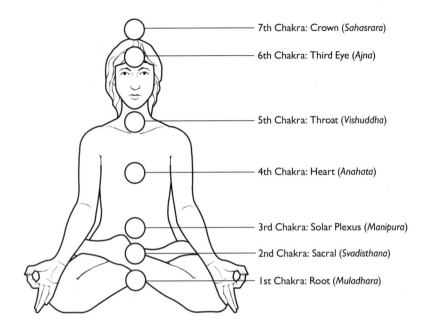

7th Chakra: Crown (*Sahasrara*)

6th Chakra: Third Eye (*Ajna*)

5th Chakra: Throat (*Vishuddha*)

4th Chakra: Heart (*Anahata*)

3rd Chakra: Solar Plexus (*Manipura*)

2nd Chakra: Sacral (*Svadisthana*)

1st Chakra: Root (*Muladhara*)

Sense: Smell

Sound: Oh

Food: Proteins

Color: Red

Element: Earth

Balanced Root Chakra: Honors and accepts family history and personal upbringing; feels grounded and balanced. Experiences a harmonious relationship with the family of origin, society, and culture. Connected to nature, facilitating spiritual growth. Stands up for oneself and feels at home in the world.

Unbalanced Root Chakra: Tendency for tightness in the anus, potentially caused by fear or other unresolved issues, inhibiting elimination. Overly intellectual lifestyle. Erratic colon function and constipation. Low back pain, sciatica, varicose veins, rectal tumors, depression, anxiety, stress, and immune-related disorders. Inability to find a place that feels like home; inability to make things happen (creative efforts blocked). Greed, hoarding, excessive weight gain, superstitious fear patterns.

Related Intention: Balance, Peace, Connection, Unity, Presence, Trust, Supported, Safety, Grounded, Nourished, Nurtured, Stillness, Security, Strength, Calm, Patience

Related Attitude: Knowledge

Yoga Poses: Focus body awareness on balance, centeredness, and presence. Feel the weight of the body over the feet, observing gravity's pull, and feeling grounded to earth. Relax the anus. Practice Root Lock to seal energy (see Step Eight).

Mountain Pose	Cradle	Crocodile
Palm Tree	Straddle, Side-	Frog
Tree Pose	ward Bend	Child's Pose
Eagle	Straddle, Foot on	Cow Face
Squat	Inner Thigh	Corpse
Root Lock	Cobra	
Butterfly	Lunge	

Breathing Exercise: Diaphragmatic breathing stretches the hips and base of the spine and helps to release root chakra blockages. Breathe deeply into the tailbone and into the root chakra.

Meditation Exercise: Imagine roots that connect you to the core of the earth. Visualize a red triangle (representing creative energy) or a yellow square (earth element).

Affirmation or Mantra: "I am safe and secure. I am grounded and stable. I belong here on earth at this time. My body is strong and healthy. Contentment with my life situation gives me abundance."

Questions for Reflection: What causes you to feel ungrounded? What helps you feel grounded? What have been your most inspired experiences—times when you felt highly connected to yourself, to others, and to the earth? How can you reignite the essence of those experiences in daily living?

Considerations: Practice outdoors, to sounds of nature, or drumming.

Case Study: As Mary learned more about yoga and the chakras, she recognized she was holding tension in her legs, especially when driving.

She first noticed the tightness during their recent move to a new neighborhood. Far from her support network of friends and family, Mary felt out of place and lonely. She began practicing root chakra–related poses with the intention of relaxing and feeling grounded through her legs. Mary decided to call her loved ones more often for support and take more walks in the woods to feel connected to her surroundings. Long-term, she planned to join a neighborhood book club and a local yoga center to establish a new support system. As a result of her actions, Mary became balanced in her new home and subsequently served as an anchor of stability for others.

SECOND CHAKRA: SACRAL (*Svadisthana*)

Energetic Anatomy: Creativity and relationships. Relationships with your partner, friends, and co-workers, and how you maintain power and control within those relationships. Enjoyment and pleasure associated with food, drink, sexuality, entertainment, desires, and emotions. The moon influences this chakra, just as the moon pulls on the earth's waters.

Physical Location: Located near the genitals. Associated with the pelvis, hips, sacrum, lower back, womb, bladder, kidneys, circulatory system, blood, lymph, gastric juices, and sperm.

Sense: Taste
Sound: Uu
Food: Liquids
Color: Orange
Element: Water

Balanced Sacral Chakra: Balanced relationships with others including personal strength and a willingness to be vulnerable. Able to give and receive. Empowered. Honoring the opportunity to learn from every relationship, even from those that are difficult. Ability to express emotions. Balanced and healthy approach to food, work, and sex. Comfortable with sensuality. Creatively inspired and fertile, able to "shoot from the hip."

Unbalanced Sacral Chakra: Addictive behavior toward food, sex, work, or relationships. Eating disorders, sexual dysfunction or disorder. Attachment to pleasure and aversion to discomfort. Financial worry or pressure—fear of not having enough. Inability to balance desires with discipline. Creatively "stuck." Fear, anger, resentment, overwork. Obsessiveness, jealous, blame, guilt. Physically or emotionally abusive or abused.

Related Intention: Creativity, Fertility, Flow, Interdependence, Collaboration, Harmony, Sensuality, Sensual Awareness, Free, Vessel for Divine Creation, Connected, Friendship, Fun, Pleasure, Fruitful, Blossoming

Related Attitude: Duty, Knowledge

Yoga Poses: Cultivate awareness of the sensual aspects of each yoga pose through the senses of sight, sound, taste, hearing, touch, and movement. Moon Salutations explore the energy of the moon and its effect on human behavior and physiology. Practice yoga with a sense of pleasure.

Forward Bend	Straddle, Side-ward Bend	Child's Pose
Angle Pose		Line (Warrior III)
Lower Spinal Twist	Straddle, Foot on Inner Thigh	Moon Salutations
Squat	Cobra	Raised Hand to Big Toe Pose
Cradle	Frog	Half Lotus

Breathing Exercise: Diaphragmatic breathing

Sensory Mastery Exercise: Yoni mudra, symbolically closing off the senses with hands on face (see Step Eight).

Meditation Exercise: The visual image and auditory sounds of water.

Affirmation or Mantra: "I allow myself to feel and experience pleasure. I am a sensual being. I embrace and celebrate my sexuality. I love and nurture myself. I embrace change. I am a part of the creation of the universe."

Questions for Reflection: In what ways do you express your creativity? Is there someone in your life you are having difficulty with? What can you learn from the relationship? What is your relationship with yourself like? Do you embrace your own sensuality? Do you like who you are?

Considerations: Listen to flowing music or the sounds of water, like the ocean, a river, or a babbling brook.

Case Study: Mary felt unattractive and feared that her husband was interested in younger women. Mary focused on her second chakra as she practiced yoga poses to get in touch with her inner sensuality and sexuality. She felt tightness in her hips and concentrated on breathing into them as she gently moved through the poses. She found herself delighting in a release of tension as she exhaled and discovered untapped reserves of energy and vitality. She began to feel her inner beauty radiate throughout her being, nourishing her in ways she normally sought in food and entertainment. Mary nurtured her body with exercise and a healthy diet. Her pre-motherhood spontaneity returned along with her laughter. Everyone, including her husband, was attracted to her rediscovered freedom.

THIRD CHAKRA: SOLAR PLEXUS (*Manipura*)

Energetic Anatomy: Manipura means "illustrious gem," reflecting the vitality and energy of the "fire chakra." Relates to self-assertion, self-esteem, ambition, and will. Ability to honor your "gut" wisdom and trust your intuition about personal and professional situations. Being the primary decision maker in your life. Self-confidence and personal empowerment.

Physical Location: Located near the stomach. Associated with the upper/small intestines, liver, kidneys, gallbladder, pancreas, adrenal glands, spleen, lower/middle back, muscles, skin, digestive system. Digestion and food metabolism (distinct from elimination, which is associated with the first chakra), the gastric glands, pancreas, and gallbladder.

Sense: Sight
Sound: Ah
Food: Starches
Color: Yellow
Element: Fire

Balanced Solar Plexus Chakra: Able to trust one's instincts and make self-empowered decisions. Balanced identity, self-esteem, and self-worth. Vital, energetic, and active.

Unbalanced Solar Plexus Chakra: Poor posture, inflated ego, self-righteous, mild depression, sad, stressed, unable to trust others or oneself. Fear and anger, reflecting lack of personal power and feeling intimidated. Weak digestion, ulcers, and production of adrenaline.

Related Intention: Honor, Integrity, Self-worth, Self-care, Illumination, Self-assertion, Ambition, Willpower, Discipline, Empowerment, Power, Strength, Fortitude, Mastery, Clarity, Focus, Determination, Persistence, Achievement

Related Attitude: Duty, Mastery

Yoga Poses: Practice poses that open the solar plexus. When posture is hunched forward, the third chakra is cut off. Stand upright with shoulders rounded back and chest out; shoulder shrugs that involve rounding shoulders back and down on the exhale. Practice poses to build confidence, building heat and energy to fuel the fire in this chakra.

Wheel	Warrior II	Camel
Side Bend	Reverse Prayer Pose	Forward Bend, hands behind the back
Sun Salutations		
Plank	Windmill	
Side Plank	Line (Warrior III)	Backbend
Warrior I	Seated Twists	Abdominal Contraction

Breathing Exercise: Breathing into solar plexus (diaphragmatic breathing) soothes the adrenal glands and releases stress. Imagine gold light filling the solar plexus.

Meditation Exercise: Visualize light, perhaps in the form of the blazing sun or a ball of fire, radiate from this area into the whole body. Or concentrate on a candle flame (real or visualized).

Affirmation or Mantra: "I am powerful and strong. I live with honor and integrity. I manifest my dreams. I am enough as I am. Whatever I do is more than good enough."

Questions for Reflection: Are there any events from childhood that damaged your self-esteem? Do you continue to engage in negative self-talk and, if so, what? When in your life did you feel the strongest and most empowered? What is a positive attribute or gift that others tend to notice about you?

Considerations: Practice meditation or yoga poses with a burning candle.

Case Study: Laura always deferred to her friends and family, and was often upset with herself that she didn't voice her thoughts to those around her. She had kept quiet for so long that it had reached the point where she often didn't even know what her own opinion was or how she was feeling. Through her yoga practice, Laura realized that her inability to think, speak, and act for herself reflected low self-confidence and a lack of trust in her innate wisdom. Focusing on third chakra poses, Laura took her time working through the emotional blocks that she encountered along the way. At first, she found it very difficult to bend backward in some of the poses because she was afraid. As she practiced, she gained inner strength, empowering her to let go of old perceptions and invite in the energy of the fire chakra. Soon she was feeling strong as she practiced her backward bends. As a result, she grew stronger in her relationships with others and radiated her own inner light and vitality.

FOURTH CHAKRA: HEART (*Anahata*)

Energetic Anatomy: This is the balance point between the world of matter and the world of spirit (the lower "physical" energy of the first three chakras with the "metaphysical" energy of the upper chakras). The heart chakra is associated with emotions like love, kindness, jealousy, anger, and hatred. Involves love for oneself and life. Relates to compassion, forgiveness, and unconditional love.

Physical Location: Located at the heart, between the solar plexus and throat. Associated with the upper chest, upper back, lungs, heart, ribs, breasts, diaphragm, shoulders, arms, hands, mid-back, skin, immune system, thymus gland, and circulatory system.

Sense: Touch

Sound: Ay

Food: Vegetables

Color: Green

Element: Air

Balanced Heart Chakra: Love, compassion, relationship, healing. Loving oneself in the form of self-acceptance.

Unbalanced Heart Chakra: Defensive, low self-esteem, egotistical, attached to outcome, needy, codependent, shy, lonely, unable to love or forgive self and/or others, fear of commitment, lack of empathy, cut off from emotions. Excessive behaviors like possessiveness and jealousy can manifest as heart disease and high blood pressure. Deficiencies express as shallow breathing, tense chest, lung disease, asthma, allergies, bronchitis, pneumonia.

Related Intention: Love, Compassion, Kindness, Generosity, Giving and Receiving Love, Unconditional Love, Forgiveness, Openness, Acceptance, Dedication, Inspiration, Hope, Trust, Healing, Humanity, Devotion, Nourishment, Surrender, Introspection

Related Attitude: Non-attachment

Yoga Poses: Develop trust; surrender to open heart fully; foster introspection.

Standing Prayer Pose	Triangle	Reclining Goddess
Palm Tree Pose	Windmill	Moon Salutations
Cow	Tree Pose	Reclining Hero
Bow Pose	Squat	Shoulder Stand
Downward Dog	Fish	Corpse
Half Moon	Bridge	

Breathing Exercise: Diaphragmatic breathing. Practice simply feeling the breath, rather than thinking about or controlling it.

Meditation Exercise: Reflect on a loving relationship that kindles positive feelings. Feel the emotion in the heart chakra and allow it to radiate throughout the body. Try mindfulness meditation focusing on breath (air element).

Affirmation or Mantra: "I am open to the deep love in my heart. I love and I am loved. I give and receive. I am worthy of love. I am compassionate, forgiving, and patient. I embrace the good and bad in the universe."

Questions for Reflection: What is your first memory involving unconditional love? Were you the giver or the receiver of this love? How did it make you feel? What do you love about life? About yourself? Finally, what ignites passion in your heart?

Considerations: Practice with air sounds, like flute music or wind through the trees.

Notes: Forgiveness is a spiritual act of perfection and can be a very physically healing act.

Case Study: Much to his surprise, Steve woke up one day and realized that his life had become rather purposeless. He had beautiful children and a lovely wife, but his passion had seemingly evaporated. Surely there was more than navigating work issues and juggling his children's schedules! Life had become "going through the motions" and he often felt he was on automatic pilot. Whenever he could connect to his emotions (which was not all that often), he felt bored and jealous of others who seemed to have rich, happy lives. Realizing this was a dead-end path, Steve dedicated himself to feeling love with his family, and discovering ways to reignite his love of life. While practicing heart-opening poses, he realized that he was protecting his heart by his usual hunched-over posture. As he explored heart chakra yoga poses, his posture transformed and he gradually connected with his emotional side. Over time Steve tried listen with his heart rather than his head, and discovered a healthy balance between the two. Balance became a key priority for Steve as he realized that he was not just a facilitator of other people's lives, but actually had his own life, which he must honor by following his heart's desires. As Steve's love of life grew through enriching experiences, his love for himself and for his family blossomed.

Fifth Chakra: Throat (*Vishuddha*)

Energetic Anatomy: Pure food, thought, and speech. Chanting, praying, or devotional singing to facilitate higher consciousness and uplift the spirit. Personal expression, thoughts, and opinions. Following one's dreams; using personal power to create, with faith and knowledge. Recognizing the power of thoughts, words, and actions in creating reality.

Physical Location: Located in the throat. Associated with the neck, jaw, mouth, teeth and gums, esophagus, hypothalamus, and thyroid glands.

Sense: Hearing

Sound: Ee

Food: Fruits

Color: Turquoise

Element: Ether / sound

Balanced Throat Chakra: Strives toward purity in food, thought, and speech. Committed to truth and honesty. Communicative and able to express feelings, thoughts, and opinions. Ability to listen objectively and inquire rather than make assumptions. Self-mastery.

Unbalanced Throat Chakra: Neck tension due to lack of communication, creativity, or harmony with others. Lack of self-assertion from being ridiculed or criticized, particularly in childhood. Inability to express emotional needs, feelings, and opinions. Dishonesty and addictions. Weak throat chakra is reflected in a chronic sore throat; mouth, gum and teeth issues; scoliosis; stiff neck; tension headache; swollen glands; and thyroid conditions. Excessive throat chakra results in excessive talking, inability to listen, hearing difficulties, stuttering, addiction, judgment, and criticism.

Related Intention: Communication, Purification, Surrender, Willpower, Personal Expression, Creativity, Faith, Knowledge, Harmony

Related Attitude: Surrender, Mastery

Yoga Poses: To release tension in neck / shoulders, open throat, stretch and strengthen muscles in shoulders and upper back. Face, neck, and jaw stretches, shoulder shrugs. Neck and shoulder tension can be released by focusing on the throat (lips relax the jaw). Practice Throat Lock in forward bending poses (see Step Eight). Shoulder Stand promotes blood flow to upper body, which nourishes the master glands, including the thyroid.

Palm Tree Pose	Cobra	Throat Lock
Forward Bend	Locust	Plough
Downward Dog	Bow Pose	Shoulder Stand
Lunge	Bridge	

Breathing Exercise: Victorious breath

Meditation Exercise: "Om" (primordial sound, universal creation).

Affirmation or Mantra: "I speak truth. I express my feelings with clarity, sensitivity, and confidence. I listen to my own voice. I allow my creativity to flow. I effortlessly manifest my ideas. I acknowledge the power of words to create."

Questions for Reflection: Do you clearly focus your intention and make choices that empower your ambition? What prevents you from communicating effectively? Why are you hard on yourself but not others?

Considerations: Practice yoga poses to music that inspires you.

Notes: Practice chanting sounds and notes that resonate with each of the chakras.

Chakra	*Sound*	*Note*
First	oh	C
Second	uu	D
Third	ah	E
Fourth	ay	F
Fifth	ee	G
Sixth	mm	A
Seventh	ng	B

Case Study: After Laura practiced with an emphasis on third chakra poses for a few months, she become more empowered but not quite able to speak her new truth to her friends and family. She therefore focused on her throat chakra to expand her self-expression and communication.

Laura discovered she was carrying the burden of her brother's illness on her shoulders and felt responsible for his happiness. At the same time, she had enabled him to take advantage of her. By practicing surrender, she was able to let go of this need to fix her brother. She decided to trust that he would be cared for and that he had his own journey to live and discover. She would continue to love him, but her responsibility was to her own spiritual growth, and she began to feel more empowered to move in a new direction with her career.

Sixth Chakra: Third Eye (*Ajna*)

Energetic Anatomy: Ajna means "to perceive or command." This chakra is the doorway through which higher wisdom and intuition enters. While the intuition of the third chakra is more practical, sixth chakra intuition is of spiritual significance, of life itself—finding the meaning and purpose inherent in all of life's cycles, including disease and death (transcending states of self-pity). The visions one sees in the third eye can be manifested into reality by willpower. The third eye chakra is about focusing energy in positive directions.

Physical Location: Located on the forehead, between and just above the eyes. Also known as the third eye. Associated with the pineal gland, brain, eyes, ears, and nose.

Sense: Sight

Sound: Mm

Food: Herbs

Color: Indigo blue

Element: Light

Balanced Third Eye Chakra: Spiritual thinking and perception—views life situations as lessons for personal development. Clear vision and possible clairvoyance. Ability to see the truth in every situation. Focused, yet open to new concepts. Introspective, inquisitive, and personally accountable. Strong in spirit and empowered to fully engage in relationships and personal endeavors.

Unbalanced Third Eye Chakra: If underdeveloped, one can experience aimlessness, headaches, nightmares, confused thinking, and depression. If overdeveloped, there's a tendency to intellectualize, to be aloof or disconnected from the heart. When unbalanced, typical indications are fear, inadequacy, insecurity, jealousy, blame, and paranoia. Also connected to brain tumors, hemorrhages and blood clots, blindness, neurological disorders, deafness, headaches, spinal difficulties, anxiety or nervousness, comas, depression, schizophrenia, grand mal seizures, emotional disorders, and learning disabilities.

Related Intention: Truth, Wisdom, Intuition, Awareness, Focus, Transcendence, Insight, Non-attachment, Spiritual thinking, Clear vision

Related Attitude: Knowledge, Non-attachment, Mastery

Yoga Poses: Poses that enhance visualization and focus attention.

Mountain Pose	Dancer	Child's Pose
Palm Tree Pose	Head to Knee	Eye Exercises
Lunge	Seated Twist	Concentration
Tree Pose	Cow	Exercises

Breathing Exercise: Alternate nostril breathing (see Step Four).

Sensory Mastery Exercise: Focus on the flame of a candle.

Meditation Exercise: Use visualization form of meditation where you concentrate on a visual image to focus the mind. Image can be real (open eye meditation) or imagined (closed eye meditation).

Affirmation or Mantra: "My mind is calm and open. I am at peace with whatever is happening in my life. I open to the wisdom within and from others. I listen to my intuition."

Questions for Reflection: What activities help focus your mind? Do you listen to your intuition? How do you define wisdom? Can you look at a current "struggle" with spiritual perception? What are the gifts that this situation has to offer?

Case Study: Steve attended a yoga retreat with the goal of escaping the stress of daily life. He felt depressed, apathetic, and burned out and experienced frequent headaches—all signs of a sixth chakra imbalance.

Arriving at the retreat, he didn't expect to work through these issues, but was simply hoping for a reprieve. While meditating on his third eye, Steve had an epiphany in the form of an overwhelming appreciation for his family and his career. He realized that he had the ability to change his life for the better, most notably his perspective and reactions to challenges. He discovered that he need only commit to daily spiritual practice to achieve balance in his life. Steve came to see his emotional turmoil as a gift, allowing him to understand his own personal responsibility more fully.

SEVENTH CHAKRA: CROWN (*Sahasrara*)

Energetic Anatomy: Associated with the highest state of enlightenment, spiritual development, and thought, and with the highest vibration on the color spectrum (violet). The crown chakra is the entry point of human life force (prana)—an invisible current of energy that endlessly pours in, nourishing every part of the body. Just as the root chakra reaches down into the earth, the crown chakra reaches upward into the spiritual world. Sense of purpose and connection to the Divine. Attitudes, values, ethics.

Physical Location: Located near the crown of the head. Associated with the cerebral cortex, central nervous system, pituitary gland, and the master gland, which regulates all other glands of body. Also, the nervous system, muscle system, skin, and skeletal structure.

Sense: Beyond the senses

Sound: Ng, silence

Food: Fasting

Color: Violet/white

Element: Thought

Balanced Crown Chakra: Spends time in spiritual company and enjoys spiritual discussions. Spends quality time with oneself. Confronts addictions and engages in nourishing activities. Healthy, vital life force reflected in healthy body and clear mind. Awareness of where one invests their energy in life and mindful of personal values.

Unbalanced Crown Chakra: Blocked crown chakra: depression, confusion, rigid belief system, lack of belief, swaying from one idea to the next. Lack of spiritual connection to oneself, others, and the environment. Lack of faith and courage, negative attitudes, self-centered or selfish, unwilling to grow and change, inability to see the larger picture of one's life. Nervous system disorders, paralysis, genetic disorders, bone problems, multiple sclerosis.

Related Intention: Awareness, Union, Wholeness, Presence, Enlightenment, Spirit, Integration, Purpose, Connection, Faith, Transcendence

Related Attitude: Knowledge, Mastery

Yoga Poses: Connect self with higher Self, balance energy of lower and upper chakras.

Mountain Pose	Tree Pose	Backbend
Sun Salutation	Squat	Shoulder Stand
Cobra	Child's Pose	Headstand*

Breathing Exercise: Observe natural breath without controlling.

Meditation Exercise: Simply observe the different states of the mind and thoughts that arise. Continue to bring the focus back to the present moment. Enjoy the moments beyond thought.

Affirmation or Mantra: "I trust in the universal good. I receive the unlimited abundance of the universe. I am one with all beings. Universal energy flows through me constantly. Everything I need to know is revealed to me at the appropriate time. I am open-minded. My beliefs are non-violent."

Questions for Reflection: What activities fuel your sense of connection to something larger than yourself? What are some ways in which we cultivate and strengthen the seventh chakra? What are some ways in which we weaken it?

---

* I don't generally recommend the practice of headstands, due to the risk of injury and increased compression of the cervical spine. If you choose to practice this pose, please do so with assistance of a trained instructor and with great care.

Case Study: After attending a yoga retreat, Mary was inspired to become a better parent and wife. Having learned about karma yoga (the yoga of action) at the weekend retreat, she began to do her daily domestic tasks as though in a moving meditation. By accepting the task at hand, she practiced being present in each moment. As she washed dishes, she enjoyed the sensation of the warm water on her hands, feeling connected to nature through this life-giving resource. By quieting the incessant complaining in her mind, Mary felt a sense of devotion and connection to God. At times she would forget this perspective, but with some deep breathing she could bring herself back to this newfound awareness. Her connection to the universe strengthened each aspect of her life.

The Circular Theory of Chakras

While it would be easier to explain the chakras as distinct and separate energy centers, it is more accurate to conceive of them as concentric circles, with the root chakra in the outermost, red ring and the crown chakra in the innermost, violet ring. Each chakra contains the other chakras within them.

For example, in Child's Pose, the root chakra energy is undeniably activated as the body rests on the ground. Curled in a fetal position, there is a strong connection to the earth. Simultaneously, the seventh chakra opens as the crown surrenders forward toward the earth. If there is a focus on the heart chakra, the relationship between the root chakra and the heart chakra is enhanced. To facilitate this you might imagine the root chakra color from the outer ring soothing the heart with a grounded quality of energy. Similarly, you could concentrate on the energy of surrender from the innermost circle of the crown chakra and imagine its violet light healing the heart.

Viewed in three dimensions, each chakra also has a front, back, and center. The front side relates to the sun or yang energy, the back to the moon or yin energy, and the center relates to balance. If you have an underdeveloped or weak chakra, focus on energizing the front/sun/yang. For the overdeveloped chakra, focus on the back/moon/yin side. Allow this level of awareness to also guide psychological explorations.

Practicing Chakra Awareness in Yoga Asanas

When practicing yoga poses, it's easy to overemphasize the physical aspects of the practice. Chakras offer us a wonderful opportunity to concentrate on the spiritual and emotional aspects of yoga, and as such, are an important part of a balanced yoga practice. As we develop subtle awareness in the poses, we practice on an entirely different level—one far more enriching and vitalizing. As you discover your chakras and begin balancing the energy in your body, you'll realize significant benefits in your daily life.

Body posture can be one of the more obvious links to the chakras. The easiest example is the heart chakra, located in the center of the chest. When someone is depressed or sad, their body slumps, shoulders round forward, and their neck rounds forward and down. From an energetic standpoint, this particular body posture blocks the flow of energy through the front of the heart chakra. A slumped-over posture lowers energy, while an upright posture uplifts the mind and facilitates deep breathing. By pulling the shoulders back and down, the heart automatically opens, improving the flow of energy through the front of the heart chakra.

Fish Pose and Heart Chakra

For example, the Fish Pose is a heart chakra pose. Lying on the back, the legs are either straight or bent, and the body lifts from the floor in an inverted posture that arches and extends the back, strengthening the lower back muscles and stretching the abdominal muscles. The body weight on the arms through the elbows and shoulders strengthens all of the supporting muscles. The head is arched back and the crown of the head rests gently on the floor. Instead of blood flowing from head to heart, gravity pushes the blood from heart to head, enhancing circulatory function. From a physiological perspective, this pose is associated with the lymphatic, circulatory, and immune systems.

Respiratory function is also enhanced in this pose. The chest cavity opens, encouraging full respiration. This opens the heart chakra, allowing the flow of energy through the front of the heart chakra. Visualizing the breath flowing in and out of the chakra can increase the effects of the pose. To do this, simply imagine the breath moving through the chakra as you inhale and exhale.

Breathing exercises can also help us connect with the emotional and spiritual qualities of a chakra. As we know, the heart chakra represents devotion, love, and compassion. By connecting the breath with feelings of love and compassion, we can discover a new level of awareness in the pose. An example of linking breath and energetic intention in Fish Pose is to view inhalation as a way of receiving love and compassion, and the exhalation as a way of giving love and compassion to others. By practicing in this way, you'll likely feel a greater sense of connection to others and to yourself. Be creative in your visualizations—they truly do enhance spiritual practice.

This simple Fish Pose now signifies multiple levels of consciousness. Without changing the outward appearance of the pose, we achieve a completely unique inner experience. This, in turn, transforms the physical experience by increasing relaxation and the sensitivity to energy flow. As we focus on each layer of our being, we enhance the natural feedback loop between these layers—each aspect of our mind, body, and spirit nourishes the others.

At this level of practice, the experience of the yoga pose is deepened, not because the pose is more physically challenging, but because of increased spiritual and emotional awareness. Interweaving multiple levels of awareness helps us to explore ourselves beyond the physical pose. When we move from the physical to the mental to the spiritual, the connections with ourselves and everything around us deepens.

Connecting to the Infinite

Step Six has introduced you to the chakra system and its role in holistic health. Chakra imbalances are responsible for a variety of physical, emotional, and spiritual ailments. Yoga poses are very effective in transforming energetic blocks in the body and restoring chakra function. Through conscious breathing and visualization exercises, you can enhance the effects of the poses on the chakras. While you may have discovered that one or several of your chakras are imbalanced, you now have the opportunity to witness just how powerful an influence the chakras are on overall health. Concentrate on poses that enhance function of your imbalanced chakra(s) as suggested in the chapter. Finally, be wary of mimicking the suggestions in this book or others; instead focus on your own process of discovery. With practice, your awareness of the chakras will grow and you'll develop the ability to consciously direct the flow of energy throughout your body.

EXERCISES

1. **Discover Your Chakras:** To identify one of your chakras, take a moment to close your eyes and imagine a loved one. Focus on someone whom you love easily and unconditionally, like a child, spouse, or pet. Spend a few moments cultivating your love and notice where you feel it in your body. Most people will feel a sense of warmth in the heart area. This is the heart chakra or energy center. Conversely, the memory of a romantic break-up or a difficult family relationship conjures up sensations of heaviness or pain in the heart.

   Butterflies in the stomach from public speaking is a common sensation related to the third chakra. This chakra is where gut feelings or intuition start, often in situations where we have to rely on senses other than our intellect to make a decision. Also related to intuition or insight is the sixth chakra, also known as the third eye. A physical headache or pressure is a typical sixth chakra response.

2. **The Chakras in Practice:** Review the information provided on each chakra. Now consider the descriptions for both the balanced and unbalanced state of each chakra. Try to pinpoint the chakras in your body that are healthy and vital and those that are unbalanced. If you find that the description for the chakra's unbalanced state matches issues you are dealing with, it's likely that it needs attention.

   Experiment with the suggested yoga poses to balance the affected chakras. As you practice, be sensitive and aware of how the poses affect you. Remember that the goal is not to develop an abundance of energy in any one area, but rather to create balance throughout the body. Focus on clear, calm, steady energy flowing through the chakra system.

Concentration

Dharana

*Use concentration to go beyond the ego
into pure experience.*

Concentration (*dharana*) stems from the Sanskrit root of *dhir*, which means "to hold or retain." When we concentrate, we cause the mind to hold firm, steady, still, and fixed on one spot, object, or idea. Concentration is the sixth step in The 8-Fold Path of Yoga, of which we have already discussed the first four steps: (1) restraints, (2) observances, (3) poses, and (4) breath control. This chapter introduces the next steps, sensory mastery (*pratyahara*), intended to minimize the distraction, and concentration (*dharana*).

Discovery

To demonstrate the power of concentration, try focusing on your right hand. Think about the hand, examine it with your eyes to trace the lines of the palm and notice the color of the skin tone. In the few brief seconds that you took to concentrate on your hand, physiological changes started to occur, the most common and perceptible change being an increase in temperature. If you compare the feeling of your right hand to your left, it is likely that the left hand feels cooler than the right.

Similarly, yoga poses transform physiology through concentration on specific body points. In Sanskrit, this concentration is called single focus (*desha*). This process often relates to the chakra system, but there is more than the chakra system to consider in the process. Mental focus on a particular point in the body takes consciousness to a deeper level. Just as a simple thought can change the temperature of the hand, concentration on specific body points can deepen the experience of a yoga pose. You will discover subtle aspects of yoga poses simply by using concentration.

"It should always be clearly understood that yoga primarily means control over the mind, and not merely control over the body. When the mind is wholly controlled, the body will certainly be brought under control. On the other hand, there may be full control over the body without the least control over the mind."

YOGA SUTRAS 2:50

Minimize Distractions to Enhance Concentration

To date, there are no other books that cover the fifth step of Patanjali's 8-Fold Path outlined in *The Yoga Sutras* (2:54). This fifth step is sensory mastery, and it enhances concentration in yoga poses as well as meditation.

Most distractions reach us through our five senses, most notably sound and sight. Distractions can easily disturb spiritual practice, whether it is a car alarm, people yelling outside the yoga studio, or a phone ringing. They can also trigger memories very easily. For example, the specific call of a bird that we heard in childhood can bring up memories when we hear that same call as an adult. Even though the memory may be pleasant, it becomes a challenge in our yoga practice. The distracted mind slips very easily out of the present-moment experience of a yoga pose and into the past or future.

The same type of distraction can happen through sight. Perhaps a picture on the wall is crooked, and it becomes bothersome to see it and not be able to correct it. The distracted mind moves from the discomfort of the crooked picture to memories, to impulsive thoughts, and then to other concerns or worries. Due to the amount of sensory stimulus in life, the mind can go from here to there and back again in a microsecond, greatly interfering with one's ability to concentrate on the task at hand. Someone arriving late to a yoga class, leaving to use the bathroom, or even coughing or breathing heavily can be very distracting to the untrained senses.

By bringing our awareness to the conscious self, we can begin to see how we perceive the world through the senses. A positive person sees everyone in a good light and puts a happy spin on everything that happens. A more negative person will always feel stressed by their negativity. While stress and negative energy interfere with concentration, the ultimate goal of sensory mastery in yoga is to rise above both positive and negative perceptions.

How to Minimize Auditory Distractions

Think about a sound that bothers you. What is it about the sound that irks you? The first step in transcending the irritation is to remove negative associations with the sound and recognize that it is just a sound, a neutral phenomenon. The same lawn mower that bothers one person may bring a smile to someone else's face. Sounds are just a part of the world and they are not inherently good or bad. Some sounds are louder than others. Can you listen to the noise without judgment? When we alter our perception, the sound of a young child whining incessantly is no different than the sound of the wind whistling through the trees.

While Suzie is in yoga class, she is faced with a fellow student who continually interrupts the flow of the class to ask questions of the instructor. At first Suzie thought the questions were somewhat interesting, but after the fifth question in fifteen minutes, she felt angry that her peaceful time was being interrupted. Every new pose had Suzie tensing up in anticipation of the next question. After some reflection, Suzie realized that she felt trapped in class, like she felt trapped in her cubicle at work. Suzie had always done the "right thing" in life. She was a good girl, a good student, and now a good member of her company. However, she's beginning to understand that she is a prisoner of her own mind. If she can learn to shift her perceptions, she won't feel trapped in any part of her life.

The key point that Suzie has recognized in her self-study and reflection is that part of her personality caused her perception to be narrow. Once she understood that, she was able to release her projections and reactionary behavior pattern, including choosing to not react to the "question man" in future yoga classes. Instead of feeling irritated, Suzie felt compassionate toward him as a new yoga student. She now has the insight to see that he may one day become a wonderful yoga teacher because of his curiosity and diligence. She smiles to herself now when he asks questions and has even grown to like him. She realizes that his nature is to question and, to him, those questions are a virtue. By understanding him, Suzie is free to accept reality as it is and remain at peace in her yoga class. This example helps us recognize how *we* are responsible for being distracted, *not* the sensory stimulus.

The goal is to understand why you react to stimuli in the way that you do. While it may take you a fair amount of time to understand each reaction, here is a short formula to help you work through this process:

Steps to minimize and eliminate sensory distraction

1. Choose one sensory stimulus that disturbs your yoga practice.

2. Notice the characteristics of this stimulus in terms of intensity, quality, and frequency.

3. Notice the feeling or emotional reaction this disturbance evokes in you.

4. Try to understand the roots of the feeling. If the sound annoys you, try to understand why it annoys you.

5. Accept that the stimulus could be interpreted in a different way.

6. Move the pre-conceived notion from a negative association to a positive. What can you focus on about the stimulus that is funny, interesting, beautiful, or inspiring?

7. Release the negative association, hear the sound for what it is, and then continue to listen or choose to ignore the stimulus. When you accomplish this last step, you will have realized freedom from sensory distraction.

Sound exercise to remove distraction and enhance concentration

Find a consistent sound. In summertime, it could be the chirp of a particular bird or the choir of crickets at night. Another common sound might be the hum of a machine or passing cars. Any sound will do, as long as it is consistent. If there is no continuous occurring sound, use an instrumental piece of music and isolate one instrument within the music. Focus your attention on the sound and then notice how other sounds pull your attention in other directions, disturbing your concentration on the original sound. Once you have started to master this exercise, it can also be done during relaxation.

Stage 1: Simply focus on the sound and maintain consistent concentration. As you continue, recognize when and how the mind wanders to think about other errant sounds. If a truck drives by, how many thoughts sprung from the mind before you returned to the original sound? Be patient and non-judgmental with this process, as it may require some time to master.

Stage 2: The next step in understanding your responses to distraction is to notice why certain sounds grip your mind's attention and others do not. In Suzie's example, the questioning student caused her to associate feelings from work with her time in yoga class. As a continuation of her self-inquiry, Suzie explored why she associated the trapped feelings from work with the question man. Each time you become aware of a new level of your emotions, you'll master the senses in a new way as well.

Stage 3: With practice, moments of unbroken concentration occur for one to three minutes at a time. At this proficient stage, you can begin to work on the sounds that you find annoying in daily life. Apply this same process to the neighbor's dog yapping or the sounds of rush hour traffic and discover that you can consciously ignore the sounds.

Stage 4: The fourth or final stage of the listening exercise occurs when you can listen to one sound and not react to other sounds that used to be disturbing. While listening to a sound and the telephone rings, you would simply notice the phone ringing and let the sound vibrate through the eardrum with no reaction. The sound is noticed but there are no thoughts attached to the sound and attention remains fixed on the original sound.

Sight exercise

To master the sense of sight, candle gazing is very helpful. To get started, sit twenty inches from a lit candle with the flame placed at eye level, in a room free of strong air currents to ensure that the flame stands straight. Avoid eye strain and consult with an optometrist if you have any pre-existing eye conditions. If for some reason candle gazing isn't an option, you can substitute a landscape to gaze at.

Look at the flame and examine it from the following perspectives:

- Note your first perception of the flame
- Relax the eyes and temples and notice the flame

- Observe deep breathing while viewing the flame
- Feel your heart while looking at the flame
- Ignore everything in your field of view except for the flame

For most candle gazers, the flame is seen in a variety of "lights." The flame will seem small at certain times and then larger at other times. The flame's heat is felt in other moments. Add your own observations to the variety of responses and realize that your eyes perceive a limited field of reality.

Flames, as well as other objects, are a complex aspect of nature and can never be fully understood by watching them. Yet, how often do we make assumptions from eyesight alone? Imagine what life could be like if we saw things with a more open mind. For example, the unspoken language of facial expressions is prime ground for misinterpreting others' thoughts and feelings. Have you ever caught yourself assuming what someone was thinking, perhaps that they were judging you in some way, only to discover that your assumption had no bearing?

After working with the candle gazing exercise, you'll find that a relaxed, soft gaze takes in more than a strained gaze does. Eyes that dart to and fro or that are squinty and tense constrict the nervous system. A soft gaze greatly reduces nervous strain and enhances concentration. In a yoga pose practice, maintaining a soft gaze with the eyes open or closed is always recommended.

The Power of Concentration in Yoga Poses

Note: In order to fully understand this section on concentration, it is important to have studied the previous step on chakras.

Concentration is extremely important in yoga practices, including the poses, breathing, and working with the chakras. Let's take the chakras as an example. There are two main approaches to working with the chakras in yoga pose practice. The first approach focuses on the chakra activated by each particular pose, as we discussed in the previous chapter. Fish

Pose, for example, is a heart chakra pose. The second approach, which requires significant concentration, is to focus on a single chakra throughout the poses, regardless of whether they are specifically reflective of that chakra. The yogi then has the opportunity to notice how their chosen chakra is affected by the dominant chakra inherent in each pose. For example, if the yogi superimposed the heart chakra in a forward bend (which generally relates to the third eye chakra), then attention would remain fixed on the heart. Because forward bends draw energy inward, practicing with a focus on the heart chakra influences the heart in a reflective, inward manner. Likewise, in a backbend, a focus on the heart causes the heart to expand and open.

Concentration in yoga poses improves our practice, stills our minds, purifies the body, and connects us to spirit. As you practice concentration in the poses, the first goal is to be aware of thoughts while in a pose. The second is to notice personal tendencies (e.g., fretting about finances, obsessing about your appearance). Then, the mind can connect to intention and empower you with greater self-realization.

Vital Zones

Swami Satyananda Saraswati, in his book, *Asana Pranayama Mudra Bandha,* recommends particular points for concentrating in yoga poses to gain the maximum physical benefits. He explains that "by directing the mind to a specific region of the body or the breath, the effect of a particular practice is increased" (Saraswati, 1991, p. 513). In *Hatha Yoga Simplified*, Shri Yogendra of The Yoga Institute of Mumbai writes, "Physiologists are agreed that the habit of such concentration produces sedative nervous effects like that of deep breathing exercises, which are conducive to the health of both the brain and the nerves. Moreover, the foundation of all success in life—whether physical, mental, moral or spiritual—depends entirely on the power of concentration" (Yogendra, 1991, p. 121).

Monastic yogis identify sixteen sensitive areas or vital zones (*marmasthanani*) that serve as focal points throughout the poses. Concentrat-

---

Marmasthanani (Sixteen Sensitive Points) and the Areas Affected

	Point on the Body	Area Affected
1.	Tips of Toes	Feet, Legs
2.	Ankles	Ankle, Heel
3.	Knees	Knee, Calf, and Thigh
4.	Fingertips	Arms
5.	Tailbone	Hips, Low Back
6.	Lower Belly	Genitals
7.	Navel	Internal Organs, Lower Back
8.	Solar Plexus	Stomach, Mid-back
9.	Heart	Heart, Chest Area
10.	Lungs	Trachea/Lungs
11.	Throat	Throat, Neck
12.	Lips	Jaw, Lower Facial Muscles
13.	Tip of Nose	Sinus, Nose
14.	Eyes	Eyes, Behind Eyes, Temples
15.	Forehead	Thoughts, Forehead
16.	Top of the Head	Skull

---

ing on the vital zones can improve our yoga pose practice dramatically, even with just a few minutes of daily practice. It is fascinating to notice the different feelings that arise when you focus on different parts of the body in the same yoga pose.

You may be interested to know that this experience is not limited to yoga poses: it can also be applied to reading. Reading can be very intellectual if the concentration is focused on the mind. If the focus is on the heart, a more emotional connection to the material can be cultivated. Reading poetry is the perfect example of these connections. Have you ever struggled to intellectually understand a poem to no avail and then had the same poem read to you by a heart-centered teacher? They are very different experiences. Reading can also be perceived by way of the chakras. Perhaps reading this book connects you to experiences that you already understood intuitively (third eye chakra), or it creates a feeling of groundedness (root chakra), and a sense of coming home to the kind of yoga practice you always wanted.

Seated Twist Pose

One unexpected pose for developing concentration is the Seated Twist Pose, which has a particular concentration point that aids the pose. To give it a try, sit on the ground, keep the spine vertical, and then twist the torso to the right and left. While detailed instructions follow in Part IV of this book, the primary thing I want to draw your attention to right now is the emphasis on turning the mid-back at the rib cage. Because the rib cage moves to the side in a twist, it might seem natural to focus on the area near the base of the sternum on the front of the body or the point between the shoulder blades on the back of the body. While this assumption makes logical sense, yogis' empirical research discovered an unexpected area for concentration in this twisting pose.

Now, concentrate on your forehead in the pose. It may seem strange to do so, since it seems unrelated to the twist. As you may already be aware, focusing on a particular area of the body tends to relax that area. A relaxed forehead means no wrinkling of the brow and soft eyebrows. If it is difficult to relax the forehead, simply smile to soften the temples and muscles surrounding the eyes.

At this point in the twist, you may feel a sense of peace that flows through the center of the body. The relaxed forehead stimulates the vagus nerve, which travels down the center of the body to the stomach. In contrast, a tight forehead, often an expression of worry or concern, can cause an upset stomach. The psychosomatic response to feelings of worry impairs the vagus nerve due to the tension. Focusing on the forehead promotes relaxation in the nervous system and further enhances the benefits of the twist.

Connecting Intention with Concentration

When focusing on the concentration point, it is helpful to align it with spiritual intention (as mentioned in Step One). As an example, we're going to work with the intention of peacefulness in a twisting pose, but you'll use your own personal intention in your practice. With this intention, visualize feeling a sense of peace flowing through the nervous system and reaching the stomach as you twist. Concentrate not just on the intention, but also on the key opening point—in this case, the forehead. Keep in mind that tension can build in other areas of the body, preventing full expression of a pose. This may mean that while you normally concentrate on the primary focus point, on occasion you'll want to concentrate on (and thus relax) the hips, back, legs, or jaw. If the forehead does not immediately relax or if it tightens again shortly after relaxation, then the tension is coming from another area. Observe where the tension is coming from and concentrate on that area with your intention. A peaceful intention will bring peace to the body, allowing you to practice the pose more fully.

CONCENTRATION USING DEEP RELAXATION

The sixteen sensitive points in the body (marmasthanani) serve as the key focal points for concentration in yoga poses. *Marman* refers to the joints, or any of the several particularly vital spots in the body. The concept of vital zones is reminiscent of Chinese medicine and acupuncture points. The yoga scriptures, the *Upanishads* (*Shandilya Upanishad* 1.8.1f), speak of the vital zones, as well, but they name of seventeen: the feet, big toes, ankles, shanks, knees, thighs, anus, penis, navel, heart, throat, palate, nose, eyes, third eye, forehead, and head. (Do not be confused by yoga scriptures that offer slightly different information. Because yoga is an unregulated ancient science with many schools of thought, minor differences will appear. Learn from both lists of sensitive points and experiment to discover what works for you.) According to the *Sshurika Upanishad* (14), one should cut through these vital spots by means of the mind's sharp blade. The underlying practice is to focus the attention and breath on each marman, freeing it from tensions so that the life force can flow freely through the subtle channels.

By cultivating a daily mental focus on these points, the body deeply relaxes. It is recommended to practice the following marman point exercise every day for a few months. Remember that it is more beneficial to practice one exercise for three months than it is to practice twenty exercises one time. Your practice can occur at the beginning, end, or middle of the day.

Lie down on the floor, bed, or couch with your feet about a foot and a half apart and the arms in a comfortable position. Close your eyes and take a moment to center. Bring your attention inward and breathe deeply. Then focus attention and breath to the first point at the tips of the toes. Focus on each area for about thirty seconds. After the tips of the toes, move sequentially to the ankles, focusing there for thirty seconds. Focus on each concentration point, moving from the lower points to the higher points one at a time. Spend thirty to forty-five seconds on each point; the total time of the exercise may be eight to twelve minutes. Notice how concentrating on the specific point relaxes the surrounding parts of the body.

Sleep is likely if you practice this for more than twelve minutes. Many people are sleep deprived, so if you doze off, accept that your body may need to rest. Use the dozing as a signal to retire earlier at night and/or reduce your daily activities. However, there are times in life (raising children, caring for elderly parents and so forth) where there is heightened strain. In that case, enjoy a refreshing, short nap!

Continued concentration on these points over time develops certain levels of awareness. First is the ability to think of the area without daydreaming. When your mind inevitably wanders during this exercise, be very gentle with yourself. Self-effacing or self-critical thoughts merely add another disturbance, whereas self-acceptance encourages deeper concentration. Know that distraction is a very normal occurrence. Rather than obsessing about doing the exercise perfectly, notice when the mind wanders and gently call it back. Even people who have practiced concentration for many years experience occasional daydreaming. The difference with the experienced yoga practitioner is that they accept the fact that the mind wanders.

With practice, begin to notice new levels of awareness. Initially, you may notice physical sensations like:

- tingling, heat, warmth, or cold
- complete stillness or a floating feeling
- sounds
- relaxation or tightness prior to tension release
- overall weightlessness, or a heavy, still feeling
- a pulse or a sensation of blood flow
- a sensation of the focal point "breathing," as if through your nose
- an electrical rush, a chill, or some type of energy movement
- color or a pure white light
- emotional release
- a feeling of compassion, optimism, love, peace, acceptance, or general well-being
- a vast sense of infinite space or of oneness with the greater whole of the universe

These sensations are based on the reports of thousands of students over years of observation while practicing this exercise. Follow the focal points and observe your own experience.

Concentration in Yoga Poses

The partial list of yoga poses I have given you here corresponds to the poses listed in detail in Part IV. As mentioned in Step Two, it is possible to discover the attitude of a pose or it is possible to superimpose an attitude on the yoga pose. The suggestions below follow the former approach of using concentration points that "go" with a specific yoga pose.

As each person is unique in their mind and body, your experience and needs in yoga practice will differ from others. A forward bend benefits the person who needs more surrender in the mind while a backbend is more suitable for someone needing more energy. Focus on the concentration points that satisfy your personal needs. The suggested points are a good introduction to understanding how concentrating on specific areas of the body can enhance yoga poses. Over time, personal experimentation is recommended. This is a tool that needs to be practiced!

Remember that this level of study in yoga poses requires effort to notice the more subtle aspects of a pose. I recommend beginning students first master the preliminary steps mentioned in this book, such as intention, attitude, breath, and alignment. As those steps begin to feel more natural, beginners can use the additional techniques offered to continue to make fresh discoveries in their yoga pose practice for many years to come.

CONNECTING TO THE POSES

Pose	Spinal Movement	Focal Point
TREE (PAGE 256)	Balance	Soles of feet, navel area, center of gravity
DANCER (PAGE 258)	Balance	Soles of feet, navel area, center of gravity
BOAT (PAGE 260)	Balance	Soles of feet, navel area, center of gravity
PALM TREE (PAGE 262)	Upward Stretch	Third eye chakra
WHEEL (PAGE 264)	Forward, Back	Solar plexus and throat chakras
SEATED FORWARD BEND (PAGE 266)	Forward Bend	Navel area, sacral chakra
CHILD'S (PAGE 268)	Forward Bend	Navel area, sacral chakra

Pose	Spinal Movement	Focal Point
CAT STRETCH (PAGE 270)	Backward, Forward	Navel area, throat chakra
COBRA (PAGE 272)	Back Bend	Top of head
BOW (PAGE 274)	Backward	Heart and throat chakras
TRIANGLE (PAGE 276)	Side Bend	Navel area, sacral chakra
EXTENDED SIDE ANGLE (PAGE 278)	Side Bend	Navel area, sacral chakra
PARTIAL SEATED TWIST (PAGE 280)	Twist	Third eye chakra, forehead
SUPINE TWIST (PAGE 282)	Twist	Base of spine, heart chakra
BUTTERFLY POSE (PAGE 284)	Extremities	Base of spine, perineum, root chakra
PIGEON (PAGE 286)	Extremities	Throat chakra, or back of neck
WARRIOR I (PAGE 288)	Extremities	Solar plexus chakra
DOWNWARD DOG (PAGE 290)	Inversion	Heart and throat chakras
SHOULDER STAND (PAGE 292)	Inversion	Throat and crown chakras
PLOUGH (PAGE 294)	Inversion	Throat and solar plexus chakras
CORPSE (PAGE 296)	Relaxation	Sixteen points
EASY POSE (PAGE 298)	Meditative	Sacrum, third eye and crown chakras
HALF LOTUS (PAGE 298)	Meditative	Sacrum, third eye and crown chakras

Connecting to the Infinite

In Indian yoga ashrams, as well as many yoga retreat centers, the ego still rears its head, even in the quest for enlightenment. Leading teachers may be brilliant lecturers with loads of charisma but also have an equally big ego. In the end, we are all human beings struggling to find inner peace. For this reason, many expert yoga teachers keep the subtle ideas of yoga secret. Only senior students are taught some of the concepts outlined in this step. This prevents eager students from becoming engrossed in perfecting the subtle aspects of yoga and thereby missing the bigger picture.

Therefore, please use these guidelines to help enhance your life in a positive direction and ultimately reduce suffering in the world. Few things are as important as accepting your strengths and faults. Acceptance, while sounding basic, is an extremely esoteric practice, and very few human beings actually accomplish it. As the songwriter mystic Eden Ahbez once said, "The greatest thing you'll ever learn is simply to love and be loved in return." The aim of self-exploration is to bring inner peace and outer harmony.

Let virtue be your superhuman feat (*siddhi*). The purpose of these exercises is to help you to have a deeper spiritual experience of yoga poses. May your yoga pose practice inspire you to be a more peaceful person with yourself and loved ones, as well as a more productive and helpful member in the whole of society.

Locks and Seals

Bandhas and *Mudras*

*Notice how awareness of subtle energy
connects you to a larger universe.*

Before beginning our study of the locks and seals, I would like to
share a story of a dedicated yoga student that illuminates the potential for extremes in this step. To honor his privacy, I'll call him Dan.
Dan's daily routine included a personal pose practice of ninety minutes every morning at sunrise. During this session an audible, forceful
breathing emanated from his sacred dormitory room into the halls of
the building. Dan would emerge from his solo practice silently every
morning and not speak for hours. He told others that he was developing
his spiritual energy, following a strict diet and heading toward enlightenment. Dan spent many of his weekends at a monastery several hours
away from school and would return from those trips with a heightened
resolve. For a yoga practitioner, Dan had an odd habit of bursting out
in anger, only to fall silent once again. One moment he was a peaceful,
vegetarian yogi, and the next, he was an angry volcano of verbal abuse.

Dan had developed his yoga practices without the instruction of a
yoga teacher. Since he had no expert to guide him, he was doing yoga

practices that did not address his personal needs. Instead of focusing on poses that would calm his nervous system and help him deal with his unresolved issues, Dan practiced more vigorous ones that built up tremendous amounts of energy in his body. This charged the unresolved aspects of his personality and fed his anger. No amount of silence was able to keep his anger at bay. A yoga student without a teacher is as dangerous as a child playing with fire; Dan's practice was a textbook example of this.

When a person practices vigorous types of yoga, energy builds. As the energy builds, both the positive and negative traits of the personality magnify. Dan had no mental problems nor was he on medication or drugs. He was simply misguided and doing practices that created an imbalance in his body and mind. While the average person may not approach yoga as vigorously as Dan did, his story serves as a warning to the few serious students who overdo their practice.

Other common issues that can stem from a misguided and intense yoga practice are a rigidity of belief, extreme seriousness, personal arrogance (e.g., believing that you are spiritually superior to others), or a martyr complex (e.g., trying to help others at the expense of your own well-being). The bottom line: you must learn yoga from a teacher. Even yoga teachers can develop these tendencies if they lack a mentor. Many of these pitfalls can be avoided if the teacher or student works consistently with an instructor. A beginning yoga student might visit or practice with a teacher on a weekly basis. At the intermediate and advanced levels, I suggest speaking with your teacher about how often you need to come to class.

In addition to seeking outside instruction, please take your time incorporating new components into your yoga practice. Each step in this book represents weeks, months, or years of practice to approach mastery. The best way of truly improving your practice is to take time getting to know yourself and addressing your personal needs. I recommend that you wait to move on to the locks and seals until you understand the previous steps in this book. This step represents the final step in yoga pose awareness.

Why Use Locks (*Bandhas*) and Seals (*Mudras*)?

I once asked my teacher, "Why should I keep practicing yoga once the mind is in such a peaceful place? Why not just relax and enjoy life without all these spiritual and physical practices?" I had reached a point where external stress had been greatly diminished and I feared losing motivation. How had my teacher practiced yoga for sixty years without a break in his practice? My teacher's response was that the mind is always in a state of change. While peace can be realized, it has to be maintained. Just as physical health needs to be addressed on a daily basis, mental health also needs to be maintained through the subtle practices of yoga. The upside of change is that there is always something new to discover and explore, making yoga consistently interesting if approached from a holistic perspective.

Exploration of locks (*bandhas*) and seals (*mudras*) in a yoga pose routine empowers students to maintain solid concentration on their practice and cultivate a beginner's mind. As boredom from years of yoga pose practice inevitably sets in, integrating the bandhas and mudras facilitates concentration and heightens your energetic experiences of poses. Many ancient yoga texts discuss bandhas and mudras together, because at times they are performed in tandem for certain practices. Although there are many similarities between the two, a sustained practice over time will illuminate the subtle differences between them.

Awakening Energy

When discussing the concepts of bandhas and mudras, we must consider *kundalini* energy. *Kundalini* is a Sanskrit word meaning "serpent power," and it refers to a mysterious force said to be located at the base of the spine. There are many different interpretations of what kundalini actually is. It is often described as latent energy at the base of the spine that awakens with purification exercises. Once awakened, kundalini energy travels through the chakras and brings about higher states of consciousness.

In this book, I'm not going to give you instructions for activating kundalini energy. Instead, I recommend that you seek out an expert teacher to learn safely and effectively. If you notice intense energy in your body while deepening your yoga practice, please consult an experienced yoga teacher or a professional psychologist with a background in yoga to balance these energies. Many people think that high energy in the body represents kundalini energy, but the majority of these incidences are actually imbalances. Energy can also be high in one part of the body and low in another, which is not healthy.

An example of an energy imbalance is Evan, a nurturing man who puts all his energy into his heart but doesn't take care himself—he often misses meals and exercise in caring for other people. He feels an overwhelming energy in his heart that he associates with love. However, after working with an experienced teacher, Evan realized that despite his copious heart energy, there's actually a lack of energy in his third chakra (see Step Six). As the third chakra relates to self-care, Evan works on balancing his time more evenly and taking care himself. After some time, Evan maintains his service to others in a balanced way, relieving him from exhaustion.

In more extreme cases, yoga students may practice poses for hours on their own, tie in intensive breathing exercises, feel extreme energies in the forehead, and think that they're on the verge of enlightenment. This type of student will often have extreme emotional swings due to surges of intense mental energy that is not emotionally integrated into the heart.

John, who has an excess of energy in his third chakra, practices yoga poses for two hours every morning regardless of any other commitment, even if it means losing sleep. He restricts his sexual activity, diet, and social life. He doesn't even take much time to relax. John has become very self-righteous, believing that all of the problems in the world would be overcome if everyone lived the same way he did. When he tries to discuss his thoughts with others, he feels misunderstood and sinks further into isolation. John's situation points to the need for guidance by an experienced yoga teacher.

The Importance of a Mentor

In yoga, one thing to remember is that you are always a student, regardless of how advanced your practice becomes. Maybe you will become a yoga teacher or you are already teaching. Even then, you must continue pursuing education and always have a mentor that guides your personal practice. Teachers experience imbalances just as students do. In Western society, we have our own unique set of imbalances; foremost among them, the ego. The individual ego is so highly regarded that few yoga teachers understand the necessity for minimizing it. Many teachers do not have a mentor to help them to maintain a healthy perspective. Finding this relationship can be challenging, as the popularity of yoga classes in the West has created an abundance of beginner teachers and fewer experienced mentors.

Yoga philosophy reiterates the importance of the teacher in a student's initiation into the practice of bandhas and mudras. It explains that awakening the kundalini energy without knowing how to channel it can be dangerous and detrimental to one's practice of yoga and overall health. The serious yoga student must learn to surrender their ego (*ahamkara*) and establish a level of understanding and trust with their teacher. This is vital for spiritual progress.

The information in this step is for the dedicated yoga student who has practiced ethical living and yoga poses for at least a year. If you are a beginner or instructing beginners, consider focusing on the basic practices first. Before you practice locks and seals, learn and experience the essence of the earlier steps of this book.

An Introduction to Locks (Bandhas)

Bandhas are internal body locks. Translated from Sanskrit, *bandha* means "to hold, lock, bind together, or close." Although the bandha is achieved through muscular movement, it is not valued for its physical effects, but rather its energetic effects. The purpose of practicing a lock is to gather and hold life force in certain areas of the body in order to redirect the energy flow for the purpose of spiritual awakening. It may be helpful to visualize the effect of the bandhas on the body as a hose being folded in half to block the flow of water, thereby increasing water pressure. Bandhas are subtle and with practice, gently tighten and redirect the body's energy.

As reviewed in Step Six, energy centers containing concentrations of life force energy are known as chakras. Extending out from the chakras are energy channels that carry the life force throughout the body, vitalizing and nourishing the entire system. When the body is held in a bandha, the breath and mind are suspended and the life force energizes the seven chakras. This elevates the level of consciousness and helps the practitioner achieve the purity of mind needed for spiritual awakening.

The role of locks in yoga's purification processes is important. The locks are used in various pranayama and pose practices to tone and cleanse the body and mind. The body's energy is circulated from the lower chakras to the higher chakras, resulting in the purification of consciousness. The physical benefits of channeling the energy are good health, substantial energy, and mental peacefulness.

There are three main bandhas in Hatha yoga:

Root Lock (*Mula Bandha*)

Abdominal Lock (*Uddiyana Bandha*)

Throat Lock (*Jalandhara Bandha*)

When all three bandhas are activated at the same time, it is called the Great Lock (*Maha Bandha*). At first, you may find it tricky to incorporate the bandhas into your yoga pose practice. With consistent effort and careful guidance by a teacher, you'll find that it gets easier to integrate them into daily routine.

Note that enlightenment is complete mastery of reality, not the continual pursuit of spiritual experiences. Once practitioners start doing advanced yoga practices, it is inevitable that they'll get in touch with subtle energies. This can manifest in any number of ways and some of these experiences can be quite pleasurable. There is the potential for the ego to surface as you realize that your practice is advancing to new levels. You must not allow the ego to stop the process, but instead continue to fulfill the responsibilities of life with commitment, love, and compassion.

Root Lock (*Mula Bandha*)

The first of three interior body locks used in asana and pranayama practice, Root Lock (mula bandha) controls the flow of energy beginning from the base of the spine. It is called Root Lock for its affiliation with the "root" of the spinal column. There are three groups of muscles around the base of the spine and in the pelvic floor—muscles around the anus, the genitals, and the perineum. On a physical level, practicing Root Lock involves drawing up the muscles of the perineum *only*. For men the area inside the perineum has to be isolated and contracted, while women have to concentrate on contracting the cervix and vaginal muscles.

To activate the Root Lock, exhale and engage the pelvic floor, drawing it up toward your navel. If you don't know how to access the pelvic floor, think of it as the space between the pubic bone and the tailbone. Initially you may need to contract the muscles around the anus and genitals, but the goal is to isolate and draw up the perineum (the area located between the anus and genitals). Do not hold your breath initially. Engaging the Root Lock while doing yoga poses gives them an extra lift.

At first this can be difficult; practice contracting and relaxing the whole of the pelvic floor until you gain muscle tone. Further exercises include drawing up and relaxing each group of muscles until you can isolate them. It takes months of practice to get fully acquainted with the Root Lock and years to perfect it.

To practice, begin by sitting crossed-legged in Easy Pose. With your spine erect and your hands resting on your knees, close your eyes and relax your whole body. Inhale deeply and observe your breath. Slowly bring your focus to the muscles of the pelvic floor. Contract the muscles and relax rhythmically a few times. Bring your attention to only the perineum muscles. Contract and release the muscles while you inhale and exhale, being mindful of not holding your breath. Repeat this exercise to learn how to isolate the correct muscles for the bandha.

Once comfortable, you may proceed to the next stage of practice where you contract and hold the muscles for up to thirty seconds. In this stage, remain aware of the physical sensation and breath. Exhale completely and then begin the Root Lock. Release the muscular contraction and when it is complete, begin to inhale. Be sure to follow this step or the inhalation will cause the release to be forceful due to the change in pressure. Always perform Root Lock in a rhythmic manner.

Root Lock's importance in yoga poses cannot be underestimated. Drawing up of the perineum is the foundation for core strength in the body. It leads to a correct tilt of the pelvis and provides a lift up through the center of the body to the top of the head.

Yoga Poses That Use Root Lock (Partial List)

Mountain Pose	Lunge	Straddle, sideward bend
Squat	Crocodile	
Butterfly Pose	Frog	Downward Dog
Child's Pose	Cow	Cobra

ABDOMINAL LOCK (Uddiyana Bandha)

The second of the three interior body locks strengthens the abdominal muscles. The Abdominal Lock (uddiyana bandha) involves pulling the muscles of the abdomen back and up. Hence it is essential that both the stomach and bowels are empty before practicing. Abdominal Lock can be practiced alone or in conjunction with the Root Lock. Perform Abdominal Lock on an empty stomach or two hours after eating.

Begin by being seated in Easy Pose with the spine elongated and palms resting on the knees. A cushion under the sit bones may be used in order to tilt the pelvis slightly forward and allow the knees to lower toward the floor. Close your eyes and bring your attention to the breath, relaxing the whole body. Let your exhalations be long and deep. Hold the breath as you lean slightly forward. Pretend to draw in a breath, meaning draw your abdomen in and up without taking in any air. Contract the abdominal muscles inward and upward toward the rib cage. Hold Abdominal Lock with the breath suspended for as long as comfortable. It is recommended that beginning students hold for five seconds or less.

To release, gradually soften the abdomen, gently straighten the spine and inhale slowly. Initially there may be a tendency to release the abdominal muscles quickly and take a jerky gulp of air, but with practice a steady and smooth inhalation can be achieved. Begin by practicing the three rounds and gradually increase to ten rounds.

The Abdominal Lock tones, massages, and cleanses the abdominal organs. It is also the seat of the gastric fire that is necessary for a healthy digestive system. The drawing in of the abdomen stokes the fire of the stomach area (solar plexus chakra). In addition to its many digestive health benefits, the Abdominal Lock can eliminate lethargy and soothe anxiety.

Advanced students can use the locks in tandem. Drawing up Root Lock automatically activates the abdominal muscles and encourages them to be drawn in toward the body. A more conscious effort may be required to maintain this subtle drawing in of the abdomen throughout the physical practice of yoga. Engaging the abdominal muscles and the perineum muscles further strengthens the body's core including the lower back, guarding against injuries to it. This is just one example of how the bandhas work together.

Yoga Poses That Use Abdominal Lock (Partial List)

Wheel	Warrior II	Forward bend from Semi-Lotus
Side Bend	Reverse Prayer Pose	
Sun Salutations		
Plank	Line (Warrior III)	Backbend
Warrior I	Camel	

CHIN LOCK (*Jalandhara Bandha*)

The third and last of the three interior body locks directs the flow of energy around the throat area. The Chin Lock (jalandhara bandha) involves the neck and upper spine to make the whole spine erect. Chin Lock can be practiced alone or in conjunction with the Root and Abdominal locks. Chin Lock has similar benefits to victorious breath (Step Four), including soothing the nervous system and calming the mind.

To engage this lock, sit in a meditative pose. Place your hands on your knees in order to extend the arms. Close your eyes and bring attention to the breath. Allow the breath to be calm and rhythmic. Exhale completely and drop the chin down toward the chest, but do not round the back of the neck. Keep the arms locked in a straight position and use the palms to press the knees down.

In this position, hold the breath for as long as it is comfortable, beginning with six to ten seconds. When you are ready to release, relax the shoulders and arms and bring the chin up to inhale. Stay seated for a few minutes to bring your breath back to a normal rhythm. You may repeat Chin Lock two to five times.

Chin Lock controls the network of energy channels around the neck. The physical aspects of these particular channels are the blood vessels and nerves of the neck. Hence this lock regulates the circulatory and respiratory systems. Once these systems are healthy, energy flows upward to the higher chakras. The practice of Chin Lock relieves stress and anxiety and produces a one-pointed concentration that will enhance meditative practices.

To practice the Chin Lock in conjunction with the other two major locks, you must first master them individually. Draw the pelvic floor upward, engaging in Root Lock. This leads to the abdomen drawing in and up under the rib cage and into the Abdominal Lock. Finally, the chin drops to the chest and draws back into the Chin Lock.

Yoga Poses That Use Chin Lock (Partial List)

Forward Bend	Child's Pose	Shoulder Stand
Seated Toe Touch	Butterfly Pose	Symbol of Yoga
Plough		

Tongue Lock (*Jihva Bandha*)

Though not considered one of the primary bandhas, the Tongue Lock (jihva bandha) still has relevance for yoga practice. During most yoga poses, meditation, and breathing exercises, it is appropriate to place the tip of the tongue directly on the roof of the mouth just behind the front central incisors. The point to focus on is where the roof of the mouth curves up. This lock aligns the energy of the front and back channels of the body by connecting energy pathways from the head to the heart. Locking the tongue symbolizes the student's attention to verbal silence while doing yoga poses. The term *mauna* represents silence in yoga and may be understood in a variety of ways ranging from verbal silence to the "silence of movement" and, ultimately, to the silence of the mind.

Most yogic breathing flows in and out of the nostrils. While there are exceptions to this rule, nasal breathing generally quiets the mind. By using the Tongue Lock while breathing, you will increase this effect. While this exercise may seem very simple, I recommend that you use the Tongue Lock in your yoga pose practice unless your instructor says otherwise.

An Introduction to Seals (Mudras)

The Sanskrit word *mudra* stems from the root word *mud,* meaning "delight or pleasure," and *dru* meaning "to draw forth." Mudras, used by yogis to regulate energy flow by sealing energy pathways, are also translated as gestures or attitudes. Some of the ancient descriptions of seals correlate to healing hand gestures and are a part of traditional Indian dance forms. Seals have evolved to become an important part of yoga pose practice.

Mudras are most accurately described as a seal to an energy pathway in order to cause the energies of the subtle body to flow in a circuit-wise fashion. Seals are similar to locks in the sense that they help channel life force, causing it to merge with the cosmic force of the universe. This is why some texts will discuss seals and locks together. The differences in the way the seal is performed can be explained in terms of physical intensity. When any of the locks are performed, a large group of muscles are contracted internally and cannot be held for long periods of time. A seal, on the other hand, may involve the whole body in a yoga pose or it may be a simple hand gesture that uses only a small group of muscles. Because of this difference, seals can be sustained for longer periods of time. Using the earlier analogy of the hose, you might visualize the effects of mudras on the body as the two ends of the hose being connected to one another, allowing water to flow in a circuit.

Seals are a combination of subtle physical movements that adjust mood, attitude, and perception and deepen awareness and concentration. There are twenty-five mudras in Hatha yoga, including hand gestures, the eyes, and body postures. The gestures are symbolic of various states of consciousness, which are incorporated into one's state of being after significant practice. Seals can help you heal, rejuvenate, balance, and connect to the voice of wisdom. The *Hatha Yoga Pradipika*, a classic Sanskrit manual written in the fifteenth century, considers seals to be a *Yoganga*, or an independent branch of yoga that requires subtle awareness.

Seals change consciousness through their powerful effect on the chakra system. As we discussed early in Step Six, there are three main energy channels, or nadis, in the body, the intersections of which are the chakras. When we connect parts of the body such as the hands and palms in certain ways, we activate, magnify, and direct the energy in the body. Each finger on the hand has meaning and significance in terms of the chakra that it activates and symbolizes a particular organ, emotion, and element. Fingers are also the ends of meridians, so there are several reasons why hand mudras are particularly effective.

Seals can be studied after the practitioner attains a certain level of proficiency and comfort in yoga pose practice and breath awareness and has started to purify the blocks in the body. This includes emotional blocks such as stress, fear, anger, hatred, and judgment. Once students have learned how to train their mind, they can achieve higher consciousness through practicing seals.

Practicing seals daily can help release old habits and unhealthy energies, helping the practitioner to feel recharged with new and vibrant life force. Some practitioners experience a strong emotional response like tears or laughter when practicing mudras, which is possibly a release of latent toxic energy. Others may experience a feeling of love, joy, happiness, peace, and/or contentment.

PRAYER SEAL (*Anjali Mudra*)

Anjali is a Sanskrit term meaning "honor or offering." While *anjali mudra* has several meanings, it is typically associated with offering an intention for yoga pose practice. It's therefore an appropriate seal to perform at the beginning of practice, though it may also be used during the Sun Salutation poses, depending on your style of yoga. The benefits of Prayer Seal include opening the heart, calming the mind, and reducing stress, anxiety, and worry. It reminds us to practice harmony, balance, and silence in our lives. Prayer Seal supports meditation practices by creating an automatic feeling of reverence.

While there are many variations, here are the most important and frequently used *mudras*:

Prayer Seal (*Anjali Mudra*)
Knowledge Seal (*Jnana Mudra*)
Consciousness Seal (*Chin Mudra*)
Horse Seal (*Ashvini Mudra*)
Womb Seal (*Yoni Mudra*)
Inverted Action Seal
(*Vipariti Karani Mudra*)
Symbol of Yoga (*Yoga Mudra*)

To practice, begin by bringing the hands in front of the chest at heart level with the palms flat and touching each other. Alternatively, you can interlace the thumbs, leaving a small hollow space between the palms. You should feel a slight heat between the palms. Keeping your spine erect, slide your shoulder blades down the back and slightly bow your head. As you practice Prayer Seal, cultivate a receptive, humble, or prayerful attitude. If you wish, set an intention for your practice. Prayer Seal can be practiced for up to five minutes at a time. You may incorporate this mudra at the beginning and ending of many poses to seal the emotional energy of the pose into your heart.

KNOWLEDGE SEAL (*Jnana Mudra*) AND CONSCIOUSNESS SEAL (*Chin Mudra*)

Jnana mudra and *chin mudra* are closely related seals in terms of physical expression and meaning. *Jnana*, meaning "knowledge or wisdom," is an effective seal for invoking wisdom and clarity. The seal is particularly meaningful in yoga pose practice as it connects us to our highest Self. *Chin*, meaning "consciousness," is a sister seal to jnana mudra. Consciousness Seal symbolizes the interconnected nature of human consciousness. Through practicing Consciousness Seal, we're reminded of our sacred relationship to others and to the world around us. The Knowledge and Consciousness seals are hand seals that help to redirect energy that is emitted from the hands back into the body.

Begin by being seated in a meditation position like Easy Pose. You are welcome to sit in any meditative pose that feels comfortable. Fold the index fingers on each hand to touch the inside root of the thumbs. Alternatively, you can just touch the tips of the index and thumb together. Straighten the other three fingers of each hand keeping them relaxed and slightly apart. Place your hands on the knees with palms facing down for Knowledge Seal and palms facing up for Consciousness Seal. Release any tension in your shoulders and relax your arms.

These seals are simple but make meditation poses more powerful. By joining the thumb and index finger, an energetic feedback loop is created between the brain and the hands, engaging the brain on a subtle level. Placing the hand on the knee creates another energy circuit that redirects the energy within the rest of the body. The effects of performing these seals are very subtle and require diligent practice and awareness to perceive the changes in consciousness.

During a long meeting or lecture, one may use these seals discretely to assist in maintaining concentration.

Horse Seal (*Ashvini Mudra*)

The word *ashvini* in Sanskrit means "horse." Horse Seal (ashvini mudra) is the controlled squeezing of the anal sphincter muscles to raise energy from the lower chakras to the higher chakras. Horse Seal alleviates intestinal disorders, regulates energy flow in the body, enhances circulation and lymphatic drainage of the prostate gland, and promotes overall vitality.

Begin by being seated in a comfortable meditative pose. Relax with your eyes closed and bring your attention to the breath. As you inhale and exhale, become aware of your sphincter muscles, the muscles around the anus. Contract on the exhalation and gently release on the inhalation. Make the contraction and release as slow and smooth as your breath. Do not hold in this mudra but learn to coordinate the muscles in this area. Repeat the practice for as many times as you are comfortable. This seal is a preparatory practice for Root Lock.

Yoga Poses That Use Horse Seal (Partial List)

Mountain Pose	Cobra	Child's Pose
Squat	Lunge	Cow
Butterfly Pose	Crocodile	Straddle,
Downward Dog	Frog	sideward bend

Womb Seal (*Yoni Mudra*)

Womb Seal (yoni mudra) uses the image of the turtle withdrawing its head and limbs as five fingertips are placed symbolically over each of the five senses, namely sight, hearing, smell, taste, and touch. The senses are symbolically "sealed" by the Womb Seal.

Begin by sitting in a comfortable meditative position. Using both hands, place your fingers in the following order—index fingers over your eyelashes, middle fingers on the bridge of your nose (don't close off the nose, but continue breathing through the nose), the ring fingers above your upper lip, the little fingers below the lower lip and thumbs over the ears. To avoid straining the shoulders, exhale deeply and lower your shoulders, relaxing the arms. The elbows may rest on the knees if a wall supports your back and your feet are placed near the hips. Hold this pose for three to fifteen minutes and observe the mind slipping into a place of inner tranquility.

After performing this pose, recognize that the pose still has an effect after the hands are lowered. Be still for at least one to two minutes before continuing on to another activity. During this transition time, notice how the mind perceives sensory information. Similar to waking in the morning after a deep sleep, use this experience to consciously understand how the mind perceives sensory stimuli. These insights can help you learn how to respond to stimuli in a neutral way. When a car alarm goes off or a baby starts crying, your perception of those sounds dictates your reaction to them. Womb Seal is a key practice to aid the sensory mastery mentioned in Step Seven, leading to inner peace and calm.

Inverted Action Seal (*Viparita Karani Mudra*)

Inverted Action Seal (viparita karani mudra) directly reverses the flow of fluids from the brain, which is done by reversing the physical body from its natural upright position. The force of gravity reverses the flow of fluids back to the brain. Gravity also allows the internal organs (e.g., prolapsed colon or uterus) to shift into their proper position. Inverted Action Seal aids the circulatory and lymphatic systems and helps the flow of energy through the body. The thyroid, pineal, and pituitary glands receive nutrients from this increased flow of the body's fluids.

The practice of Inverted Action Seal is similar to Shoulder Stand. The major difference is the angle of the back and legs on the floor. In Shoulder Stand the upper back and legs are perpendicular to each other (90-degree angle), while in Inverted Action Seal the upper back and legs are held at respective 45-degree angles.

Begin in a relaxed position lying down on the floor with your legs bent. Lift your legs at a 90-degree angle to your torso and back, which remains firmly on the ground. Follow the steps for Shoulder Stand, except placing the back and legs at a 45-degree angle. Bring your attention to the throat chakra and visualize the color blue surrounding your body.

Remain in the pose as long as you are breathing normally. If you feel strained, release the seal gently by bending knees to the chest and then slowly lowering the legs down to the floor. Alternatively, you can do the pose with your legs up the side of a wall.

It is recommended to practice Inverted Action Seal every day at the same time, preferably in the morning on an empty stomach or two hours after a meal. Hold the final position for a few minutes or until you feel discomfort. Gradually progress to longer periods of time as the body becomes familiar with the seal.

Symbol of Yoga (*Yoga Mudra*)

Yoga mudra refers to the union of individual consciousness with the universal consciousness (the life force that pervades all living beings). It is sometimes referred to as an attitude of reverence, gratitude, or humility wherein the thinking mind surrenders to the feeling heart. The Symbol of Yoga is an excellent practice for relieving anger and tension. It creates tranquility in the mind and reminds us to uphold the principles of gratitude and humility in daily life.

Although advanced yoga students begin with full Lotus Pose, I recommend practicing yoga mudra seated in Easy Pose when you are first learning. To perform, hold one wrist with the opposite hand behind your back or grab the opposite elbows. Breathe deeply and relax your whole body. Bring awareness to the root chakra or the base of the spine. You can perform Root Lock if you wish. Inhale slowly, allowing the breath to rise up in the body. Exhale slowly while bending forward. Complete the exhalation as the forehead touches the floor or when you've achieved a stretch that feels challenging but not overdone. While your head is below the heart, visualize the color violet surrounding the body.

Inhale slowly, raise the trunk, and return to an upright position. Remain aware of your breath. Exhale and bow forward to repeat the mudra. Observe the flow of breath from the crown of the head to root of the tailbone. Perform three to ten rounds (one exhale/inhale cycle), based on your flexibility and personal practice.

Using the Bandhas and Mudras in Daily Life

As we discussed in Step Two on attitude, body posture reflects one's emotional state. At every moment, you are communicating nonverbally that your energy is positive or negative, high or low. Through cultivating your yoga practice, you can transform the way you perceive and react to life's circumstances. Yoga helps us to become aware of our patterns, giving us more power to transcend them. When we take control of our thoughts and emotions, life takes on new meaning and depth.

Locks and seals are an important aspect of managing our emotions so that we can achieve higher consciousness. Think, for a moment, about how you react to daily situations. Are you taken in by the negativity of a co-worker and overwhelmed by your children's high energy, or are you able to handle both types of energies, remaining centered and grounded? There is an associated energy pattern with each perception and reaction—meaning that if you're feeling overwhelmed, anxious, or irritated, there's a negative energy connected with those feelings. Conversely, approaching challenges with vigor, neutrality, and confidence connects you to positive energies. If you've ever caught yourself continuing to think the same thought over and over, you have likely noticed that it affects your energy, for better or worse.

Negative emotions like worry, fear, and guilt create negative energy that hurts the prana system of the body and ultimately compromises your health. To reverse the energy flow to positive levels, you must first become aware of your state of mind and then consciously direct the flow of energy in your body. This means you will need to police what enters your body and treat it like a temple. Begin by avoiding the sources of negative energy. If this is not an option, then turn your thoughts to different aspects of your yoga practice. You can use restraints, observances, poses, pranayama, or mudras to slowly release the old habits that deplete your energy. Diligently practicing positivity will create a gradual change in consciousness and ultimately an incredible lightness of being.

Cautions and Dangers

There are many yoga practitioners who are well versed in locks and seals and enjoy the positive benefits they confer. People who have a daily practice of locks and seals have noticed changes such as converting old, exhausting, unhealthy habits or energies into new positive ones, and being recharged with a new perspective and healthier life force. They may experience love, happiness, joy, peace, and contentment.

While it is natural to enjoy these benefits, it is important to be aware of potential dangers. For instance, awakening spiritual energy without connecting it to a higher intention can cause the energy to manifest in the ego. Without an intention, it's fairly easy to ride the feelings of accomplishment ("Wow, I'm getting really advanced in my practice!") rather than go even deeper. A person who practices locks and seals without an intention may develop a self-righteous attitude. The danger here is that the wisdom of the practices becomes lost when the ego takes over. When the ego is unbalanced, the practitioner can wander off the spiritual path without even knowing it.

Fixating on the energetic sensations is another common danger. It is important to remember that no matter what sensations you experience, it is best to not affix too much meaning to them, as assigning meaning may lead to creating attachments to the sensations. Once you feel the need to perform intense practices in order to create a specific experience, it is imperative to recognize that you are creating a dependency on the result of the practice. It's a type of addiction, strange as it may seem. This type of unbalanced practice creates a yo-yo effect of highs and lows. The highs are great, but if you do not have a disciplined practice, the accompanying low feelings may lead you to stop practicing altogether. Use other people as a gauge of your spiritual development. Your spouse, children, co-workers, and friends should find you a kinder, more peaceful, more focused, and gentler person after yoga practice, not spaced out, angry, or agitated.

First learn to cultivate the qualities of non-violence, purity, kindness, love, charity, and forgiveness. Once nurtured, understanding the ethical norms will allow the ego to become silent. When the ego is silent, the mind is clear and open to receiving instructions for the higher practices like the locks and seals. When the ego enters into submission, the mind is able to manage the emotional effects of a yoga practice in a constructive and spiritual way.

One of the dangerous misconceptions about practicing yoga is that it will remove certain problems from life. For example, certain yogic texts may say, "Practice the Womb Pose and your mind will be introverted." This is not always true—we can work to quiet and focus the mind in Womb Pose, but the pose itself is not a magical formula. We may feel the physical benefits when we practice yoga, but ultimately it is the willingness to explore and understand ourselves, as well as the adherence to ethical norms and positive behaviors that will ultimately offer the most long-term benefits.

Connecting to the Infinite

The bandhas and mudras are the most esoteric topics in this book. These practices have the potential to catapult you to an entirely new level of sensitivity to subtle energy. Like the power of fire, these exercises can burn or they can harness newfound sources of enthusiasm. The suggestion to practice the bandhas and mudras with an instructor is meant to help clarify personal questions. You are now ready to continue into the psychological facets of life that are revealed when traveling beyond the physical to fully understand that which separates you from the infinite.

PART III

Self-Exploration
and Psychology
Steps 9–10

Psychological Blocks

Klesas

*Discover the roots of your tension to gain
physical and psychological freedom.*

Before yoga, I thought I was a happy person," Sue said with a smile that reflected the soul of someone who has faced pain and risen above it. "In the midst of my journey, I realized areas of my life that I had buried from my consciousness. I actually felt hatred toward my brother. A few months ago, I would have told you that I was a completely happy person. At the beginning, I would have said, 'Of course I love my siblings.' Later on I realized that I close my heart at family functions. Prior to yoga, I didn't notice that I came home with neck tension or that I tensed my jaw when I was angry.

"At first, I blamed my new awareness on yoga and stopped practicing. After time, and with the help of my mentor, I was able to realize that yoga has helped me understand who I truly am and allowed me to heal. Since my discovery, I have spent the past month asking forgiveness from God for my hypocrisy. My brother has done nothing wrong. He is conservative and I am liberal. In my arrogance, I thought he was a bad person for being so strict with my son. It took me some time to release my anger, but when I did, I understood how truly free I am when I apply yoga principles to every part of my life. I say this with humility, as I realize there must be other hidden blocks like this one. By re-establishing my yoga practice, I realized that yoga can and will continue to take me to profound levels of consciousness and healing."

Sue discovered a psychological block that she was unaware of, one that was governing her behavior and experience of life. Furthermore, she experienced a mind-body connection and recognized that her anger manifested into jaw and neck tension. Sue exemplifies the transformative power of yoga psychology, the subject we will explore in this step. If we live controlled by our minds, we are slaves to ourselves. Yoga shows us how to master our minds, so that we can be the person we wish to be and live the life we want to live.

The Honeymoon Stage of Yoga and Beyond

Even in my yoga teacher-training course, I often see dedicated yoga students who find reasons to resist a consistent practice. Often toward the middle of the year-long program, the teacher-in-training will stop coming to training seminars, repeatedly miss classes, and avoid yoga practice. When I finally catch up with the students, they will often share that they are feeling despondent from all of the big discoveries they have made about themselves. Unlike the first few months of the program when they are still experiencing the euphoria of their initial studies, some students become scared to face their psychological issues. This experience is common among all yoga students, not just teachers-in-training.

In the honeymoon stage of yoga practice, students often feel motivated as they realize tangible benefits such as less tension and stress, and an increase in vital energy and flexibility. Overall the intensity of minor aches and pains start to become less and less acute. Students become more emotionally stable and their dispositions improve. The yoga pose purification process works its magic on the digestive system and toxins start releasing from the body. A student may start to make dietary choices based on healthy nourishment instead of some kind of emotional impulse. It is because of this that some students lose or begin to normalize weight.

Once the student has passed through this first phase of a yoga pose practice, things start to shift. This is not unlike the initial happiness of a marriage, a new friendship, or even a new job. After six months or more of yoga practice, many students encounter a mental block or hurdle, typically associated with the problem of trying to maintain a consistent and disciplined practice. As we'll explore shortly, we each have our own challenges, and experiencing them isn't usually perceived as fun. Yoga illuminates these challenges and requires us to deal with them. Some students resist facing their pain and it feels safer to stop practicing. They blame the problems and emotions that are surfacing on the practice, not realizing that the problems existed in some kind of masked form all along. Or perhaps they are already aware of the issue but it feels too overwhelming to address. Another common block is having certain expectations in yoga practice that, if not met, cause the students to give up. The ego suggests that they have taken yoga as far as it can go and it is time to experience a new form of exercise. The excuses for not practicing consistently are plentiful.

Throughout the psychological healing process that happens in yoga, we inevitably face emotions that feel uncomfortable or scary. The mistake, however, is to run away from these experiences. Personal growth takes courage, discipline, and self-love; if we're to embody the person we want to be, we must persevere in the face of challenges. Remember that the mind fights hardest to cling to old negative patterns right before it is about to make a real shift in perception.

One of the most interesting examples I have of this phenomenon is a personal one. My leg was broken at the age of nine and my right hip had been tight ever since the full-length cast was removed. As an athlete, my stretches on the right side were always limited. Even after practicing yoga poses for ten years twice daily and teaching yoga for five years, my right hip was still tight. So tight, in fact, that I had given up hope that it would ever relax. During a session with one of my Ph.D. mentors, Dr. Larry Scherwitz, I explored vigorous yoga poses. Larry noticed my tight right hip and my protective stance when I was in the hip-opening Pigeon Pose. He helped me to understand how my protectiveness was actually contributing to the physical condition, and coached me on releasing my emotions so that I could begin addressing the hip. After a few agonizing minutes, I chose to release the fear and see what happened. My body dropped into a stretch that equaled the left side! I immediately realized that my right leg had been as healthy and strong as my left leg for twenty years. The limit of my flexibility was a mental construction. Through this experience I developed a much deeper appreciation for the gifts that yoga can provide.

The key is in understanding that self-realization through yoga is a life-long process. Intention feeds motivation in yoga practice. If your intention is self-centered, you must connect it with something deeper and stronger to carry you through the many dimensions of transformation. An intention of losing weight or developing muscular strength will only take you so far in your practice. But if you expand that intention to improving your health and cultivating a caring attitude for yourself, your intention integrates a spiritual perspective focused on personal development. It is only through a long-term, sustained, and personally meaningful approach to yoga that you'll be able to move through its many highs and lows.

Yoga Psychology: Overview of Key Concepts

Western psychology addresses our mental thoughts and processes, which represents only one part of yoga's understanding of psychology. The Sanskrit term *citta* includes the concept of mind; however, it's defined more broadly by Classical Yoga as "consciousness." This consciousness encompasses all physical reality including bodily awareness, breath, senses, emotions, ego, and thought processes. The concept of citta demonstrates how

Eastern psychology considers the mind, body, and spirit as a whole. In the English language, there is no equivalent.

In yoga philosophy, matter is defined as all things perceived by consciousness. One of the qualities of matter is that it is constantly changing. Matter is defined by the three gunas mentioned in Step One: active, inactive, and balanced. The mind shares these same characteristics. One day, with the mind jumping here and there, the mind is active. On another day, when unmotivated, depressed, sad, or afraid, the mind is in an inactive state.

Matter (*Prakriti*)
Always changing
Active (*Rajasic*)
Inactive (*Tamasic*)
Balanced (*Sattva*)

After yoga class, meditation, or a walk on the beach or in the woods, the mind resides in a balanced state—quiet, pure, clear, and insightful. Both matter and the mind are constantly changing, which is an unstable state of existence.

Unlike matter, which constantly changes, the true Self is eternal and constant. Yoga's goal of accessing the highest state of awareness, *samadhi*, is realized through purifying every part of the self. Samadhi exists beyond language, though many have tried to de-

Spirit (*Purusha*)
Unchanging
Transcendental Self
Enlightened Mind

scribe it with words like *union, oneness, bliss, ecstasy, nirvana*, or "the peace that passeth understanding." It is a constant awareness of spirit in which one understands the limited nature of material objects and has learned how to remain free from suffering.

Afflictions of the Mind (*Klesas*)

Yoga psychology offers a path to the true Self through mastering mental afflictions, known in Sanskrit as *klesas*. The klesas have been described by yoga texts such as *The Yoga Sutras* as obstacles, hindrances, troubles, and suffering. Born of the mind, the klesas are mental constructs associated with the "real world" (i.e., matter)—things such as our appearance, belief systems, physical body, jobs, possessions, and relationships. They are all things that change as we age. If we identify with the material world, we experience constant inner turmoil and are separated from our true Self—the soul that remains unaffected by life's constant changes.

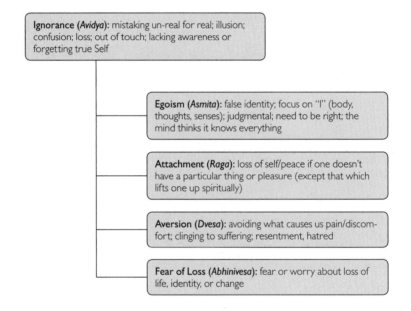

The klesas are a mental chain reaction that is best learned in the order found in the yoga philosophy text, *The Yoga Sutras*. Ignorance is when the mind is unaware of the higher Self, identifying only with material reality. A state of discontent and/or confusion exists. Without knowing the true Self, the mind wanders and the Ego takes over. As the mind wanders, it forms Attachments in an attempt to feel happy. The ego wants to be fed so it seeks material objects. The ego rejects anything that makes it unhappy or uncomfortable, and Aversions develop. The ultimate attachment is to the physical body and its pleasures, and from that attachment a Fear of Loss grows.

IGNORANCE (*Avidya*)

Avidya is translated as "ignorance." It is not a reference to the uneducated or illiterate person; in fact, higher education has nothing to do with this kind of ignorance. In yogic philosophy, ignorance is a state of existence in which we don't know who we truly are. We are more than our body, thoughts, jobs, relationships, and all the other changing aspects in life, yet many of us define ourselves by these types of external variables. We mistakenly believe that our value as an individual is based on our appearance, career, intellect, athletic capabilities, or accomplishments. Yoga philosophy and practice demonstrates that these passing conditions have nothing to do with our inherent essence—that eternal, timeless, ever-present spark of consciousness that exists in all living beings. Ignorance fuels false identification with pain in the body and feeds suffering.

> Ignorance is seeing the impermanent as permanent, the impure as pure, the painful as pleasurable and the non-Self as Self.
> YOGA SUTRAS 2:5

For a few moments, imagine yourself at the age of one hundred. Ask yourself, "Who do I want to be when I am one hundred years old? What will be important to me at that stage in my life? Will my physical appearance be important? What about my job?" Slowly work your way back from the age of one hundred to the present and ask, "Who am I when I take away all that I think defines me?" As you remove the illusions attached

> Avidya (Ignorance) is the breeding ground for the others whether they be dormant, attenuated, interrupted or active.
> YOGA SUTRAS 2:4

to your identity, the true Self is revealed. The process of removing those illusions, of peeling back the layers of your created reality, is yoga's path to liberation.

The five classes of ignorance described in *The Yoga Sutras* are listed in terms of strength, with the first class being the area that takes the most effort to overcome:

1. **Dormant:** This is ignorance that hasn't yet manifested or is suppressed in some way. For example, a newborn baby has not yet had the time to experience life and allow the klesas to become active. An aged, experienced yogi may practice yoga without ever realizing the true Self.

2. **Sustained:** Those who are content to live their lives in total ignorance. They are absorbed in the material world and do not explore spirituality. As a result, people in a state of sustained ignorance experience life like a roller coaster.

3. **Interrupted:** The majority of yogis fall into this category. They are aware of the hindrances; however, they continue to be dominated by them, often feeling mental agitation as a result. The student attempts to recognize these disturbances and tries to overcome them every day with diligent practice.

4. **Attenuated:** This is a state of muted ignorance experienced by yogis who have cultivated the opposite virtue related to the particular hindrance, but have not completely worked through it. The person can maintain a stable state of mind in trying situations and is gradually weakening the klesa. This can occur after years of dedicated practice.

5. **Parched:** This state considers the hindrance to be like a parched seed that is incapable of sprouting. The yogi has achieved self-mastery. Situations that would normally evoke the response of an attached mind have no effect on the wise mind of the experienced yogi.

Central to ignorance are the concepts of permanence and impermanence—those aspects of our nature that are eternal and those that are transitory. A way of visualizing these concepts is to imagine two objects sitting on the floor. One is a spinning top, representing impermanence, and the other is a book, representing permanence. The top is always changing its speed, moving, and altering its course until it eventually comes to a stop in a different location each time it is spun. How can this changing top be the true Self? If a breeze enters the room, it changes. If someone jumps on the floor, it changes. If a child sees it and decides that he wants the top, he grabs it. Can you see how unstable the top is? The book is just sitting on the floor, not moving, not changing. It just exists. When we identify with things that constantly change, we find ourselves in a vortex of instability.

Many people worry about the effects of aging. *What disease will I get? How long will I be able to work? Will I be able to enjoy retirement?* These are all spinning tops! As we're about to discover, identifying with external circumstances sets the stage for other mental afflictions. Play any of these questions out in your mind and you'll quickly see why. If you define your happiness and fulfillment as being able to work, for example, what happens if you can't? How would you feel if you were hoping for a wealthy retirement, only to arrive at its doorstep with a nickel in your pocket? While there's nothing wrong with goals, we must not confuse them with who we actually are. Yoga teaches us how to find stability in an uncertain and unsettling world.

The remaining four klesas stem from this first misunderstanding of our true nature. This means that if we remember the true Self, we won't suffer from the remaining afflictions! While we will still experience pain in our lives, our perception of suffering will be different. In other words, we can experience pain without suffering. The pain is just a passing sensation. Similarly, when there is celebration, there is joy in the moment, but no loss when the celebration ends.

For a human being to achieve a constant awareness of the divine is a most difficult feat. The material world pulls us in many directions.

Constant vigilance and study are required to prevent the mind from being overcome by life's twists, turns, ups, and downs. Daily yoga pose practice and meditation are key to staying centered and stable. It helps us to recognize the changing aspects of life so that we don't mistakenly identify with them. From a place of clear understanding, we can focus on the common themes that reflect a pure state of being—love, patience, faith, hope, and joy. Living with an awareness of these unchanging virtues greatly energizes and inspires our lives.

Egoism (*Asmita*)

Egoism is the "You" that you fabricate and present to the world: body, personality, behavior, thoughts, and intellect. Thought processes and hair and skin color are all manifestations of the body, not of true consciousness. Think of the ego as the costume we wear to hide who we truly are.

> Egoism is the identification, as it were, of the powers of the Seer (*Purusha*) with that of the instrument of seeing (body-mind).
> Yoga Sutras 2:6

A typical example of egoism is when a person's sense of self is tied to their physical attractiveness. We saw this with Mary, whom we read about in Step One. When her body changed after having two children, she no longer felt good about herself. She feared her husband was no longer attracted to her. Perhaps more significant is the value Mary had placed on herself as a vibrant, successful woman, prior to becoming a mother. When that changed, she lost her identity and self-esteem. If Mary related to her true Self, rather than her "changing self" or ego, she would be content and at peace. And she'd likely be more attractive as her vibrant energy would shine through in her physical appearance.

Egoism is in full force when we believe that our thoughts, beliefs, and behaviors are superior to those of other people. In thinking it knows everything, the mind completely overrules the spirit. This klesa is evident when someone talks about him- or herself all the time, is judgmental or has to "be right" all the time. The ego is in charge when we feel proud about being complimented or flattered, when we expect credit for our accomplishments, or become jealous when others succeed. Egoism can also express itself in the opposite manner by being weak and disempowered. When we believe we are not good enough, feel like a victim, are overly concerned with others' opinions and acceptance of us, or are constantly giving without caring for ourselves, our ego is still in charge. A healthy ego senses a connection to all of reality, which includes the welfare of all people.

While those who come to yoga for personal growth may already have some notion that the ego is not the center of the universe, it is difficult to remove egoism completely. It is subtle and challenging territory, especially for the highly educated person who can reason and argue his or her point of view. Yoga helps reduce the ego by stilling the mind to better reflect pure consciousness. Who can you not forgive? Is there someone who challenges your ability to love unconditionally? Are you unable to love the criminal, the liberal, the conservative, the smoker, the meat-eater, the television, the corporations, or the military leaders? Why? Can you already hear your mind, your "self," justifying your beliefs around this? What if we all let down our mental justifications and loved one another? Can you feel how this brings us closer to true Self and to a greater peace, wisdom, and understanding?

Consider the analogy of the movie projector. The light equals pure consciousness. The projector is the material world. Normally, we are consumed with the drama of life. We spend very little time examining the light of pure consciousness, because we are absorbed in life's dramas, unless a catastrophe hits. As soon as there is a malfunction in the movie projector or material world, people seek help. In the middle of an earthquake, most people pray for God's mercy. Yoga helps us to remember that in each moment, the light of consciousness—not our ego—is the source of our lives.

In yoga class, how often does the ego try to surface? Some studios are surrounded with mirrors. Certainly you can use them to correct your posture so you appreciate all of the benefits of the asana. But, how many people use them to see if they look good compared to the other students?

We can inflict violence upon our bodies by allowing the ego to prevail in yoga class. For example, Steve's friend Joe encouraged him to attend an intermediate yoga class with him. Steve had only attended a few beginning yoga classes at that point, but decided to go anyway. Joe felt like showing off for Steve, so he did a particularly challenging pose for the knees in warming up. Steve's ego kicked in and before he knew it, Steve forced his body into the pose. The asana was extremely uncomfortable for Steve, but he did it to show his friend that he could. Later that day, Steve had to ice his knees because of how badly they hurt. It took Steve several weeks to get back into to the yoga studio due to the knee injury. Steve's situation is extremely common and demonstrates just how powerful the ego is that we are willing to injure ourselves lest we appear weak or inferior.

ATTACHMENT (*Raga*)

We experience attachment when we base our happiness on external influences, such as food, sex, drugs, money, or material things. These addictions, which are often fueled by the desire to avoid pain, only make us feel good momentarily. The mistaken belief that pleasurable things will bring us happiness is devastating to our well-being. When we look within and eliminate attachments, bliss remains constant. If we confuse bliss with a set of outside influences, we become attached. We cling to our attachments, and when we inevitably lose them, we suffer.

> Attachment is the clinging to pleasure.
> YOGA SUTRAS 2:7

Some other examples of attachment include being possessive or trying to control another person. Depending on others for our own happiness is a form of attachment, whether it is a partner, friend, family member, teacher, or minister. Negating other religions and points of view is an attachment to our own beliefs, usually fueled by fear and the need to control reality. There are positive forms of attachment that lift us up, inspire us, or increase our spiritual connection. Family members can foster an ability to love unconditionally. While there is pain with death, attachment here teaches a person to reduce ego, overcome self-ishness, and grow in faith.

In terms of a yoga practice, there are many examples of attachment. How many times have you said, "I love this pose"? Or, "I love coming to this studio to practice when Lucy teaches"? To explore your motivations, try asking yourself, "Why do I love this pose?" "What is it about this studio or teacher that makes me love to come here?" You will begin to see that your attachments interfere with your connection to the true Self and that pleasure must come from within.

Attachments change with time. Loved ones pass away. Issues and concerns around children change as they develop, grow, and eventually leave the house. Money is gained and lost. Health improves and declines. By recognizing attachments to "changing things," a person can learn to find happiness within. Make a list of all that you own and ask, "What can I live without?" Then make a list of your beliefs and ask yourself, "What am I attached to? Do I feel superior to others?"

Consider this passage from the Jain religion's list of sixteen reflections on the impermanence of this world. Read the paragraph below a few times and then close your eyes to consider the ideas. Be in a position to relax the body with the head supported by a chair or by lying down comfortably. Make sure to be warm and undisturbed for eight to ten minutes. If your mind wanders, re-read the passage.

Anitya Bhavana

What was in the morning is not at the midday; what was at the midday is not at night; for all things are transitory. Our body, which is really the cause for all kinds of human efforts, is as transitory as the scattering clouds. All our objects of pleasure are changing. Wealth is as transitory as a wave; youth like a cotton particle blown off in a whirlwind; and opportunities like the fleeting dreams. Why should I be attached to anything when nothing is permanent and everything is changing?

AVERSION (*Dvesa*)

Aversion is the opposite of attachment; it a dislike for anything unpleasant. It rightfully follows attachment because when an object of attachment is removed, we develop an aversion to what took it away. We want to avoid suffering and be happy.

Some of the aversions that are easier to overcome include mundane daily tasks. With these types of aversions, a relatively small shift in attitude can make a dreaded activity into a consciousness-raising time. For example, washing the dishes, usually considered a burden or a chore, can become a symbolic washing of the soul. It can be a mindful practice where, similar to meditation, we become very present with every moment, from the sensation of water on the hands to the movement of the dishcloth over the plate. This practice, if done with intent, can calm the mind and bring peace. A red light can be annoying or it can be a time to repeat your favorite prayer. Traffic is a chance to practice deep breathing. Disturbing noises in the house during a meditation practice are an opportunity to practice appreciation for family members. Music blasting from our neighbor's yard gives us the opportunity to hear the sound without asserting judgment. As we begin to find happiness from a life centered on a transcendent reality, we can easily accept external situations.

More difficult, perhaps, are aversions to people or situations we perceive to be unjust, immoral, or harmful. While healthy aversions help us avoid danger,

> Aversion is clinging to suffering.
> YOGA SUTRAS 2:8

> The mind becomes purified by the cultivation of feelings of amity, compassion, goodwill and indifference, respectively, towards happy, miserable, virtuous, and sinful creatures.
> YOGA SUTRAS 1:33

unhealthy aversions foster feelings of hatred and contempt. When we are angry with someone, we experience an aversion to what that person said, did, or thought. When we think of that person, our disgust rips through any existing stability in the mind. These aversions toward others are often projections that mirror our dislike of ourselves. We may have an aversion to our own personality and engage in negative self-talk or self-criticism. Aversion exists when we don't accept ourselves. Aversions prevent us from facing a situation, whether it is something that involves ourselves or another person. Once it is expressed, an aversion can be understood, accepted, and transformed.

Let's consider the example of Claire, who had an aversion to television. At first, she felt righteous in her disgust with the television (egoism). She became angry whenever her husband watched it. Her anger grew and she became agitated whenever she saw a TV on in stores or in other people's homes. Upon reflection, she realized that her feelings were related to her dislike for consumerism, objectification of women, and competition, all of which were constantly broadcast on television. Going deeper, she realized that she had been hurt by these messages and struggled as a young woman to find self-esteem amidst the mass media projections that she was never going to be good enough, have enough, or achieve enough. Claire realized the television itself was not to blame and in fact, there was some decent programming out there. Her husband didn't have the same experience of television because he had not been hurt by it. Healing her old wounds helped Claire release her aversion to television, and in particular, her anger toward her husband for enjoying it.

When studying aversion, many students are surprised at the number and strength of the aversions they have in their own lives. Here are some classic examples that might help you notice your own aversions:

- Laura was angry with her friend for not recycling and composting, something she felt very strongly about doing.

- Steve judged his brother for working too long and not spending time with his children.

- Mary complained about her neighbor who smoked, indignant that he was polluting the air with the smell and setting a bad example with his unhealthy behavior.

The key for all of these people is to first understand that their aversions are self-created. Beyond large injustices that may take more time to heal, I recommend trying to resolve personal dislikes in the moment you discover them. At the root of every aversion lies an attachment to a specific outcome and an ignorance of our essential truth. If you can remember that as you experience aversions, it may help you figure out why you experience them. For example, do you "hate" it when your spouse doesn't call to let you know he'll be late for dinner? Why is this? Perhaps you look to him to make you feel attractive or special (a form of attachment). If that's the case, you've forgotten that your beauty, truth, and value doesn't lie in your appearance, but in the love, kindness, and peace found only in the true Self. Aversions, however insignificant they may seem, usually have a deeper emotional basis and can offer a window into ourselves.

One of our goals in yoga is to release the situations that are out of our control. Yet, this doesn't imply passivity. We must still practice stewardship, ethical behavior, and compassion. The great spiritual teacher and leader Gandhi is a good example of transforming aversion into compassion and recognizing injustice without distress. He was extremely disturbed by the British rule of India, yet he also had a deep empathy for British people. He transformed anger into love while maintaining his stance against British oppression.

In yoga class, you have probably thought to yourself or heard someone say, "I hate that pose!" or, "I hope we don't do many Sun Salutations!" Why do we "hate" a pose? Again, the answer is within. Does the pose remind you of a bad memory? Can you not do that pose "perfectly," and it therefore upsets your ego? Is the pose uncomfortable? Whatever the reason, can you recognize that a pose is just a pose? The time that you spend practicing that pose will pass, just as when you are doing a pose that you "love." Each and every pose feeds the mind and body. It is only when you accept the poses for what they are that you can begin to discover your true Self.

Aversion Exercise

Make a list of all the things you dislike. Include chores, people, difficult situations, and anything you dread. Distinguish two categories in the list: Things that harm you and things that don't (you can think of these as "neutral" dislikes). Washing the dishes is neutral, while passing a dark area at night is potentially dangerous. Return to the list of neutral activities. As you read through them, can you notice how none of these activities are actually bad? Rather, it's simply your perception that makes them appear so. Consider that other people might love those activities. What is it about the activities that makes you resistant to them? Find creative ways to release resistance to the activity, something as simple as singing or even smiling. Notice how a negative attitude creates more stress surrounding the activity, and how a positive or neutral attitude makes the activity much easier.

FEAR OF LOSS (*Abhinivesa*)

Fear creeps into life without us even knowing. Let's consider Mike, who gravely feared public speaking. Mike's job required him to give presentations and the buildup in his mind prior to giving them caused him to lose sleep. Mike imagined that his coworkers made fun of him as he spoke. He was afraid that everyone would see his weakness and that it would

> Clinging to life (which) is self-sustaining, arises even in the wise.
> YOGA SUTRAS 2:9

lead to being fired. Thinking through this overwhelming fear of public speaking, Mike traced it to a deeper fear of losing all of his money and becoming homeless. After a week of deep reflection, Mike distilled the fear further, realizing that he was afraid of losing his family's love. Mike decided that in all situations, he would focus on feeling love in his heart in order to feel close to God (as he put it) and that his faith would carry him through life.

Fear is a form of attachment; we fear losing something, someone, or some part of ourselves. Fear of losing one's identity (i.e., death) may be the largest fear that exists for humankind. And it's fairly easy to see why: if we are our bodies, minds, and external reality, death destroys our identity. We fear the finality of death with all its mysteries, questions, and implications. We fear the process of dying with its pain and suffering. We watch loved ones age and die ungracefully, and we avoid thinking about our own demise. At the base of these fears is a false identification with the physical body. This is the ultimate attachment. We must realize that we are not our bodies, minds, careers, or life roles. The only thing that we are, and ever have been, is love. This constant truth, that of our true Self, has always been and always will be the same.

Another common fear is incessant preoccupation with the future. We worry that things aren't going to turn out the way we want them to. "Is he going to ask me to marry him? Will I have money to go back to school? What will I look like when I'm fifty? What if I don't have enough money for retirement?" These types of questions, from the seemingly trivial to life-and-death importance, are mental constructs with little basis in reality. They pull us away from the present moment and into a fabricated world of worry, dread, and anxiety. By living in a constant state of fear over the future, we're not truly living.

Fear of making mistakes is one of the most debilitating types of mental afflictions. And unfortunately, it's all too common. Many people are so concerned about making a mistake that they never even try to achieve their goals. We avoid potential failure so that we don't have to face the ridicule and embarrassment that might follow it. But without the risk, where's the reward?

Think for a moment about that 100-year-old version of yourself that you imagined earlier in the chapter. Would that person want to look back and see a life penned in by fear? Or a person that soared, followed their dreams, and lived in their integrity? If we're open to it, life gives us the opportunity to experience joyful and difficult moments without being attached to or fearful of them. One thing is for certain: we all die. When you do, who do you want to have been in this life?

As you go through daily life, become aware of your fears. If it helps to see them on paper, make a list of the things you fear. Accept these feelings and remain aware. Notice if fear causes you to behave in an unhealthy way. As you practice yoga, you will gradually release your attachments, including your attachment to being alive. Those who have had near-death experiences often report that they are no longer afraid of death, remembering their experience as one of great peace and comfort. Others who have survived major illnesses learn not to take life for granted and appreciate the joy of being alive each day. As the Shaker saying goes, "Live each day as if it were your last, and as if you had a thousand more."

Understanding Klesas in a Yoga Practice

In each person's individual yoga practice, there are poses that we tend to emphasize and others that we avoid. As highlighted earlier, our pose preferences are connected to attachment and aversion. It can be insightful to consider why we prefer certain poses over others and to notice if there are any changes over time. It is quite common to avoid poses that create an uncomfortable physical or emotional experience. For example, the feeling of an exposed heart and stomach in Camel Pose can bring up issues of vulnerability and fear. Those who have tightness in their hamstrings or calves find that forward bends can be uncomfortable, and staying in those poses may cause feelings of frustration and anger.

Klesas typically manifest as physical tension. Thus, tense areas of the body often reveal emotional blocks such as grief, fear, denial, and guilt.

If you can get a muscle to relax in yoga but it quickly tenses up again, it is likely related to an emotional issue. Common trigger points include neck, jaw, shoulders, lower back, and sometimes the sciatic nerve. Psychological tension should not be confused with tightness caused by a physical injury. In the case of a pulled muscle in the neck, be aware of the muscle and also how you might be compensating to protect the neck. As you practice yoga, open yourself fully to the experience of each pose, even those that you don't like. Breathe deeply in every moment and allow yourself to receive physical and emotional healing from the poses.

A daily practice is essential in order to achieve the level of self-awareness required for transforming the klesas. As you perform each pose, begin by isolating the area of tension. Make sure that you have identified the primary area of tightness (hint—you may need to explore beyond the obvious area). In a forward bend, Laura thought there was tightness in her hips. After she gently explored the pose, she realized that the tightness actually originated in her hamstrings. As she breathed into the muscles, she recalled a childhood injury. Suddenly all the feelings of frustration and insecurity she experienced at that time flooded back into her awareness. While she had not thought about this memory in a long time, her body had stored it in the hamstring muscles. Laura also remembered that she was playing soccer when the injury occurred, something she did for approval from her father. This memory helped her revisit her need for approval from others. When she was able to process and release the emotion, her hamstring tension disappeared.

Yogic Inquiry of Psychological Blocks

Once we isolate the tension, the task is to accept it. Easier said than done! Acceptance becomes more natural when we realize that life experiences, including bodily pain, help us to learn more about ourselves. Each physical limitation or emotional block is an opportunity to discover that which is holding you back from freedom, joy, and love. You may find it helpful to visualize the klesas as a lock on the door to your true Self and acceptance as the key. We cannot move beyond personal blocks without first accepting that they exist. How can you transform something that you resist? In every situation, look for the underlying lesson and cultivate gratitude for the experience.

The more aware we are of the subtle physical, energetic, or psychological tensions in the body, the less the body needs to communicate with pain. A slight feeling in the throat signifies an oncoming cold and will encourage you to rest to prevent a full-blown cold. A weakness in the arm signals that it is time to re-evaluate a practice to prevent injury. Recognizing subtle body signals helps us to understand our needs and develop a nurturing yoga practice.

Ongoing tension in a yoga pose calls for deep reflection. Is the tension related to a present life situation?

Commit to daily practice
Isolate the tension
Accept the "block"
Relate it to life issues
Identify feelings
Identify emotions
Identify klesas
Take responsibility

Does tightness in the legs relate to a recent move into a new place and your root chakra telling you to get grounded? Is the tension a result of a physical activity? Did you work too hard raking leaves yesterday? Did you sit too long in an airplane? Try to identify when the tightness began. Is it surface tension or does it feel like it has been there for years?

Next, try to identify the feelings and sensations associated with the tension. Is there a sense of heat or cold? Is there a color that comes to mind? Can you relate the tension to a particular element like water, fire, air, or metal? Does a certain chakra make itself evident? Is there a visual image associated with the tension? As you associate feelings with the tension you will begin to be able to name the tension more specifically.

Consider how emotions are related to the tension. Does a particular memory come to mind? Do you feel like crying? Are you angry, frustrated, or irritable? Do you feel disempowered or weak? Do you feel afraid? At this point, if you uncover a deep issue you may wish to discuss it with a counselor or trusted yoga teacher. Use the power of positivity to visualize that you are free from the block. How do you feel? What positive emotion or intention would help you transform the block? Concentrate on opening and relaxing the area with your intention.

As you continue to explore, see if you can identify situations in your life where you experience the block. Pick one situation where you feel the tension. Be honest and allow yourself to tell the story in blame mode for five minutes, but no longer. For example "My boss is such and such," "My commute is too long," "My kids show no respect," etc. From the complaints, pick one particular incident you can concentrate on and journal about it. After you are finished with journaling, turn the situation around by taking responsibility for your actions. How are you giving your power away to the situation? What are you failing to learn by looking at it from this perspective? How does what you have written about that person or situation relate to you? Are you embodying the traits that drive you crazy? Think these questions over, create your own questions, and journal from your new perspective. As you find yourself in challenging situations, remember that you have a choice whether or not to respond to the situation in a stressed-out manner.

CASE STUDY Mary's Neck Tension

Mary, the 36-year-old mother, came to yoga class to turn her life around. *She committed to a daily practice.* With the help of her yoga instructor, *she isolated the tension* she held in her shoulders. Mary hadn't really noticed just how tight they were and it came as a shock to her how difficult it was to get them to relax. In time, Mary worked her way back to the source of the tension, which developed after having her first child. Ready for change, she *accepted the block* and became grateful for her new insight. As she explored it more and *related it to life issues*, she realized that the tension is most pronounced when she is stressed or overwhelmed with her responsibilities as a mother.

Mary then *identified the feeling* associated with her shoulder pain—it is a sensation of tightness and burning in the shoulders that sometimes moves into her neck and back. It feels red and pulsing. Mary went even deeper and realized that she felt angry and frustrated. She *identified the emotion*. She was angry because she perceived that her responsibilities as a mother prohibited her self-care and ultimately made her look and feel bad. In talking with her yoga teacher, Mary *recognized the mental hindrance* underlying her thought patterns. Because her ego revolved around other people's opinions of her (and her looks), she was attached to her good looks and approval from others in order to feel happy.

These revelations, along with her desire to bring about change in her life, empowered Mary to release her old patterns of thinking. *She took responsibility*. She realized that her top priority was being a good mother. This involves developing a strong character and finding time for herself in her busy schedule with the girls. Mary realized that what others thought of her really didn't matter and that she needed to start living a life that she could be proud of. For Mary, this meant embracing motherhood, taking better care of herself, and not basing her value and worth on her appearance. Now, she is uncovering her true Self and allowing love, joy, and passion back into her life. She has returned to her original excitement of being a mother, which has transformed her relationship with her daughters.

CASE STUDY **Steve's Lower Back Pain**

Steve, the 40-year-old businessman, recognized that his stress response caused him lower back pain. He was aware that his career and home life took a toll on him, but he didn't know how to shift his perceptions. Steve *committed to daily practice* of yoga, *isolated the tension pattern*, and worked to release it. He also *accepted the block* as a sign that something needed to change.

Steve *related his pain to life issues*. He felt a heavy responsibility to provide a good lifestyle for his wife and children, and worked in overdrive to succeed at his high-paying job. Steve's back pain was sharp and unpredictable, and he recognized that he felt afraid. He has *identified the underlying feeling and emotion*. Steve identified an imbalance of the second chakra, which relates to attachments; the greatest being his attachment to money. He deeply feared not having the resources to provide for his family. When he learned about the klesas, he immediately saw how he was operating under the afflictions of attachment (to making money) and fear (of not being able to care for his family).

To take responsibility, Steve recognized that he was creating unnecessary stress by putting pressure on himself to be something he didn't have to be. He shared his realizations with his wife and they talked about ways to reduce their cost of living so that Steve could spend more time with the family. Steve reduced his workload, enjoyed his work more, became more successful, and even earned a raise. He remains aware of the fact that the pain in his back returns when he is under stress. When he starts to feel the stress coming on, he does some deep breathing and stretching to manage it. These actions also help him to maintain a healthy perspective.

Connecting to the Infinite

We have discovered how yoga psychology can help us to deepen our experience of yoga poses and empower us to transform our lives, reduce suffering, and create greater well-being. It may feel overwhelming to realize there are so many aspects of yoga practice beyond the physical poses, but take comfort in knowing that yoga is a lifelong journey. There's no need to tackle everything today. Quite to the contrary, yoga is best explored steadily. Our practice reveals everything we need when we are ready to experience it. Yoga students dedicate many years of their lives to learning, understanding, and practicing the principles presented in this book. The essence of these teachings extends far beyond yoga into all aspects of life, particularly to our duties to Self, family, and work. Through such a holistic approach to yoga, life takes on more meaning and peace. This is the essence of being a yogi.

As you discover and work with your own afflictions of the mind, remember to keep it simple. Complete understanding of the mind-body can seem impossible. Take it one step at a time—narrow down your growth goals to one area and then commit to understanding it. Suggested areas include close relationships (family or friends), personal discipline for health or spiritual practice, and attitude at work. If you choose attitude at work, make the goal more specific, like relationships at work. When you identify the klesa, think of the opposite state and use that as a mantra for the situation. For example, Mary identified egoism and attachment to others' approval, and created a mantra of "As a mother I fulfill my greatest potential." Steve identified attachment and fear, and repeated his mantra of "Success comes when I am balanced and take care of myself." Practicing mantras in yoga poses is good preparation for practicing them in daily life.

Mental afflictions present an opportunity for growth and must be viewed as such. Practicing yoga means cultivating positive states of mind. A purified mind remains in a balanced state and is continually aware of a larger reality—it remembers life's bigger purpose at all times. To develop this purity of mind, you must practice yoga daily. Through awareness, we can train the mind to remember the meaningful aspects of reality. Just as a traumatic experience may leave behind intense emotional responses to situations, positive experiences based on faith in a larger reality also become ingrained in the mind. Thus, yoga tradition encourages consistent practice until the consciousness is completely purified. As the Buddha said, "No one is enlightened until all sentient beings are enlightened." In other words, one discovers that there is more than his or her self in the universe, and a sense of compassion for others blossoms. From this place of compassion, the enlightened mind is both infinite in scope and endless in time.

Exercises

Consider each of the following questions; you may wish to review these periodically to check back on your progress.

1. Review your week, pick a klesa, and reflect on how it affected you. For example, on Monday, did ignorance disturb your day? On Tuesday, did your ego interfere with any decisions you may have made?

2. Which yoga poses do you "like"? Why?

3. Which yoga poses do you "dislike"? Why?

4. How do you find equanimity in your yoga poses?

5. Do your "likes" and "dislikes" change? If so, why?

6. Do you compare yourself to others in yoga class? If so, why?

7. Are you upset if there is a substitute teacher for your yoga class? If so, why?

8. Are you upset if someone's mat is in "your" spot when you get to class? If so, why?

9. When you are in yoga class and the teacher plays music, does it affect your practice? If so, how?

10. Are you truly practicing selfless service if you seek praise for your work?

11. Think about the qualities of active, inactive, and pure. Are you free of the hindrances of the mind? How are you working toward a balanced lifestyle?

12. Has there been a period of your life that seemed to be dominated by a particular klesa? Spend some time journaling about what was going on in your life, how you felt, and what you learned.

Reflect on all of your answers. Can you see how each response is rooted in ignorance?

Emotional Transformation

Bhavana

Transform emotions to master the ego and
merge with the infinite.

Traditionally, yoga students were required to demonstrate ethical living, which involved exploring and positively transforming their emotions. The head teacher observed how the students handled adversity, often testing their resolve. Students had to demonstrate that they understood yoga philosophy before they ever began yoga practices. In today's yoga culture, students don't typically receive this type of mentoring. Most students pay their class fees and learn the basic yoga practices, but without a philosophical understanding. Many never even hear of the yogic principles of ethical living, a vital aspect of emotional transformation.

In Step One, we learned about intention, the restraints, and observances. These are all guidelines for ethical behavior. We also learned that practicing the opposite of negative emotions is a tool to steer the mind toward emotional balance. To further our understanding of emotional transformation, this step outlines the healthy and appropriate role of the following opposing emotional states: laziness/discipline, fear/

courage, anger/kindness, sadness/joy, worry/faith, despair/hope, and selfishness/selflessness.

Emotional transformation is a process of awareness, acceptance, and transformation of negative or limiting emotions. The word *negative* does not intend to label emotions as good or bad, it simply refers to emotions that we typically try to avoid. We may resist feeling sad because we don't want to accept the fact that a good friend moved away. Or, we may cling to the feeling of a happy situation, like being a new parent. When we cling to an emotion, we don't allow the emotion to pass and this ultimately causes suffering.

CASE STUDY Steve's Transformation

Let's examine Steve's process as an example. Steve discovered that his lower back pain was related to the klesa of fear (Step Nine). As Steve focused on transforming his emotions, he thought about the opposite of fear. This is generally regarded as faith, but Steve did not feel connected to this emotion. Instead, the concept of courage gave Steve a feeling of energy and vitality. As a provider, his faith was expressed as courage. Courage evoked a feeling of warmth and love in his heart.

Ultimately, Steve came to understand that providing for his family was his way of expressing love to them. These actions were well intended but displaced—they caused Steve to feel the stress that manifested in his back. Steve's mistake was in correlating providing material wealth and stability for his family with love. In his yoga practice, Steve focused on feeling love and receiving love without having to do anything to earn it. As he learned to unconditionally receive love, he no longer associated it with success at work. Steve practiced these ideas at his job and noticed that he felt less pressured and was able to think clearly. Feeling renewed, Steve's productivity at work increased dramatically. More importantly, Steve relaxed into a state of unconditional love with his family. He realized that he did not need to do anything to win his family's love, which transformed his outlook and his relationships with his wife and children.

Steve's example of transforming his fear by practicing courage reflects an additional step in overcoming the klesas. In this chapter, we'll cover a variety of emotions, their role in personal growth, and how to cultivate their positive opposite. These ideas expand the discussion of mental attitude from Step Two. While that chapter focused on how yoga poses positively affect attitude, we're about to learn how to transform our attitude through cultivating emotional responses.

Emotions Change

Of the many qualities that all emotions share is their constant state of change. An event as simple as a new person walking into the room requires some sort of adjustment. The mind remains in an emotional state until the new situation is accepted. The mind is only able to rest when it becomes accustomed to the new situation. On any given day, you are likely to experience hundreds of emotions, subtle as some of them may be. Sometimes it seems like emotional states never change, such as feelings of depression or anger. Repressed emotions are deeper-seated feelings that have yet to be fully understood. While they are more difficult to change, it is possible to transform all emotional responses. It can be overwhelming to face one's emotions, and some students will find that yoga poses cause continued emotional upset. If this is the case, you should seek help from a counselor who specializes in emotional healing. A yoga practice coupled with counseling can be very effective.

As you have likely experienced in your own practice, exploring "negative" emotions is not always easy. It can be painful and uncomfortable. That is why so many of us, even longtime yoga practitioners, do our best to avoid them. However, it's the resistance that causes much of the pain. When we are able to greet our emotions, resistance falls and new understandings can be formed. This practice helps us to accept life as it is.

There are seven emotional states reviewed in this step, but keep in mind that every emotion has multiple expressions. Some emotions are painful and will have several layers that must be processed in order to be fully understood. Regardless of how challenging it may be, don't lose sight of the fact that you *will* be able to transform your emotional patterns. The purpose of studying our emotions is to comprehend where they are coming from and release any blocks that might keep us from connecting to the infinite.

The process of emotional transformation is imperative for yoga students. Remember that it can take a lot of time and practice to work through challenging emotions. Many of us have spent years nurturing the klesas. Start with small changes at first and allow the transformation to happen with an organic flow, rather than rigid force.

Emotional transformation can be compared to the yogic breath. As we become aware of the breath, it naturally slows and deepens. When we gently allow the breath to expand, it becomes free and full, rather than forced. Remember non-violence and be gentle in the process. Just like balance in Tree Pose, cultivating balanced emotions takes practice. In time, stronger states of mind will develop, balancing your emotions through life's ebbs and flows.

Opposing Emotional States

LAZINESS (*Alasya*) AND DISCIPLINE (*Tapas*)

Laziness and discipline are both healthy when expressed in appropriate situations. An old story speaks to this truth: a yoga master reprimands one of his students because of his habit of staying out too late at night. That same yoga master recommends to a somewhat rigid and well-behaved student that he should go to a party. As the master was well aware, what is good for one person may not be good for another. Laziness helped the overworked student and discipline balanced the lazy student. The key is to discover what is needed in order to bring individual balance.

Let's think for a moment about discipline and laziness from the perspective of non-violence. When does discipline cause violence to you or others? Yoga students are classic examples of folks who are usually very kind and peaceful toward others, while often being very critical of their own actions. For example, it is quite common for students to give themselves a hard time about missing a yoga class. If you're consistently missing your practice, you may need to develop more discipline. But beating yourself up over it does little good. Likewise, if you're only missing the occasional class, then what's the point of criticizing yourself? When we are too rigid in our lives, whether it is our dietary habits, pose practice, or otherwise, we're creating an imbalance. Other misuses of discipline include overworking in general, often as a means or excuse to avoid some kind of pain. Exaggerated discipline can be an avoidance technique or it can be used to control others.

Examples of positive discipline include a daily yoga practice, reading inspirational or spiritual books, having a positive attitude about work, refraining from gossip, and breathing deeply while driving. Discipline is personal: only you know what you truly need and what you don't. It's a process of abstaining from those activities that negatively affect you and engaging in those that enrich you. Being disciplined in your diet does not mean just accepting the rules handed down to you from a dietician or yoga teacher. It comes from cultivating internal awareness; noticing the effects of things like sugar, alcohol, caffeine, and white flour on the body; and avoiding substances that foster imbalance. Discipline should always be tempered with love and compassion. A positive and balanced practice of discipline leads to Self-realization.

The opposite of discipline, laziness, can also disrupt balance. Failing to meet commitments, for example, causes harm to all of the people involved. Being too lazy to do yoga practice decreases its benefits. On the other hand, laziness can be positive if it means having a relaxed approach to life. Making time to sit, play music, socialize, and take a walk, especially in a fast-paced culture, is very important. While it is normally a pejorative term, laziness is positive when it fosters balance.

Somewhere between rigid discipline and laziness lies balanced discipline. A balanced discipline requires a certain fire from within. This fire is what motivates a daily yoga practice. Often the ego clings to past behaviors and creates all types of excuses that contradict healthy behaviors.

Many teachings emphasize eliminating the ego, but I recommend embracing it. The ego says, "Today is a good day to rest and talk a walk, why do more yoga poses?" The higher self replies, "Yes, ego, you are right, how about a focus on relaxation in poses today?" In this inner-dialogue, the ego is not resisted, but honored. By walking the path of non-resistance, you can achieve a non-violent approach to yoga practice.

In each yoga pose, there is a delicate dance between effort and release. This process is often called "finding the edge." Heat-producing asanas like Sun Salutations and third chakra poses help in achieving balance. These poses emphasize the dance between effort and surrender, teaching us valuable lessons that we can use in life. Just as the expert in meditation can find silence amidst the noise, the expert in discipline relaxes in the midst of effort. The ability to go deeper in a yoga practice often has more to do with relaxation than effort. By relaxing into a challenging yoga pose or surrendering to the sounds of construction outside while trying to meditate, you go deeper into pure consciousness.

The key to finding balance is to pay attention to your behavior. Be non-judgmental and honest with yourself, discover your motivational blocks, and notice your thoughts. While you honor the ego, be aware of how it justifies behavior that isn't healthy or balanced. Keep your yoga practice disciplined and fun, just as you would in any artistic venture. If yoga is on the proverbial "to do" list, then take it off and put it on the fun list. If you can't change a situation, then change your mind. This is what bhavana, or emotional transformation, is all about.

Fear (*Bhaya*) and Courage (*Dhairya*)

A yoga fable shares the following story about fear: Once a swami was traveling with his guru. Each day when they would bathe in the remote rivers, the guru would ask the student, "Is there anything to fear here?" Perplexed at why the enlightened master had fear, the student searched the guru's clothes and discovered a carving in gold given to the guru from a disciple. The next day when the guru asked if there was anything to fear, the student said, "No, I threw fear away at the last river." The student had thrown the gold piece in the water, symbolically removing the potential for fear. As this story demonstrates, when you have nothing to lose, you have nothing to fear.

Is there anything that you are afraid of? Fears can be large or small, personal or universal. Many people are afraid of personal failure, of being alone, and of not belonging. When we look at these fears more closely, it becomes clear that the underlying fear is of not feeling love, of not being worthy of love, and of not being good enough. Whatever your fears are, be aware that there may be deeper layers than you initially realize.

There are three recommended steps for approaching fear. The first is self-understanding. Through developing awareness of our fears, we can often recognize an inherent illusion. When we understand the fear, it loses its power. Steve's surface fear was losing his job. As he explored this issue, he discovered his deeper fear was losing his family's love. Empowered by his self-knowledge, the fear no longer gripped Steve.

Fears can actually be healthy and prevent potentially dangerous or harmful choices. The fear of crossing the street without looking, of pushing too far in a yoga pose, or of standing too close to the edge of a cliff saves us from injury or greater harm. Fear doesn't need to be demonized, because it can be a vehicle for transformation. Many people come to yoga through a great pain or sickness that prompted them to ask, "What am I supposed to be learning from this situation?"

The second step is personal effort. This may be through direct action, such as taking a scuba diving course in order to overcome a fear of deep waters. The effort may involve a shift in perception or talking to others about the fear. The "effort" can be made in a myriad of ways, but the point is that you are taking conscious steps to transform the fear.

The third step in approaching fear is self-realization. This is particularly important in regard to the greatest fear, the fear of death (*The Yoga Sutras*, 2:9). Some people are faced with a very real and imminent death, whether they are aging or experiencing a life-threatening illness. This fear might include the fear of pain, fear of losing contact with loved ones, or the fear of the unknown. Fearing death is part of our survival mechanism as human beings; it is wired into our genetic code. Overcoming this fear, and others, requires a deep understanding of our spiritual nature. Only when we have realized that we are neither body nor mind do we learn how to live free of fear.

Yoga poses offer the opportunity to examine fear and practice courage. Balance poses, as well as heart- and throat-opening poses, often bring up fear in students. The throat is the center of communication and the heart is the center of feeling—when challenged, we round to protect the throat or cross our arms to protect the heart. It is natural to feel vulnerable and afraid while exposing the heart and throat. Backward bending poses can have this effect, particularly Camel Pose and Bow Pose. All of these opening poses have transformative potential if they are used to cultivate courage in the face of fear. Cultivating such courage can take years. The courageous person knows fear intimately, but continues to function in the world. Unlike other, less primal emotions, it may be a long, long time before you completely resolve fear. Remember that success is in the practice, not the end result.

Anger (*Krodha*) and Kindness (*Daya*)

Gandhi's anger against the British government provides an excellent example about anger and kindness. Though he was passive in his resistance, Gandhi's strength of will was so strong that those who tried to hurt him stood no chance of doing so. Gandhi tells the story of a man who tried to strangle him: "I summoned up all the love within me and looked into his eyes." The man crumbled to his knees and became one of Gandhi's followers. As Gandhi's life demonstrates, anger can be directed in positive ways and become fuel for truth, love, and kindness.

A fundamental question in yoga psychology is "Who am I?" When you are angry, ask yourself this question repeatedly until the anger changes to love. When you experience this blissful state of anger transformed into unchanging reality, you will have experiential proof of how powerful yoga psychology is in creating mental stability. Gandhi maintained his composure in tense situations by focusing on virtuous concepts that transformed his anger into a kind and peaceful righteousness.

When we forget the unchanging reality of who we are, egoism leads us into tumultuous emotional states like anger and possessiveness. If how we feel depends on external factors like whether someone was nice to us or how much traffic we encounter during the commute home from work, we will be in a continual state of change. If we live this way, life becomes one big drama after another.

Anger reveals a strong feeling of displeasure or antagonism. In situations where we feel angry, we need to ask ourselves, "Does this response stem from an attachment or an aversion?" "Does the anger speak to a need to change something?" Anger can be experienced without having to be expressed in harsh words. Similarly, repressed anger only makes the feeling explosive. Repression usually leads to unpredictable lashing out, self-destructive behaviors, or cold detachment. These different disguises for anger are not transformative or healing. If anger is not expressed in a healthy way, it will manifest in the body as eruptions in the skin, ulcers, or other fiery conditions.

At times, our anger may be like that force that makes the bulbs come up in the springtime. In other words, anger can be a positive force when it is understood and directed appropriately.

A helpful three-step process is to accept the anger, acknowledge and understand the feelings behind it, and then respond in a positive way. Once we understand the root of the anger, it is possible to practice the opposite. Gandhi expressed his feelings of anger about the occupation of India, but he acted from a place of power rather than victimhood. Gandhi's anger manifested as firm love.

When you are afflicted with anger, notice where you feel it in your body and how it affects your breath. The old adage about taking ten breaths before speaking when angry is a good one. Simply breathing changes your emotional reaction. With a calm and full breath, you are more open to understanding the reason for the anger and you are more likely to react in a way that is in line with the higher Self, rather than the ego.

Anger usually creates discomfort in the body or breath. As a result, we can use discomfort as a cue to explore anger issues in yoga pose practice. The breath (air) is the element of the fourth chakra, which is also the energetic center for emotions in general. Practicing heart-opening poses when feeling anger may provide some useful insight. Perceiving with the heart instead of the head is a great way of connecting with the higher Self. Heart-opening poses like Downward Dog, Windmill, Cow Face, Lion, and Wheel encourage empowered responses to heated emotions.

Relaxation poses such as Corpse or Crocodile can aid in the release of anger. Twisting poses like Seated Twist offer a new perspective. To find the strength and courage to express anger, practice poses that stimulate the third chakra and activate a sense of personal power. Forward bending poses like Wheel or Forward Bend encourage ego-driven feelings of anger to surrender.

It can be an interesting exercise to relate the issue of anger to the seven chakras. If you notice a feeling of "being stuck" with anger in one of your chakras, you may want to focus on that chakra during yoga pose practice.

> *Root chakra:* Am I lacking grounding or balance?
> Are those feelings contributing to my anger?
> Am I suppressing anger toward a specific person?

> *Sacral chakra:* Do I have anger about my relationships to
> co-workers or friends?
> Am I frustrated with my creative endeavors?

> *Solar plexus chakra:* Can my anger help me make empowered
> choices and changes?
> Do I need to better manifest integrity and personal power in
> the world?

> *Heart chakra:* How can love transform my anger?

Throat chakra: Can I express my anger in an enlightened, empowered way?

How can I transform my anger into creativity?

Third eye chakra: Can I sublimate the energy of my anger into something positive?

Crown chakra: How can I remain continually aware of my divine self?

Am I focused on a larger perspective?

Am I living to my highest potential?

SADNESS (*Dukha*) AND JOY (*Sukha*)

Emotional transformation purifies the mind by eliminating toxic emotions. Mastering the senses and emotions leads to a pure state of equilibrium, peace, balance, poise, and brightness. This process of purification results in a joy or delight that is independent of outer circumstance. A pure state of being is what brings us to self-realization.

Sadness may express itself as grief, unhappiness, or depression. It is normal to feel sad when we lose something or someone. As with all emotions, there are lessons to be learned from feeling sad. In the death of a loved one, sadness teaches us about forgiveness, the nature of life and love, and helps us discover deeper aspects of ourselves. Recognizing the positive allows us to feel blessed by their presence in our life, however fleeting it might have been.

When sadness is repressed or ignored, any situation where strong feelings surface can also cause fear. In this state the immune system is compromised, as is the ability to regain emotional balance. If self-pity develops from an overanalyzed sad situation, a form of attachment to the sadness can happen. The sadness becomes familiar and comfortable. Helpful ways to cope with sadness include talking with a friend, journaling, walking in the woods, or meditating on the transitory nature of life. In some cases, the help of a professional counselor is required.

When you are feeling sad, focus on relaxing. Notice how relaxing affects the body, breath, and mind. Become a witness to yourself and to the emotion. Observing yourself without judgment is a high form of spiritual practice. Yoga poses offer an opportunity to accept sadness. The Wheel Pose reflects the cycles of life. Twisting poses and inversions offer a new perspective. If you are sad about a breakup, your heart probably needs attention, so practicing heart chakra poses will be helpful. If you have lost a loved one, focus on their positive, loving presence by doing Sun Salutations with a devotional attitude. Poses don't affect everyone in the same way, so experiment with them as you work through your sadness. Child's Pose, for example, can provoke feelings of pure joy for some and can be torturous for others. Take the time to notice which yoga poses give you joy and where you feel that joy in the body.

If you are practicing yoga poses or meditation on your own, be careful not to let your sadness multiply. Sadness has a way of turning itself inward and spiraling out of control into deep depression. When you are sad, seek out others for support and model your behavior after that of joyful people to develop a balanced state of mind.

WORRY (*Chinta*) AND FAITH (*Sraddha*)

Worry is a draining, disempowering form of fear that is usually not based in reality. Worry is a habitual response that focuses on a negative or worst possible outcome. We worry that we are going to be late for work, even though this fear doesn't actually help us get there faster. It is unfortunate that many people are stuck in a state of constant worry about things that they cannot change or control.

Worry often relates to an attachment of being in control of life events or other people. Without a connection to the true Self, the ego thinks that it is in charge. Worry also reflects a lack of faith that the universe will provide and support us. Without faith, worry consumes us at life's every twist and turn that goes in a seemingly "wrong" direction. Faith helps us to realize that life may not always go the way we want, but it gives us exactly what we need in order to learn the appropriate lessons.

Ask yourself, "Do I have faith?" If the answer is yes, in what do you have faith? Now write down one to three worries you experience. Look at your worries and ask yourself the first question: Do you have faith? If you really have faith, then you would have no worries!

CASE STUDY **Megan's Worry**

Megan was a yoga student who was crippled by worry. She was very frail and worried about most everything and everyone in her life. During a yoga class, she was able to quiet her mind, allowing her to be worry-free for an entire hour. Inspired, Megan summoned up the courage to go on a yoga retreat, though she worried about what it would be like and felt quite uncomfortable about her decision. During the first class of the retreat, the instructor guided the group into Tree Pose and asked the students to close their eyes. Megan noticed that when she focused on balancing, she stopped worrying. If her mind wandered and started worrying again, she lost her balance. Megan found that by momentarily escaping her worrying, its power over her was greatly reduced. Megan decided to begin a daily practice of balancing with her eyes closed. In time, she was able to stand on one foot for five minutes without moving! She learned to transfer this ability to concentrate to all tasks in her life and transformed her worry into faith.

DESPAIR (*Vishada*) AND HOPE (*Aasha*)

Despair is an emotion related to dejection, exhaustion, confusion, and a complete loss of hope. A classic example of this comes from the sacred Hindu scripture, the *Bhagavad Gita,* when Prince Arjuna expresses his despair about killing on the battlefield. The key principle of yoga philosophy is non-violence, which can make it difficult to understand why there is a battle in the *Bhagavad Gita.* In this situation, Arjuna had to honor his role as a leader on the battlefield. He may not have wanted to be in that position, but turning away from his obligations would have done more harm than fighting the battle.

Despair is often the result of not having things go our way. Efforts that we make are met with multiple obstacles. Doors seem to be shut in our face. Events around us seem cursed, we fail at our endeavors, and feel at a loss. Despair often occurs when we're living ethically, working hard and trying to be healthy, yet things don't seem to work in our favor. Life doesn't seem fair. We feel as if we have no control.

Yoga offers a unique and highly effective strategy for cultivating hope in the face of despair. Central to finding hope is the concept of selflessness. This involves aspiring to the greatest good for all people rather than a specific good we think is best (there's that ego again). Through selflessness, we realize greater success and peace. For example, if we are interviewing for a job we want, we can hope for "the best outcome for all" rather than a specific hope to "get the job." We can hope for experiences that will further us along on our spiritual journey. If a good friend is sick in the hospital, we can hope for healing, rather than a specific outcome. This might require a new understanding of healing as a spiritual process of transformation rather than the elimination of symptoms, disease, or even death.

While many people believe the meaning of life is finding happiness, the true meaning of life is finding knowledge. What we think is going to make us happy does not always end up doing so. Happiness, as it is, is a fleeting state. We are reminded of the yogic ethic of non-attachment. If we are attached to a specific outcome, we are on the road to suffering. It is also likely that we are engaging in egoism and forgetting the truth of who we really are. Through knowledge we discover our own truth. This discovery is what brings meaning to life, whether our path be painful or joyous, or both.

Learning to move beyond feelings of despair is necessary as we encounter obstacles in the course of practicing yoga. Beginning yoga students may despair as they struggle to bring their mind to focus in meditation or experience stiffness and tension within a yoga pose. Longtime yoga practitioners may overcome these obstacles only to face other crises of the mind when they uncover deep-seated emotional pain. It is in these moments that despair or hopelessness takes form in thoughts like "I am never going to be able to do a forward bend right" or "My mind is never going to be quiet—what is wrong with me?" or "Am I ever going to be able to let go of my attachments?"

During these times it is important to focus on the goal of gaining self-knowledge, rather than perfection or happiness. The mind is usually most resistant when it is about to make a shift—in the darker moments the light is really near! Transformation is a bit like childbirth, there are labor pains that happen before something new and wonderful is born. Stay with despair. Accept it, acknowledge it, and hope for understanding. Strive for knowledge and awareness on the spiritual journey. In life, there is always something to learn. If we don't learn it now, we will have to repeat the lesson to learn it later, so why not do so now?

Yoga poses help us to develop hope. Practice Palm Tree Pose and think about reaching your highest potential. Are you trying too hard? Can you soften into the journey by relaxing your shoulders? As you lower your arms and your feet sink into the ground, can you feel your connection to the energy of the earth? Can you allow yourself to feel supported? Practice Child's Pose and ask your inner child if it needs love and care.

Forward bending poses offer the opportunity to practice surrendering to a larger reality, one of the observances discussed in Step One. Can you release your desire for a specific outcome? Can you let go of what you wished for or feel that you deserve in favor of faith that everything is as it should be?

Try practicing a beginner inversion or Shoulder Stand where you can turn despair on its head and focus on what you are grateful for. Experiment with other poses, like heart-opening poses (see heart chakra, Step Six) to get you out of your head, or twisting poses to help you see life from a different perspective.

Most importantly, observe your breath. Deeper breaths change the flow of prana in the body. As you simply breathe in and out, the muscles, glands, and organs are soothed by the flow of energy. The increase in oxygen and blood flow calms the mind. Deep breathing relaxes the nervous system and allows the frontal lobe of the brain to engage in higher thought processes like humanitarian and spiritual conceptualization, such as faith and hope.

SELFISHNESS AND SELFLESSNESS

The difference between the small individual self and the universal Self is the difference between suffering and bliss! As Govindan writes, "The ordinary person who has not yet begun to practice yoga is involved in desires which are activated by the three constituent forces of nature, with little or no control and only fleeting glimpses of happiness" (p. 18). The typical person goes from day to day driven by their self, by their ego, and by their illusion of separateness. They attempt to find happiness through the fulfillment of their desires and cravings.

> When we permanently realize the Self, the joy and peace is so fulfilling that automatically we gain discrimination between the Self and the non-Self, and with this we lose desire for involvement even in subconscious motivated desires, memories and fantasies. They lose their force and wither away.
>
> KRIYA YOGA SUTRAS 1:16

It is this type of selfishness, with a small *s*, that causes suffering for all. It likens us to the characters in the movie *The Matrix*, who live their lives completely unaware that they are controlled by a vast computer system. When we relate to the individual self, we are slaves to our senses and cravings. We suffer because of our lack of awareness. Once we move beyond selfish desires, consciousness expands and we connect to a higher reality.

Welcome in the Self with a big *S*, also know as Selfishness, or selflessness. This is not selfishness in the traditional sense of the word; instead we are talking about the true Self. This is the Self that cares not for passing fancy, for changing states of desire or pleasure, but exists in continual peace and bliss. This Self is not attached to any particular outcome—it is content regardless of external factors.

Selfishness in this definition involves engaging in activities that get us closer to the true Self. We care for the true Self by nurturing the body, the "temple" that embodies the Self in this lifetime. Healthy eating habits, exercise, adequate rest, and a daily yoga practice encourage physical vitality, allowing the true Self to emerge. As we create and perpetuate this Self-care, we are mindful of what we need in order to function at our highest level. At any given point, this may mean taking personal time for reflection, volunteering to help your community, going on a long bike ride, or enjoying a movie. Casting judgment to the side, you are the only person who is capable of evaluating your needs. When you take care of them in a balanced, healthy manner, you're aligned with the true Self as you honor the body. This isn't selfish in the traditional sense, but Selfish in terms of pure consciousness.

Karma, literally meaning "action," is central to this concept of Selfishness. Karma says that every action has a consequence or reaction. When we help others, we also help ourselves. In truth, our actions nourish the collective Self, of which we are all a part. In the words of karma, when we help another, we plant a seed from which future similar acts of kindness grow. When we help an old woman across the road, it doesn't necessarily mean someone will help us in the same way or even that someone will help us at all. Instead, our actions spread kindness around the world, transforming reality and allowing humanity to grow closer to its true nature.

There will be many times in life when you will have to choose between your own needs and another person's needs. There is no rule for this situation. It depends on the person and the circumstance. When in this position, you might ask yourself, "Why do I want to give to this person?" If you give to another person out of a place of guilt, obligation, or fear, then you are not giving from the Self. Instead, you are giving from your self. If you recycle, but do so with a feeling of righteousness and expectation of reward, then you are motivated by the self, not the Self. If you ignore another person's needs because you want to get in line first, then you are operating from the self. If you say no to someone's request because you need rest, then you are caring for the Self. It is crucial to understand where your motivations come from!

Transformation (Bhavana)

So far, we have approached emotional transformation from the perspective of conscious emotions including laziness, fear, anger, sadness, worry, despair, and selfishness. Emotional transformation (bhavana) is the practice of accepting, understanding, and shifting an emotion into a positive form. As you are unique in your experiences and feelings, your transformation will take its own distinct path. Use the guidelines in steps Two and Ten to explore your emotional struggles. Ask yourself what opposite emotion would help you to move forward in a more empowered way. Bring this into your yoga pose practice and daily life, and watch your own transformation toward healing and balance!

Bhavana
Acceptance
Understanding
Transformation

CASE STUDY **Mary's Stored Memories**

Unconscious emotions are usually stored in our body. Thinking back to Step Six on the chakras, remember the example of Mary and the tension she held in her legs. When Mary practiced a forward bend, she noticed that she had very little flexibility in her hips as she bent forward. She focused on breathing through the tension and **accepted the feeling** rather than running away or ignoring it. Many people would stop doing the pose because it was uncomfortable, but Mary knew the difference between discomfort and pain. Mary always stopped doing a pose that caused her pain, but she knew that she had something to learn by exploring poses that caused her discomfort.

As Mary breathed into the tension, her exhale helped her come more fully into the stretch. At the same time, she noticed feelings of frustration and anger. Not understanding where these emotions were coming from, she continued to accept them. Rather than fighting the emotions, she stayed with them and allowed them to inform her. The tension shifted, as did her understanding of it, when she realized the tension was actually originating in her hamstrings and not her hips. As she brought breath and awareness to her hamstrings, she reflected on her first chakra (her root, including her legs). Mary recognized that her move to a new home was causing her to hold on tight with her legs in order to feel grounded and safe.

Though this did not immediately change the muscular tension, Mary came to **understand** what was causing it. From this realization, she **transformed** her emotions by practicing poses that made her feel more grounded and comforted, as well as engaging in activities that fostered a sense of safety and belonging. Mary's practice of yoga poses has become a key tool in emotional transformation.

Connecting to the Infinite

Emotional transformation is a vital aspect of the yoga journey. Yoga doesn't seek to deny the emotions, but rather to be aware of them. Our goal is to achieve balance, which we find by being mindful of ourselves. As this chapter has demonstrated, there is a place for every emotional experience. Anger is not bad, nor is laziness. However, feeling and expressing emotions can be either beneficial or destructive, depending on our situation. Your individual needs are unique, so what may be good for you may not be appropriate for others. If your intention is to connect to your true Self, you will find solutions that point you in its direction.

Remember that the first step in emotional transformation is recognizing the need for it. Physical tension and pain can signal hidden emotions, so remain aware throughout your yoga pose practice. As you discover deep-seated patterns, you may notice them surfacing frequently. You'll see your life in a new light and become empowered to transform emotional imbalances. Through awareness, understanding, and positive transformation, you can overcome challenges and find the light and love of the true Self.

EXERCISE

As an exercise to learn more about your own patterns, consider these questions:

1. What do you worry about?

2. If you probe deeper, what is the underlying fear?

3. Can you determine which klesa you are afflicted with?

4. Can you discover an opposite emotional response? As with any emotion, practice acceptance and listen for its message. Practice small acts of faith. Pray when you start to worry.

Practice faith during your yoga practice. The poses have been practiced by countless yogis for thousands of years, so let their ancient wisdom transform your life. Have faith in the process and reverence for those who have gone before you on the path. Practice yoga poses with a positive intention in your mind.

PART IV

Practice and Poses

Putting It into Practice

This final chapter offers guidance for successfully applying the information of the ten previous steps to your yoga pose practice. Integrating all the information can be overwhelming at first, but please remember to be patient with yourself, enjoy the process, stay connected to your intention for yoga, and take things one step at time. There are varying styles, practices, and guidelines to help you apply this information to your yoga pose practice, and I encourage you to work with your teacher and yoga community.

CASE STUDY Sally Faces Her Self

After practicing yoga for a few years on her own without instruction from a teacher, Sally came to our studio to practice poses and study yoga philosophy. Studying yoga from a holistic perspective clarified aspects of the practice that she had intuitively considered but did not know how to explain. After a few weeks of exploring yoga in this new way, Sally came to the studio to express how overwhelmed she felt from what she was learning about herself. She shared that her home practice had previously

239

given her peace of mind and the new ideas that she was working with were causing her to feel anxious.

Sally's experience is not that uncommon. It is uncomfortable to confront our issues, patterns, pains, and fears. Some of them are harder than others to transform. Remember to start at the beginning! As a great Chinese sage once said, "The journey of a lifetime begins with just one step." You are on a lifelong journey with your practice and there's no reason to fret about all the things that need attention. You'll have plenty of time to develop your practice. When you're just starting out, don't do anything more complicated than creating an intention to guide your basic yoga pose practice.

Practice One Aspect at a Time

As a student of yoga, focus on learning one new principle at a time. It can be very challenging to take this slower approach; however, it will result in the greatest progress over time. The desire to know all about yoga is real—after all, who wouldn't want the benefits that follow? To receive yoga's benefits, you must go one step at a time. Let the joy of discovery be the primary benefit and your journey will be fun as well as rewarding.

If you are new to yoga, you will find that proper physical alignment demands a lot of attention at first. This is normal. You have to learn the appropriate physical actions for each pose, which requires focus and concentration on the teacher's instructions. As you settle into the pose, come back to your breath and your intention. Having a teacher guide you through poses is invaluable, as he or she can give you helpful feedback that a video or picture book cannot. Follow instructions in class as long as they suit your level of physical fitness, and back off when you need to. A good teacher will offer you pose modifications based on your body type, level of experience, and flexibility.

Keep in mind that you do not have to match the perfect physical form of a pose. You only need to activate the areas of the body that relate to the pose. The key to a simple toe touch is not touching the toes but activating the spine in a forward bend. Your teacher should honor your capabilities in the poses and never suggest that you must be as flexible as a gymnast or contorting yogi. Where you are at in your journey is exactly where you should be; the right teacher challenges you without compromising your safety.

For students at any level, yoga practice can be compared to the building of a stone house. First, you dig the foundation through proper mental alignment. Each new aspect that you learn is a stone that fortifies the shelter of knowledge. A good mason knows two stones cannot be placed at once. Rather, he takes his time carefully setting each stone. In the same way, a beginning student may spend six months to a year just on alignment and breathing before moving on to other practices.

Whatever your level of experience, take one step of the ten-step program at a time. The beauty of this program is that you can adapt it to your level of yoga education. Eventually, you will have memorized the steps and you can build on what you have mastered. Mastering one step at a time will eventually coalesce into a balanced and focused yoga practice. Finally, it's important to note that we all need to go back to the beginning sometimes. In this way, the journey can be cyclical.

Two Yoga Practices:
Vinyasa and Traditional Hatha Yoga

The historical practice of yoga as recorded in the *Hatha Yoga Pradipika* outlines each pose as its own program. This means that the student performs one pose at a time and then moves into another pose. There is a slight pause between poses in a traditional Hatha yoga program. This is often the method used for beginners and those who have some physical limits or are advancing in age.

A second form of yoga is a flow (*vinyasa*) where yoga poses are linked together into one flowing series of movements. While there are many forms of vinyasa, it is typically faster paced and quite energetic.

The vinyasa style of yoga often increases body heat and purification through perspiration.

If you are considering what type of practice will suit your needs, take into account your physical ability and what it is you want to achieve. Do you want to create heat and energy in the body, or do you want to go slow and calm yourself down? Though most people have a preference, one practice does not prohibit the other. You may find that one type of practice suits you well on one day, while you prefer a different style of yoga the next. For most students, it is harder to go slow than it is to go fast. This is no different from martial arts, where the younger practitioners enjoy the fast paced aspects of the arts (similar to the vinyasa flow practice). As the students progress, the master requires them to practice their art in slow motion in order to understand the powerful, subtle aspects of the practice. Whatever your choice, develop a yoga practice that fully addresses the mind, body, and spirit.

It may require some trial and error to discover the best form of yoga poses for your body type. Remember, no form is better than another. Some teachers may feel strongly about the benefits of their particular style of yoga and project that opinion onto you. It is natural for a teacher to believe in their practice, as they have seen it help many people. However, it is most important that you find the style that suits your disposition and needs.

It is true that the more psychological aspects of yoga poses are revealed clearly when the poses are held for longer periods of time. However, this can be challenging for many students whose thoughts are easily distracted, also known as the "monkey mind" or "puppy mind." When we move slowly, it is easy to daydream or lose concentration. Remind yourself to focus on deeper intentions when you are doing long-held, slow poses.

If you practice the vinyasa style of yoga, I recommend warming up slowly and allowing your mind to sink deeper into the experience. This awakens the spiritual, heart-centered component of yoga and minimizes the ego. When initiated in this way, practice requires less effort and struggle. Flowing movements minimize distractions as you focus on the task at hand. At times, you may wish to slow down even if that means being out of sync with the class. Your teacher should be fine with you following your own rhythm; if not, their ego may be dominating their teaching style. In home practice, you may wish to work on a handful of poses in more depth to gain more subtle awareness.

Conversely, if you tend to practice a slower Hatha style of yoga, experiment with vinyasa and notice its effects on minimizing distraction. If you have physical challenges that prevent you from practicing vigorous types of yoga, you can do other activities like taking a walk with mindful intention, attitude, and breathing. In this case, the activity becomes the yoga pose.

Practice Themes

I train yoga teachers and often take the opportunity to experiment with them in class. In certain specialty intermediate classes, I ask students to hold poses for a longer duration of time, sometimes only doing twelve poses in a ninety-minute class. After each pose, I poll the students about how they feel. While individual experiences vary, they typically fall under two categories: one group of students has a similar energetic state after every pose and the other group experiences different feelings after each and every pose.

Students who experience the same energy state in each pose commonly share feeling grounded and having an open heart or a clear mind. Regardless of what pose they are practicing, students in this category always vocalize the same feeling. These students superimpose their own state of mind onto the poses. The second category of students has different responses to each pose. Using their intuition, they discover the archetype and energy of the specific poses. They apply the essence of the pose to their lives from a different viewpoint than the first group.

Neither experience is better than the other—both of the groups are correct in their approaches to the psychology of yoga. The generalization is that students in the first group will likely relate better to a vinyasa style of practice, doing poses sequentially without breaks. Students from the second group are likely to savor the essence of each pose in a slower Hatha style of practice, where each pose is held independently.

Focus on What You Need

If you are a beginner, start out with the first step and try to follow the program in a sequential order. Once you have been doing yoga poses for six to twelve months, you can progress on to the more advanced practices presented in this book. Some steps will inevitably require more time, effort, and focus. If you feel called to work on a step, then go ahead and do so, even if it is out of the order provided here.

No matter what, make sure that your yoga practice addresses your needs. Understand that life will throw you curve balls and you must work within your own parameters. Depending on what is going on in your life, how much time you spend on your pose practice may vary from week to week, month to month, or year to year. At specific times in your life, relaxation may be more important, or breathing, or meditation. Trust your inner guide to tell you what you need.

Processing Your Experience

Yoga experiences vary between students. But one thing is certain: yoga is an incredible journey. At times, it is exhilarating and uplifting, and at others, challenging and overwhelming. It is vital that you find ways to process your experience, such as finding an instructor and creating a yoga community with a small group of serious students. If you do not have access to a yoga community or instructor, surf the Internet and research reputable yoga blogs and online communities and teachers to correspond with. Journaling is a good way to keep track of your progress and work through emotions. Attending yoga retreats or joining extended seminars can also inspire your practice. If you are isolated, make plans to go away and study at a retreat center for a weekend or longer.

Many yoga students make the mistake of going to extremes. Students sometimes put too much effort into their practice and neglect other responsibilities, which can actually slow progress. Extended periods of individual practice can give way to daydreaming or alienate students from their daily affairs. Yoga requires time, but remember that it should enhance your personal experiences and responsibilities to family and work, not take away from them. As in any situation, cultivating balance is key.

Find a Teacher

If appropriate, ask your yoga teacher to work with you individually. Learning one-on-one with a teacher may trigger some creative insight into your own practice. The teacher's fees should be reasonable, perhaps in line with paying for bodywork and commensurate to his or her level of experience. Some general rules of the student-teacher relationship follow.

- Though some styles of yoga involve physical adjustments by the teacher, they should not overly manipulate a student by pushing or forcing the student to stretch into the most limber position.

- The teacher and student should be in a semi-public situation with others present.

- Yoga teacher-student ethics should be of the highest standard and should maintain professional boundaries. No sexual advances or relations should occur between teacher and student.

- The student should strive to remain self-reliant and be careful not to become dependent on the teacher. Likewise, the teacher should give the student space to make independent discoveries in the yoga poses.

Journaling

Journaling can be a good way to tap into your emotions. Use your journal as a tool to examine and explore your pose, meditation, or pranayama practice. Just like a diary, a journal is a place to express your experiences and discovered truths on paper. There are so many things that the mind can dance with during practice: the breath, sensations in the body, mental focus, psychological aspects, chakras, archetypes, and more. When you consider that this menu of choices is true for each and every posture that you practice, including Child's Pose and relaxation, there is a potential to be swept away by continual thoughts.

Journaling will help you process feelings that arise during yoga. The things you write about may be a direct expression of your practice or about how it affects your life. By putting your thoughts to paper, you can go deeper into your practice. Keep the journal near your mat during pose routines. If you practice outside of your home, have the journal in your car and keep it in the same location, so that know where to find it. Writing before going to sleep is a good way to review the events of the day and allow the mind to shut down and rest. For some, the early-morning hours are when they are the most clear. If you choose to journal in the morning, be careful that your daily responsibilities don't take precedence over writing. Find a time of day to journal that allows you do it with some consistency.

Components of a Daily Practice

Establishing **consistency of practice** is important if you want to achieve yoga's multiple benefits. Though they can be helpful, tools, tapes, or television programs make it difficult to fully realize these benefits. Attending a regular class with a qualified yoga instructor is the best way to receive comprehensive instruction. Your individual home practice is where you explore and enhance the skills you learn in class. A home practice is very important to progressing in yoga, but it is not a substitute for classroom interaction.

Setting **a regular schedule for your practice** is also important. Yoga poses may be practiced at any time of day except after meals. To help develop consistency, try to practice at the same time every day. In setting a schedule for yoga practice, consider your responsibilities and lifestyle. It is better to accommodate your multiple demands than to attempt practicing at a time of the day when your focus may be scattered. Picking the wrong time of day to practice may cause additional stress and anxiety. Recommended times for your practice are early in the morning when things tend to be quiet and calm or in the early evening around sunset. These two times are particularly auspicious, helping you build a reservoir of positive feelings and reduce stress.

In selecting the **length of your practice** you should use the same guidelines as selecting the time of your practice. Choose a length of time that will allow you to practice the physical asanas and have some quiet time for relaxation and/or meditation at the end. Be realistic so that you stick with your practice. It is better to have a consistent yoga practice that is shorter in duration than a longer practice that becomes erratic and stressful. The benefits of yoga can be achieved in a shorter time period if practice is consistent.

The **location** of your practice is also important. Select a well-ventilated, clean room. Stay away from practicing in an area with strong winds or a fan that blows full force on the mat. The temperature of the room should be warm and comfortable. Place your mat away from furniture and other objects that may cause injury if you lose your balance. Select a place that is reasonably quiet. You may also practice outdoors in an environment that is pleasant and comfortable.

The **sequence** of a yoga practice begins with centering and/or breathing exercises that often lead into the following progression of poses: standing, seated, lying, inversion, relaxation, and meditation. After warming up, you'll want to start with more vigorous poses, then gradually move on to relaxing poses, leading to stillness in Corpse Pose or meditation. Include poses that move the spine in five directions—upward, forward, backward, sideward, and twisting. It is beneficial to practice balancing, stretching for the extremities, and inversions. Remember that there are no hard rules when it comes to sequencing. As you progress in yoga practice, tune in with awareness and let your body tell you which poses you need.

In the beginning, **developing awareness** of tension and relaxation in your body is like going into uncharted territory. We're not usually taught subtle body awareness, and it takes practice to begin noticing how your body works and feels at any given moment. With time, you'll start to recognize when you are holding tension in your neck, shoulders, jaw, belly, or low back, and you will try to avoid postures or activities that make your muscles tense. You can relax your body by simply taking a deep breath, releasing tension in the shoulders, or sitting up straight. With many years of practice, you will become greatly tuned in to the workings of your whole being, including the internal organs and systems of the body, the connection between the emotions and body, and the flow of breath and energy.

It can be very helpful to **cultivate a feeling of "fun" around yoga** discipline. If yoga is on the to-do list, then take it off! The way we perceive our practice will make or break the ability to come back to it each day. By connecting to the bliss that results from daily practice, we can more easily stay dedicated to it. Most students say, "When I do my yoga practice in the morning, everything in my day just goes better, from traffic lights being green, to completing tasks, to smooth relations with my partner." Studies with children show that yoga practice increases their ability to anticipate and cope with challenges. Child yogis are more prepared to face problems, are more flexible in carrying out plans effectively and efficiently, concentrate better, have less fear of failure, have good memory, are able to plan and set priorities, and have healthy self-esteem and a positive social circle.

On the days when you're not feeling disciplined or motivated, the role of **community** becomes paramount. Monastic people recognize the importance of joining together to help one another in the same way that extended family members care for one another. Within a community, it is also helpful to have a personal mentor who takes on the role of personal motivator. A mentor or close friend in the community understands our personal intentions to have a daily yoga practice. These support people help us transform our lives into an expression of our deepest intentions.

Guidelines for Yoga Practice

- Do not force, strain, or stretch further if any pain is noticed. Success in yoga poses is not measured by flexibility. Learn to find inner peace from yoga.

- Do not eat a heavy meal within two hours of practicing yoga poses.

- Do not hold your breath for longer than six seconds in any pose. Breathe normally anytime you need air.

- If your back hurts from sitting on the floor, please use a chair; no extreme discomfort should be felt.

- During group discussion, speak only from your own experience. Do not give advice to others in the group unless a question is addressed to you. If you strongly disagree with a person in the class or the instructor, discuss your issue in private.

- For beginners, try six to eight yoga classes to determine if you plan to continue with yoga over the long term. Remember that there are a variety of yoga styles, so what you experience in one class will be different in another class. Normally, it requires one year to integrate the first level of yoga principles into your life: relaxation, deep breathing, stress management, and flexibility. Ten minutes to an hour of daily practice at home is recommended for maximum benefits.

- Classical yoga is a non-sectarian, non-dogmatic, philosophical approach to healthy living. People of all faiths are welcome to learn yoga as well as those who considers themselves atheist or agnostic.

- For women:
  - In the case of pregnancy, please notify the instructor at any stage. Forward bending, backward bending, inverted poses, and twists may need to be modified or avoided during pregnancy. Yoga's relaxation is beneficial, but stretching must be adapted to pregnancy.
  - During menstruation, inverted poses (Shoulder Stand) are to be modified due to the shift of blood flow that may disturb the natural process of the body. Also, any position that causes strain may be modified.

Catalog of Yoga Poses

This section offers descriptions and pictures of twenty-three poses designed to support your exploration of the ten steps. The description for each pose highlights the ten-step approach for mastering yoga poses. The following information is intended to guide you in applying the information from the book into your yoga pose practice. You may also visit www.pureheartofyoga.com/23poses to view online video instructions of the twenty-three poses. One or two poses are highlighted from these basic categories: balance, meditative, extremities, inversions, relaxation, and spinal stretches (upward, sideward, forward, backward, and twisting). You may already know other poses, or will learn more poses in the future. In those cases, you can apply the principles outlined in this book to any pose in your repertoire.

This text intentionally does not offer an entire yoga pose routine. The focus of this particular work is to illuminate the practices and concepts of a holistic yoga pose practice, not to outline pose routines. Learning from a teacher is of foremost priority. The information here may enrich your practice and your understanding of yoga poses, but it cannot substitute for a class. Finally, individual needs vary and there are no one-size-fits-all yoga programs.

The Sun and Moon Salutations are not outlined here because this approach studies poses from the psychological aspect requiring holding the pose for a longer duration. Once you begin to understand your poses in a deeper manner, you will be able to automatically apply your knowledge to any Sun or Moon Salutation series.

Please note that the instructions beside each pose are suggestions only. Ultimately, the process is subjective. Focus on using the guidelines to create your own approach. In time, this will change. Some periods of life will demand a more introverted approach, and at other times energy will flow freely. The instructions listed are purposefully brief to inspire you to develop your own approach to the poses. For yoga teachers, I recommend acting as a mentor to your students by helping them to enjoy their own personal discovery in yoga pose practice.

There is more than one possibility for each pose. Most poses have multiple areas where the mind may focus. If you do not connect with the suggestions, then just follow what you are experiencing.

May these ideas deepen your existing practice and honor your existing student-teacher relationship as well as your existing yoga tradition. Yoga offers a lifetime of self-exploration, growth, and transcendence. As you get in touch with your creative, loving, and unchanging Self, your life will become richer and more fulfilling. Savor the journey and remember, have fun!

Categories of Poses

These categories describe the effect the poses have on different areas of the body. A balanced yoga routine covers each of these categories, so you may use them as another tool to gauge and design your yoga practice.

- Upward
- Sideward
- Forward
- Backward
- Twisting

- Balance
- Extremities
- Inversion
- Relaxation
- Meditative

These categories are mainly based on the way in which the pose stretches the spine: upward, sideward, forward, backward, and twist. The movement of the spine directly impacts the nervous system that is the bridge in the mind-body connection. Balancing poses cultivate coordination and concentration. Poses for the extremities open the shoulders, hips, arms, and legs. Inversion poses are superior for overall health. Relaxation and meditation poses cover internal experiences. This is one rough practice guideline to memorize and apply to your practice to ensure that you have a well-balanced routine:

- The directions of the spine (upward, sideward, forward, backward, and twist)
- Balance
- Extremities
- Inversion
- Relaxation and meditation

To simplify our discussions in this book, I highlighted only twenty-three of the hundreds of popular yoga poses. From these basic poses, you can detect similarities and further classify and organize some of your daily yoga poses. The complexity of a pose changes based on the many variations available. For example, simply positioning the hands in an upward versus downward position slightly alters the experience of that pose. One book may never be able to conclusively cover every yoga pose, so I encourage you to see the universality of the poses and apply the principles of this book to your practice.

In addition, for intermediate to advanced students, below is a list of additional poses that are not included in this book. Please apply the ten steps of this book to these poses as well:

- **Balance:** Eagle Pose, Toe to Finger Pose, Warrior III or Line Pose
- **Upward:** Stick Pose, Mountain Pose
- **Forward:** Arm-leg Pose, Head to Knee, Three Limbs Pose, Symbol of Yoga Pose, Standing Forward Bend, Throat Lock, Yoga Mudra, Maha Mudra
- **Backward:** Fish, Bridge, Upward Dog, Peacock Pose, Camel, Reclining Goddess, Reclining Hero, Locust, Cricket
- **Sideward:** Gate Pose, Half Moon Pose, Angle, Straddle, Sideward Bend
- **Twist:** Torso Twist, Windmill Pose
- **Extremities:** Warrior II, Warrior III or Line Pose, Bound Ankle Pose, Cow Pose, Chair Pose, Cow Face, Fish, Cradle, Crow Pose, Root Lock or Squat, Simple Throne, Seated Straddle Forward Bend, Spiraled Head-to-Knee Pose, Quadriceps Pose, Plank, Side Plank, Lion, Cradle, Lunge, Frog, Reverse Prayer Pose, Goddess Pose
- **Inversion:** Dead Bug, Ball, Half Plough, Half Fish, Arch Pose, Legs on Wall Pose, Happy Baby Pose, Headstand (not recommended), Handstand
- **Relaxation:** Crocodile
- **Meditative:** Lotus, Adamant Pose, Open Pose, Perfect Pose, Auspicious Pose, Bull Pose, Standing Prayer Pose, Womb Pose

One final explanation. You may also debate my category choices, as certain poses have multiple effects on the body. For example, a pose like the Downward Dog stretches and strengthens the extremities, inverts the head below the heart, and offers a mild backward bend! I chose inversion as a category rather than extremities, but both are valid.

The twenty-three poses are categorized as follows:

Balance

1. Tree Pose
2. Dancer Pose
3. Boat Pose

Upward

4. Palm Tree Pose

Forward

5. Wheel Pose
6. Seated Forward Bend
7. Child's Pose

Backward

8. Cat Stretch
9. Cobra
10. Bow Pose

Sideward

11. Triangle Pose
12. Extended Side Angle

Twist

13. Partial Seated Twist
14. Supine Twist

Extremities

15. Butterfly Pose
16. Pigeon Pose
17. Warrior I

Inversion

18. Downward Dog
19. Shoulder Stand
20. Plough Pose

Relaxation

21. Corpse Pose

Meditative

22. Easy Pose
23. Half Lotus Pose

Visit www.pureheartofyoga.com/23poses for free video instructions of these poses.

I. TREE POSE
Vrikshasana

1. Intention
- Personal intention based on individual growth

2. Attitude
- Giving
- The abundance of a tree

3. Archetype
- Deeply rooted while reaching for the sky

4. Posture Alignment
- Rest foot on ankle, calf, or inner thigh
- Lifted knee turns out to the side
- Press foot into leg and leg into foot
- Lengthen spine upward, relax shoulders
- Upper arms close to ears

5. Breathing
- Natural deep breathing

6. Mental Focus
- Root—one foot beneath the floor
- Heart—feeling the giving nature of tree

7. Energy Center
- Root chakra (1st)
- Heart chakra (4th)

8. Locks and Seals
- Prayer mudra, hands above head or hands at heart
- Root Lock

9. Psychological Block
- Challenges attachment to balance
- Aversion to imbalance
- Fear of falling

10. Emotional Transformation
- Worry vs. Faith

2. DANCER POSE
Natarajasana

1. Intention

- Openness

2. Attitude

- Grace of the dancer
- Confidence and self-esteem

3. Archetype

- Transformation
- Connection in the dance of life
- Balance and completion

4. Posture Alignment

- Hold inside of the foot with same-side hand, press the foot into the hand to extend the arm
- Lean slightly forward from the hips
- Opposite arm curves upward and creates circular energy up the hand
- Reach up and back with the opposite extended arm, toward the lifted foot
- Visualize the foot touching the head

5. Breathing

- Natural deep breathing

6. Mental Focus

- Navel or top of head

7. Energy Center

- Sacral chakra (2nd)

8. Locks and Seals

- Fix eyes on one stable point
- Visualize foot touching head to seal energy loop

9. Psychological Block

- Ignorance of the "dance" of life
- Not flowing in life, like a dam in a river

10. Emotional Transformation

- Seek a balanced expression of emotions
- Learning from effort

3. BOAT POSE
Navasana

1. Intention

- Strength

2. Attitude

- Faith

3. Archetype

- A boat navigating the currents of life

4. Posture Alignment

- Balance body on buttocks and keep spine straight
- Extend legs forward in a bent or elongated position
- Engage abdominal muscles to sustain the posture
- Bring lower back to floor or hold the back of the legs for modified boat

5. Breathing

- Inhale first, raise body
- Suspend breath in pose
- Continue natural deep breathing if holding pose

6. Mental Focus

- Center of body, just above the navel

7. Energy Center

- Solar plexus chakra (3rd)

8. Locks and Seals

- Root Lock

9. Psychological Block

- Aversion to difficulty, challenge, struggle, or change

10. Emotional Transformation

- Looking forward
- Facing the "waves" of life with courage

4. PALM TREE POSE
Talasana III

1. Intention
- Gaining higher awareness through dedication
- Reaching for your higher Self

2. Attitude
- Faith

3. Archetype
- The palm tree has a strong trunk that reaches for the sun
- The palm tree bears one of earth's most nutritious fruits

4. Posture Alignment
- Raise arms over head, palms facing each other (touching or not), keep shoulders relaxed
- Lift up onto toes (for modification, keep feet flat on the floor)
- Reach the spine upward and then release arms to starting point
- Keep head straight, gaze at an object eye level (do not look up or arch the back)
- Tuck hips to flatten lower spine and touch chin to the chest to flatten neck curvature, creating a straight spine to feel energy movement up and down the body
- As the arms rise up and down, bring shoulder blades together so that the heart is open and the upper arms rise up to the side of the ears

5. Breathing
- Inhale while raising the arms
- Retain breath while holding the pose
- Exhale when lowering arms

6. Mental Focus
- Top of head
- Advanced—top of head and twelve inches below the ground (simultaneously)

7. Energy Center
- Crown chakra (7th)

8. Locks and Seals
- Root Lock
- Abdominal Lock
- Chin Lock
- Great Lock (all of the above in tandem)

9. Psychological Block
- Examine the ego in relation to striving
- Balance excess or deficiency

10. Emotional Transformation
- Reach your highest potential
- Face life with open arms

5. WHEEL POSE
Cakrasana

1. Intention
- Surrender of emotional issues

2. Attitude
- Letting go, detaching

3. Archetype
- Circle of life
- The essence of the wheel
- The power of motion

4. Posture Alignment
- With feet shoulder-width apart, raise arms up over the head
- Extend up and out of the lower back
- Do not strain the head or hips backward
- Exhale and bend forward from the hips, extend out through fingertips as you fold forward
- Circle arms like a wheel and clasp them behind the back in the forward fold
- Extend arms toward the ceiling (to modify, let them rest on the lower back)

5. Breathing
- Inhale as you stretch upward, exhale as you bend forward
- Equal breath while holding pose
- Exhale relaxing arms
- Inhale while rising back to standing

6. Mental Focus
- Center of the body, just above the navel

7. Energy Center
- Solar plexus chakra (3rd)
- Opens the back side (moon side) of all chakras

8. Locks and Seals
- Abdominal Lock

9. Psychological Block

- Ego domination
- Identifying with difficulty and strife

10. Emotional Transformation

- Let go of impediments
- Surrendering and releasing the past

6. SEATED FORWARD BEND
Pascimottanasana

1. Intention
- Surrender personal limitations

2. Attitude
- Non-attachment to dreams

3. Archetype
- Introspection

4. Posture Alignment
- From seated position with legs outstretched and arms raised, bend forward from the hips
- Keep back straight as far forward as you can and then surrender head, spine, and hands to rest on legs or feet
- Relax head and tuck the chin

5. Breathing
- Exhale as you bend forward
- Intermediate students may suspend breath while in the pose, then breathe normally if held longer
- Inhale rising back up

6. Mental Focus
- Base of spine
- Back of throat

7. Energy Center
- Third eye chakra (6th)

8. Locks and Seals
- Root Lock
- Abdominal Lock
- Chin Lock
- Great Lock (all of the above in tandem)

9. Psychological Block
- Surrendering egoistic ideas and future fantasies

10. Emotional Transformation
- Find stillness within

7. CHILD'S POSE
Balasana

1. Intention

- Openness
- Connection to the infinite
- Receiving

2. Attitude

- Humility by consciously receiving

3. Archetype

- Return to the womb

4. Posture Alignment

- On all fours, sit back onto (or toward) the heels, bending forward. If the buttocks do not touch the heels, tuck a blanket in between for support.
- Touch forehead to floor if possible with arms resting at sides (modification is to rest the forehead on crossed arms or double-stacked fists)

5. Breathing

- Breathe into the diaphragm area to loosen the lower torso

6. Mental Focus

- Arms and legs touching the earth
- The point between kidneys on the back of the body

7. Energy Center

- Sacral chakra (2nd)

8. Locks and Seals

- The pose itself is a seal
- Throat Lock

9. Psychological Block

- Avoiding life

10. Emotional Transformation

- Feel the freedom of infant who is cared for by the larger universe without worry

8. CAT STRETCH
Marjariasana

1. Intention

- Honesty

2. Attitude

- Self-inquiry in terms of the higher Self

3. Archetype

- Curious cat exploring reality

4. Posture Alignment

- Start on all fours, with hands and knees shoulder-width apart
- Hands under the shoulders and knees under the hips
- Notice weight distributed equally through all four limbs
- Arch into backbend-like stretch, tipping the tailbone up, dropping the belly and stretch the throat by reaching the chin out first and looking up (do not overly compress the neck) (Cow position)
- Follow by rounding the back, dropping the tailbone and tucking the chin toward the chest, and pull the belly in toward the spine (Cat position)

5. Breathing

- Inhale as you stretch up and back
- Exhale as you round forward
- Intermediate students may hold breath while arching and suspend breath while rounding

6. Mental Focus

- Crown while arching
- Center of back opposite solar plexus when rounding

7. Energy Center

- Crown chakra (7th) when arching
- Solar plexus chakra (3rd) when rounding
- Notice which chakra your attention is drawn to, as this pose activates all of the chakras

8. Locks and Seals
- Abdominal Lock after breath suspension while rounding
- Throat Lock while rounding

9. Psychological Block
- Ignorance
- Rigid view of life
- Narrow-mindedness

10. Emotional Transformation
- Courage to seek the truth
- Faith and hope
- Overcoming fear

9. COBRA POSE
Bhujangasana

1. Intention

- Transcendence

2. Attitude

- Achievement

3. Archetype

- Snake shedding its skin is symbolic of transformation
- Release old patterns and allow new energy to flow

4. Posture Alignment

- Lying on your belly, rest your forehead, arms, and the tops of your feet on the ground
- Lift up the chest (while resting the arms on the floor) as far as is comfortable (modify by supporting the upper body with forearms and palms on the floor)
- Relax the arms, buttocks, and leg muscles
- Head follows the spine (one long line of energy)

5. Breathing

- Inhale as you lift the spine
- For intermediate students, retain breath while holding the pose
- Exhale as you lower the spine

6. Mental Focus

- Top of the head

7. Energy Center

- Crown chakra (7th)

8. Locks and Seals

- Root Lock
- Tongue Seal

9. Psychological Block

- Ignorance of the changing nature of life

10. Emotional Transformation

- Recognizing comfort in the growth process

10. BOW POSE
Dhanurvakrasana

1. Intention
- Focus

2. Attitude
- Fortitude
- Discipline

3. Archetype
- Honing the strength and skill to aim the bow

4. Posture Alignment
- While lying on the stomach, reach back for toes or ankles
- Lift chest off of the floor as the hands and feet lift toward the sky
- Modification is to reach arms back toward toes (by the side of the body) and lift upper body and legs simultaneously

5. Breathing
- Inhale while moving into pose
- Intermediate, retain breath while in the pose
- Exhale while returning

6. Mental Focus
- Heart or throat

7. Energy Center
- Third eye chakra (6th)

8. Locks and Seals
- Eye Seal with eyes focused inward toward third eye

9. Psychological Block
- Attachment to perfection

10. Emotional Transformation
- Concentrate and remain committed to practice

II. TRIANGLE POSE
Trikonasana

1. Intention
- Harmony

2. Attitude
- Honesty

3. Archetype
- The triangle has powerful historical meaning in different cultures—the triad, the trinity, the pyramid

4. Posture Alignment
- Stand with legs spread apart, back foot is at a 45-degree angle, toes of the front foot point forward. Both the front and back legs are extended. Line up the front foot with the arch of the back foot and open the hips to the side of the room
- Raise arms to shoulder height. Reach from the waist, out through the fingertips as far as you can. Keeping hips and lower body steady, extend front arm to reach down toward the thigh, shin, or foot. If you feel the back hip coming forward, ease up on the stretch. Reach up through the fingertips of the back hand as it extends toward the ceiling. If the neck is flexible, turn to look up at the ceiling
- Keep hips open; lower arm hangs with gravity and the core muscles engage to hold the posture (or the lowered arm can be used for support by holding onto the shin or thigh)

5. Breathing
- Diaphragmatic breathing

6. Mental Focus
- Sacrum

7. Energy Center
- Sacral chakra (2nd)
- Heart chakra (4th)

8. Locks and Seals
- Root Lock

9. Psychological Block

- Categorize qualities of reality as pure, energetic, or dull
- Egoism and attachment tend to be of an energetic nature
- Aversion and fear fall under the dull category

10. Emotional Transformation

- Notice the poles of the triangle each have tendencies and each support the other; negative qualities have positive counterbalances and both are connected to a pure outcome
- Cultivating a pure state in all aspects of our lives helps us to rise above ignorance

12. EXTENDED SIDE ANGLE
Stthita Parsvakonasana

1. Intention
- Trust

2. Attitude
- Flexibility

3. Archetype
- Rootedness

4. Posture Alignment
- Similar to triangle pose, stand with legs spread apart, back foot at a 45-degree angle, toes of the front foot pointed forward. The back leg is extended and the front leg bends so that the knee is over the ankle
- Raise arms to shoulder height. Reach from the waist, out through the fingertips
- Keeping hips and lower body steady, let the elbow of the front arm come down and rest on the thigh
- Keep hips open as the back arm comes to reach up

and over the head, feel the pose as one long line of the energy, from the fingertips of the extended arm all the way through the hip and into the leg and foot of the extended leg

5. Breathing
- Diaphragmatic breathing

6. Mental Focus
- Sacrum

7. Energy Center
- Root chakra (1st)

8. Locks and Seals
- Root Lock

9. Psychological Block
- Aversion to change

10. Emotional Transformation
- A strong base supports transformation. Challenge yourself while recognizing limits for stretching in yoga poses, and in life

13. PARTIAL SEATED TWIST
Ardha Matsyendrasana

1. Intention

- Joy

2. Attitude

- Peacefulness

3. Archetype

- Fire; purification

4. Posture Alignment

- Choose from the different
  modifications pictured
- Twist from core muscles,
  not shoulders
- Keep spine erect
- Relax forehead

5. Breathing

- Exhale while entering the
  twist
- Intermediate students,
  suspend breath
- Diaphragmatic breathing to
  hold pose longer

6. Mental Focus

- Third eye

7. Energy Center

- Solar plexus chakra (3rd)
- Third eye chakra (6th)

8. Locks and Seals

- Abdominal Lock

9. Psychological Block

- Fear manifested as worry

10. Emotional Transformation

- Release doubt and worry
  to allow the body's energy
  to flow
- Cultivate joy in the body,
  mind, and spirit

14. SUPINE TWIST
Supta Matsyendrasana

1. Intention

- Release of past
- Forgiveness

2. Attitude

- Effort
- Objectivity

3. Archetype

- Yogi or spiritual master. Supine twist is named after the famed tenth-century yogi Matsyendra
- Purification

4. Posture Alignment

- Lie on the back and lift the knees to the chest
- Start on the right side by lowering the knees to the floor. Keep the knees in line with the hips
- Place your arms to your sides straight out from the shoulders
- Turn your head away from the knees to twist the neck

5. Breathing

- Release into twist with the exhale

6. Mental Focus

- Sacrum
- Point between the kidneys

7. Energy Center

- Sacral chakra (2nd)

8. Locks and Seals

- Abdominal Lock

9. Psychological Block

- Ego; are you able to see another perspective, or are you attached to your own view? Can you release the past?

10. Emotional Transformation

- Recognize that past issues can be released and healed

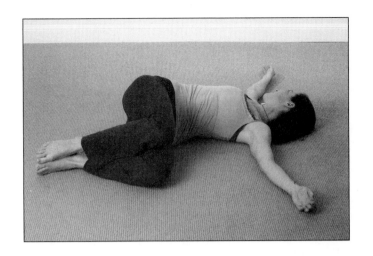

15. BUTTERFLY POSE
Poorna Titali Asana

1. Intention
- Freedom through transformation

2. Attitude
- Openness

3. Archetype
- Butterfly (metamorphosis)
- Freedom from suffering
- Transformation through spiritual cocoon

4. Posture Alignment
- Draw the soles of the feet together from seated position and hold on to the toes, ankles, or shins
- Sit up straight
- Slowly butterfly the knees up and down

5. Breathing
- Inhale as you lift the knees, exhale as you lower

6. Mental Focus
- Root
- Base of spine
- Sacrum

7. Energy Center
- Root chakra (1st)
- Sacral chakra (2nd)

8. Locks and Seals
- Root Lock
- Horse Seal

9. Psychological Block
- Fear of change
- Attachment to life

10. Emotional Transformation
- Like the caterpillar's transformation into the butterfly, our negative emotions can be transformed in order to serve our highest potential and the greater good

16. PIGEON POSE
Eka Pada Kapotasana

1. Intention

- Communication within one's self (inner dialogue)

2. Attitude

- Self-awareness and self-understanding

3. Archetype

- Relationship to ego, pride, gifts and talents, power (puffing out of the chest like a pigeon)

4. Posture Alignment

- While seated, bring the leg in front of the body, the knee at a 90-degree angle (if this is not possible or comfortable, draw the foot closer to the groin)
- The back leg is bent behind in a comfortable way
- If able to straighten the back leg, do so as long as the corresponding sit bone doesn't pop up

- Begin with a backward bend, shoulders rounded back, heart and throat open
- Bend forward, using arms out in front to lower body and the forehead to the floor (modify by slightly bending the elbows and using the hands to hold you up, or resting on the forearms or double-stacked fists)

5. Breathing

- Inhale into the backward opening stretch
- Intermediate students may retain breath while arched upward
- Exhale in forward bending and release into pose
- Intermediate students may suspend breath while forward

6. Mental Focus
- Throat while arching back
- Back of neck while in forward bending

7. Energy Center
- Throat chakra (5th)

8. Locks and Seals
- Chin Lock in forward bend

9. Psychological Block
- Ego
- Ignorance about the true Self

10. Emotional Transformation
- Notice the balance between effort (upward stretch) and detachment (forward bend) in terms of personal growth
- Surrender the mind to the heart

17. WARRIOR I
Virabhadrasana I

1. Intention

- Power
- Courage

2. Attitude

- Self-esteem
- Perseverance

3. Archetype

- Spiritual warrior
- The strength to face blocks and transform

4. Posture Alignment

- From standing position, step one foot back three to four feet and turn the foot outward 45 to 90 degrees
- Lunge with front knee until it is over the ankle, square hips to the front
- Raise arms up above head, palms together
- Back is slightly arched from the stomach, eyes gaze forward

5. Breathing

- Equal diaphragmatic breathing for prolonged practice
- Breath retention for shorter durations

6. Mental Focus

- Solar plexus

7. Energy Center

- Solar plexus chakra (3rd)

8. Locks and Seals

- Root Lock
- Abdominal Lock

9. Psychological Block

- Fear
- Aversion to emotional issues

10. Emotional Transformation

- With effort, positive emotions are cultivated
- As a spiritual warrior, act with confidence and an open heart

18. DOWNWARD DOG
Adho Mukha Svanasana

1. Intention

- Joy

2. Attitude

- Optimism

3. Archetype

- Relax, stretch, and feel the joy of your own body
- Playfulness

4. Posture Alignment

- From all fours, open up the fingers to create a stable base, tuck your toes under to put weight on the balls of your feet, and send the hips back as you lift your knees off the floor
- Relax the head and neck as you send the chest toward the legs
- Stretch the spine as you lengthen and extend the arms and guide the tailbone backward and upward
- Heels toward the floor (they may or may not touch the floor)

5. Breathing

- Diaphragmatic breath, bring stomach muscles back toward spine for complete exhalation

6. Mental Focus

- Heart
- Throat

7. Energy Center

- Heart chakra (4th)

8. Locks and Seals

- Root Lock
- Abdominal Lock

9. Psychological Block

- Attachment, possessiveness

10. Emotional Transformation

- A symbol of unconditional love, man's best friend teaches us how to transform our emotions with loyalty and devotion to the human race

19. SHOULDER STAND
Sarvangasana

1. Intention

- Introspection

2. Attitude

- Wisdom

3. Archetype

- Turning upside down, viewing reality from a new perspective

4. Posture Alignment

- While on your back, rock your knees and lift the hips, supporting them with your hands
- Tuck your chin and be mindful of the pressure your spine
- Half Shoulder Stand keeps the legs angled at 45 degrees
- Full Shoulder Stand extends the legs toward the ceiling
- For modification, keep the low back on floor and hold behind knees, feet up in the air

5. Breathing

- Normal deep breathing

6. Mental Focus

- Crown

7. Energy Center

- Crown chakra (7th)

8. Locks and Seals

- Chin Lock

9. Psychological Block

- Ego, fear of change

10. Emotional Transformation

- Recognizing the limited nature of perspective
- Sensing the distinction between selfishness and selflessness
- Seeing things from a new perspective

20. PLOUGH POSE
Halasana

1. Intention

- Silence

2. Attitude

- Humility

3. Archetype

- Furrowing, reaping bounty
- Pushing new boundaries
- Planting seeds for new growth

4. Posture Alignment

- On back, lift legs up over head and down toward the floor behind head
- To activate the legs, extend through the toes as they lower to the floor
- Be careful of spinal compression by supporting torso with the hands on the floor or back, or above the head
- Modify by pressing the feet into a wall behind you

5. Breathing

- Inhale while on back
- Exhale bringing legs overhead
- Intermediates may suspend breath in the pose

6. Mental Focus

- Throat

7. Energy Center

- Throat chakra (5th)

8. Locks and Seals

- Chin Lock
- Tongue Seal

9. Psychological Block

- Fear

10. Emotional Transformation

- Willingness to be quiet and reflective
- Overcoming the need of external justification

21. CORPSE POSE
Shavasana

1. Intention

- Faith

2. Attitude

- Acceptance
- Letting go
- Release

3. Archetype

- Rebirth
- Rest or rejuvenation

4. Posture Alignment

- Lay on your back with feet a foot and a half apart, arms at your side, or any comfortable pose for relaxing the body
- To modify for low back pain, place a rolled blanket beneath the thighs or knees

5. Breathing

- Natural breathing, notice the diaphragm activate in this position

6. Mental Focus

- The sixteen concentration points help release tension in the nearby areas of the body:
  1. Tips of toes
  2. Ankles
  3. Back of knees
  4. Thighs
  5. Anus
  6. Reproductive organs
  7. Navel
  8. Stomach
  9. Heart
  10. Throat
  11. Lips
  12. Tip of the nose
  13. Eyes
  14. Third eye (space between eyebrows)
  15. Forehead
  16. Top of the head

7. Energy Center

- The activated chakra relates to the area(s) of release, may be one individual chakra or multiple chakras. Follow your intuition

8. Locks and Seals

- The pose itself is a seal, as the supine position symbolically seals you from activity

9. Psychological Block

- Fear of death and change
- Attachments

10. Emotional Transformation

- Surrendering ego-consciousness in preparation for returning to original form.
- Self-realization; who are we beyond body and mind?

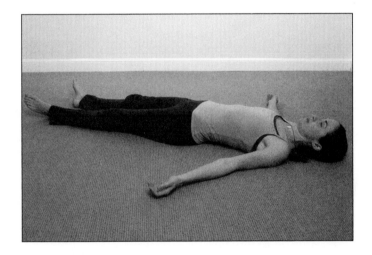

22. EASY POSE
Sukhasana

and

23. HALF LOTUS POSE
Ardha Padmasana

1. Intention
- Clarity

2. Attitude
- Reaching for true Self, grounded in the earth while reaching for the sky

3. Archetype
- Lotus flower seed contains a perfect flower within, the inherent Divine nature
- Beauty in turbid conditions

4. Posture Alignment
- From sitting position, sit with erect spine and sacral mutation (lumbar curve)
- Relaxed shoulders, arms, hands, face, smile
- Half-lotus brings one foot up onto thigh
- Use wall, pillow, or chair for support or comfort

- Bottom half of the body feels heavy, rooted
- Upper half of the body feels light and airy

5. Breathing
- Natural breath (in meditation)
- Many different breathing exercises can be performed in this position

6. Mental Focus
- Common areas are root, solar plexus, heart, third eye, and crown

7. Energy Center
- Third eye chakra (6th) for concentration of mind
- Chakras related to specific meditation exercise

8. Locks and Seals

- Cross-legged position acts as a seal symbolizing a still body and mind
- Knowledge Seal
- Consciousness Seal
- Locks as they relate to specific exercises

9. Psychological Block

- Ignorance

10. Emotional Transformation

- If experiencing negative emotion, meditate upon the opposite
- Meditative poses create space to discern the real from the unreal

Glossary of Sanskrit Terms

Aasha . . . . hope

Abhinivesa . . . . fear of death/change

Adho Mukha Svanasana . . . . Downward Facing Dog Pose

Ahamkara . . . . ego

Ahimsa . . . . non-violence

Ajna . . . . command wheel; sixth or third eye chakra

Alasya . . . . laziness

Anahata . . . . wheel of the unstruck sound; fourth or heart chakra

Ananta-samapatti . . . . connecting to the infinite

Anitya bhavana . . . . passage describing all things as transitory

Anjali mudra . . . . Prayer Seal

Aparigraha . . . . non-attachment

Ardha Chandrasana . . . . Half Moon Pose

Ardha Matsyendrasana . . . . Partial Seated Twist

301

Ardha Padamasana . . . . Half Lotus Pose

Asana . . . . physical posture or pose in yoga

Ashvini mudra . . . . Horse Seal in which the sphincter
muscles are contracted

Ashwa Sanchalanasana . . . . Lunge Pose

Asmita . . . . egoism

Asteya . . . . non-stealing

Avidya . . . . spiritual ignorance

Ayurveda . . . . an ancient Indian system of holistic
medicine

Balasana . . . . Child's Pose

Bandhas . . . . physical locks of energy in the body

Bhagavad Gita . . . . foundational spiritual text of yoga

Bhava . . . . attitude or state of mind

Bhavana . . . . emotional transformation

Bhaya . . . . fear

Bhujangasana . . . . Cobra Pose

Brahman . . . . unified energetic field

Bramacharya . . . . moderation

Cakrasana . . . . Wheel Pose

Cakrasana III . . . . Backbend

Chakras . . . . energy centers

Chandra Namaskara . . . . Moon Salutations

Chin mudra . . . . gesture of consciousness, palms
face up

Chinta . . . . worry

Citta . . . . consciousness

Daya . . . . kindness

Desha . . . . single focus

Dhairya . . . . courage

Dhanurvakrasana . . . . Bow Pose

Dharana . . . . concentration

Dharma . . . . duty

Dhyana	meditation
Dukha	sadness, suffering
Dvesa	aversion
Eka Pada Kapotasana	Pigeon Pose
Ekapadasana	One Foot Pose
Garudasana	Eagle Pose
Gomukhasana	Cow Pose
Guna	quality of existence
Guru	teacher
Halasana	Plough Pose
Hastapadangustasana	Toe-Finger Pose
Hastapadasana	Standing Forward Bend
Hatha Yoga	path of yoga by which self-realization occurs via the body
Hatha Yoga Pradipika	ancient Hindu yoga pose practice book
Ida	the left energetic channel
Ishvara aisvarya	mastery
Ishvara pranidhana	surrender
Jalandhara bandha	Throat Lock
Janu-Sirshasana	Head to Knee
Jihva bandha	Tongue Lock
Jnana	knowledge
Jnana mudra	gesture of knowledge, palms face down
Kapha	earth
Karma	action or notion that every action brings about a reaction
Karma Yoga	path of yoga by which self-realization occurs through work / selfless service
Klesa	affliction or hindrance of the mind
Konasana I	Angle Pose
Konasana III	Windmill Pose
Kosha	sheath or layer

Krodha . . . . anger

Kumbhaka . . . . breath retention

Kundalini . . . . serpent power or latent force at the base of the spine

Maha bandha . . . . Great Lock

Makarasana . . . . Crocodile Pose

Mandukasana . . . . Frog Pose

Manipura . . . . wheel of the jeweled city; third or solar plexus chakra

Marjariasana . . . . Cat Pose

Marmasthanani . . . . sixteen concentration points in the body

Matsyasana . . . . Fish

Matsyendrasana . . . . Supine Twist

Mauna . . . . silence

Maya . . . . external world

Mayurasana . . . . Peacock Pose

Mudra . . . . physical seal created by the body to enhance energy flow

Mula bandha . . . . Root Lock

Muladhara . . . . root prop wheel; first or root chakra

Nadi . . . . energy channel

Nadi shodhanam . . . . channel purification

Natarajasana . . . . Great Dancer Pose

Navasana . . . . Boat Pose

Niyama . . . . observance

Om . . . . primordial sound of the universe; universal creation

Pada Prasar Paschimottanasana . . Seated Straddle Forward Bend Pose

Padahastasana . . . . Standing Forward Bend Pose

Padmasana . . . . Lotus Pose

Parsvottanasana . . . . Reverse Prayer Pose

Parvatasana . . . . Seated Mountain Pose

Pascimottanasana. . . . . Seated Forward Bend Pose

Pingala. . . . . the right energetic channel

Pitta. fire

Poorna Titali Asana . . . . Butterfly Pose

Prajna . . . . wisdom, realized knowledge

Prakriti . . . . Nature, the physical world

Prana. bio-energy or life force

Pranayama. . . . . breath control

Pratipaksa bhavana . . . . practice the opposite intention

Pratyahara. . . . . sensory mastery

Puraka. . . . . prolonged inhale

Purusha . . . . Consciousness; transcendental Self

Purvaja . . . . archetype

Raga . . . . attachment

Rajas . . . . active, energetic, hyper, obsessive

Recaka . . . . prolonged exhale

Sadhana. . . . . remembrance, daily practice

Sahasrara. . . . . thousand-spoked wheel; seventh or
crown chakra

Samadhi. . . . . union, enlightenment

Samkalpa. . . . . intention

Santolanasana . . . . Plank Pose

Santosha . . . . contentment

Sarvangasana. . . . . Shoulder Stand Pose

Sattva. . . . . balanced, pure, calm, clear, focused

Satya . . . . truthfulness

Saucha. . . . . purity

Shakti . . . . creative energy

Shalabasana. . . . . Locust Pose

Shavasana . . . . Corpse Pose

Shishya . . . . disciple

Siddhi . . . . superhuman feat

Simhasana . . . . Lion Pose

Sirshasana . . . . Headstand Pose

Sraddha . . . . faith

Sthitaprarthanasana . . . . Standing Prayer Pose

Stthita Parsvakonasana . . . . Extended Side Angle

Sukha . . . . joy

Sukhasana . . . . Easy Pose

Sunyaka . . . . breath suspension

Supta Matsyendrasana . . . . Supine Twist

Surya Namaskara . . . . Sun Salutation

Sushumna . . . . the central energetic channel

Svadhyaya . . . . study of self or scripture

Svadisthana . . . . own base center; second or sacral
chakra

Svarodaya . . . . the science of breath

Taittiriya Upanishad . . . . from food to joy

Talasana III . . . . Palm Tree Pose

Tamas . . . . inactive, dull, depressed

Tapas . . . . discipline

Trataka . . . . eye exercises

Trikonasana . . . . Triangle Pose

Uddiyana bandha . . . . Abdominal Lock

Ujjayi . . . . victorious breath, partial closure of the
glottis while breathing

Urdhva Muhka Svanasana . . . . . . Upward Dog Pose

Ustrasana . . . . Camel Pose

Utkatasana . . . . Chair Pose

Utthanasana . . . . Squat Pose

Vata . . . . air

Viaragya . . . . non-attachment

Vinyasa . . . . flow

Viparita karani mudra . . . . Inverted Action Seal (a modified form
of Shoulder Stand)

Virabhadrasana I . . . . Warrior I Pose

Virabhadrasana II	Warrior II Pose
Virabhadrasana III	Warrior III Pose or Line Pose
Vishada	despair
Vishuddha	pure wheel; fifth or throat chakra
Vrikshasana	Tree Pose
Yama	restraint
Yastikasana	Stick Pose
Yoga mudra	Symbol of Yoga Pose; union with Supreme consciousness
Yoganga	independent branch of yoga requiring subtle awareness
Yoni mudra	Womb Seal, five fingertips placed symbolically over senses

Bibliography

Anodea, Judith, and Selene Vega. *The Sevenfold Journey.* Freedom, CA: Crossing Press, 1993.

Aranya, Swami Hariharananda. *Yoga Philosophy of Patanjali.* Albany, NY: State University of New York Press, 1983.
  (Referred to herein as *Yoga Sutras.*)

Butera, Robert. *The Classical Yoga Lifestyle.* Devon, PA: YogaLife Institute, 2000.

Coulter, H. David. *Anatomy of Hatha Yoga: A Manual for Students, Teachers and Practitioners.* Honesdale, PA: Body and Breath, 2001.

Coward, Harold. *Jung and Eastern Thought.* Albany, NY: State University of New York Press, 1985.

Easwaran, Eknath, tr. *The Upanishads.* Petaluma, CA: Nilgiri Press, 1987.

Feuerstein, Georg. *The Shambhala Encyclopedia of Yoga.* Boston, MA: Shambhala Publications, 1997.

Gerber, Richard. *A Practical Guide to Vibrational Medicine.* New York: HarperCollins, 2001.

Govindan, Marshall. *Kriya Yoga Sutras of Patanjali and the Siddhas*. Eastman, Quebec: Kriya Yoga Publications, 2000.

Herrigel, Eugen, and D. T. Suzuki. *Zen in the Art of Archery*. Tr. R. F. C. Hull. New York: Vintage Books, 1989.

Mercier, Patricia. *Chakras: Balance your Body's Energy for Health and Harmony*. New York: Godsfield Press: Distributed by Sterling Pub., 2000.

Mitchell, Stephen. *Bhagavad Gita: A New Translation*. New York: Harmony Books, 2000.

Motoyama, Hiroshi. *Theories of the Chakras: Bridge to Higher Consciousness*. Wheaton, IL: Theosophical Publishing House, 1981.

Muktibodhananda, Swami. *Hatha Yoga Pradipika*. Munger, Bihar, India: Bihar School of Yoga, 1993.

Myss, Caroline. *Why People Don't Heal and How They Can*. New York: Harmony Books, 1997.

Ornish, Dean. *Dr. Dean Ornish's Program for Reversing Heart Disease*. New York: Random House, 1990.

Radha, Swami Sivananda. *Hatha Yoga: The Hidden Language, Symbols, Secrets, and Metaphor*. Spokane, WA: Timeless Books, 1995.

Rama, Swami, Rudolph Ballentine, and Alan Hymes. *Science of Breath: A Practical Guide*. Honesdale, PA: Himalayan Institute Press, 1998.

Satyananda Saraswati, Swami. *Asana Pranayama Mudra Bandha*. Monghyr, India: Bihar School of Yoga, 1991.

Yogendra, Jayadeva, ed. *Cyclopaedia Yoga*. Vol. 1, *All about Asanas and 100 More Topics of Yoga*. Santacruz, Mumbai, India: Yoga Institute, 1993.

———. *Cyclopaedia Yoga*. Vol. 2, *A Systematic Programme on Yoga Education for the Child and the Adult*. Santacruz, Mumbai, India: Yoga Institute, 1989.

Yogendra, Shri. *Guide to Yoga Meditation*. Bombay, India: Yogendra Publications Fund, 1986.

———. *Hatha Yoga Simplified*. Bombay, India: Yogendra Publications Fund, 1991.

Resources

YogaLife Institute

Robert Butera, Ph.D., and Kristen Butera
821 W. Lancaster Ave.
Wayne, PA 19087
Phone: 610-688-7030
Email: yogalifeinstitute@comcast.net
Web: www.yogalifeinstitute.com

YogaLife New Hampshire

Julie Rost
8 Clifford Street
Exeter, NH 03833
Phone: 603-686-5435
Email: julierost@yogalifenh.com
Web: www.yogalifeNH.com

Welkin Wellness Center

Erin Byron

45 Dalkeith Drive, Unit 13

Brantford, Ontario N3P 1M1

Canada

Phone: 519-751-1368

Email: yoga@welkin.ca

Web: www.welkin.com

The Yoga Institute of Mumbai

Shri Yogendra Marg

Prabhat Colony, Santacruz (East)

Mumbai 400 055 India

Phone: 91 22 2611 0506

Email: yogainstitute@gmail.com

Web: www.theyogainstitute.org

International Association of Yoga Therapists (IAYT)

115 S. McCormick, Suite 3

Prescott, AZ 86303

Phone: 928-541-0004

Email: mail@iayt.org

Web: www.iayt.org

About the Author

Robert Butera, MDiv, Ph.D., directs the YogaLife Institute in Wayne, Pennsylvania, where he trains teachers and leads seminars, online courses, and yoga and meditation retreats for the public. All of the programs YogaLife offers follow Dr. Butera's self-published book, *The Classical Yoga Study Guide*. Dr. Butera is also publisher of the popular holistic magazine for the greater Philadelphia area, *Yoga Living*, a free publication that shares resources with the community about how to live a holistic lifestyle.

Dr. Butera is certified by The Yoga Institute in Mumbai, India, where he studied a non-sectarian style of classical yoga with Dr. Jayadeva Yogendra. His Ph.D. studies at The California Institute of Integral Studies focused on developing a yoga-based healing program for the immune system. Dr. Butera holds a Masters of Divinity from The Earlham School of Religion and has studied Buddhist psychotherapy, meditation, and personal growth in Japan, Taiwan, and India. He is certified as an E-RYT (Experienced Registered Yoga Teacher) from the Yoga Alliance, reserved for those with extensive teaching experience.

With more than twenty-five years of experience, Dr. Butera approaches his teaching with knowledge and passion. Emphasizing education and simple language in his courses, he teaches clients how to create a yoga practice based on their personal needs. It is a simple, yet transformative process that helps many students learn to live to their fullest potential. The thriving community at the YogaLife Institute is a reflection of Dr. Butera's dedication and expertise.

You can learn more about Dr. Butera's approach to yoga by visiting www.YogaLifeInstitute.com and www.pureheartofyoga.com.

Free Catalog

Get the latest
information on our
body, mind, and spirit products!
To receive a **free** copy of Llewellyn's consumer
catalog, *New Worlds of Mind & Spirit,* simply
call 1-877-NEW-WRLD or visit our website at
www.llewellyn.com and click on *New Worlds.*

☾ LLEWELLYN ORDERING INFORMATION

Order Online:
Visit our website at www.llewellyn.com, select your books, and order
them on our secure server.

Order by Phone:
- Call toll-free within the U.S. at 1-877-NEW-WRLD
  (1-877-639-9753). Call toll-free within Canada at
  1-866-NEW-WRLD (1-866-639-9753)
- We accept VISA, MasterCard, and American Express

Order by Mail:
Send the full price of your order (MN residents add 6.875% sales tax) in
U.S. funds, plus postage & handling to:

> **Llewellyn Worldwide**
> **2143 Wooddale Drive, Dept. 978-0-7387-1487-5**
> **Woodbury, MN 55125-2989**

Postage & Handling:

Standard (U.S., Mexico, & Canada). If your order is:
$24.99 and under, add $4.00
$25.00 and over, FREE STANDARD SHIPPING

AK, HI, PR: $16.00 for one book plus $2.00 for
each additional book.

International Orders (airmail only):
$16.00 for one book plus $3.00 for each additional book

Orders are processed within 2 business days.
Please allow for normal shipping time. Postage and handling rates subject to change.

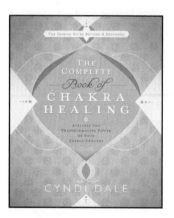

THE COMPLETE BOOK OF CHAKRA HEALING
Activate the Transformative Power of Your Energy Centers
CYNDI DALE

When first published in 1996, Cyndi Dale's guide to the chakras established a new standard for healers, intuitives, and energy workers worldwide. This groundbreaking book quickly became a bestseller. It expanded the seven-chakra system to thirty-two chakras, explained spiritual points available for dynamic change, and outlined the energetic system so anyone could use it for health, prosperity, and happiness.

Presented here for the first time is the updated and expanded edition, now titled *The Complete Book of Chakra Healing*. With nearly 150 more pages than the original book, this groundbreaking edition is poised to become the next classic guide to the chakras.

978-0-7387-1502-5
456 pp., 7½ x 9⅛ $24.95

CHAKRAS FOR BEGINNERS
A Guide to Balancing Your Chakra Energies
DAVID POND

The chakras are spinning vortexes of energy located just in front of your spine and positioned from the tailbone to the crown of the head. They are a map of your inner world—your relationship to yourself and how you experience energy. They are also the batteries for the various levels of your life energy. The freedom with which energy can flow back and forth between you and the universe correlates directly to your total health and well-being.

Blocks or restrictions in this energy flow expresses itself as disease, discomfort, lack of energy, fear, or an emotional imbalance. By acquainting yourself with the chakra system, how they work and how they should operate optimally, you can perceive your own blocks and restrictions and develop guidelines for relieving entanglements.

The chakras stand out as the most useful model for you to identify how your energy is expressing itself. With *Chakras for Beginners* you will discover what is causing any imbalances, how to bring your energies back into alignment, and how to achieve higher levels of consciousness.

978-1-56718-537-9
192 pp., 5³⁄₁₆ x 8 $11.95

Spanish edition:
Chakras para principiantes
978-1-56718-536-2   **$12.95**

HEALING BODY, MIND & SPIRIT
A Guide to Energy-Based Healing
HOWARD F. BATIE

Remove diseased energy patterns before they make you sick. Want to know the root cause of physical disease? Look to the faulty patterns in the etheric body (aura) or higher energy bodies. Performing healing work on these energy levels can often keep disease from becoming a physical problem.

Energy healer Howard Batie discusses several energy-based healing techniques that have repeatedly demonstrated a positive effect on his clients. You will learn how to develop your own sensitivity to energy and open yourself as a channel for healing energy. You'll discover the surprising origins of disease, including infections, viruses, trauma of injuries, and emotional and mental illness.

978-0-7387-0398-5
312 pp., 6 x 9 $16.95

YOGA
Anytime, Anywhere
CAROL BLACKMAN & ELISE BROWNING MILLER

Carol Blackman and Elise Browning Miller offer step-by-step instructions for learning traditional yoga poses to improve strength and flexibility. Based on their original book, *Life Is a Stretch*, this new edition gives readers more information about using yoga stretching practices to reduce stress and increase vitality. These simple tension-relieving routines—that can be done at home or in the office—are easy to incorporate into everyday life.

Yoga: Anytime, Anywhere presents new practices, such as a 15-minute routine to stretch the whole body. Also presented are seven routines, one for every day of the week, each focusing on a specific body area or on particular poses, such as backbends and twists. The authors demonstrate how readers can use these routines to work out their entire body, or personalize their yoga practice by repeating selected exercises.

978-0-7387-0635-1
288 pp., 8½ x 10⅞ $17.95

TO ORDER, CALL 1-877-NEW-WRLD
Prices subject to change without notice
Order at Llewellyn.com 24 hours a day, 7 days a week!

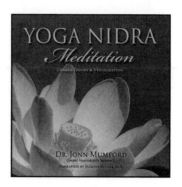

YOGA NIDRA MEDITATION
Chakra Theory & Visualization
JONN MUMFORD
NARRATION BY JASMINE RIDDLE

Yoga nidra is a life-changing technique practiced by sages and yogis for thousands of years. Available for the first time as a digitally remastered compact disc, *Yoga Nidra Meditation* can help you achieve a unique state of consciousness conducive to self-healing and spiritual growth.

Dr. Jonn Mumford, a world-renowned authority on Tantra and yoga, and Jasmine Riddle will guide you through Tantric meditation and visualization exercises. Accompanied by music and mantras, your conscious awareness will rotate through your physical body, mental images and sensations, and the chakras—ultimately ending with "psychic sleep." During this special state of consciousness between wakefulness and sleep, you can communicate with your subconscious.

Full relaxation—physical, mental and emotional—is just one of the many benefits of yoga nidra. The enclosed sixteen-page booklet explores how this technique is a catalyst for efficient sleep, deep meditation, healing childhood traumas, awakening the chakras, and spiritual enlightenment.

978-0-7387-1446-2
A digitally-remastered audio CD and 16-page booklet $16.95

YOGA
The Ultimate Spiritual Path
SWAMI RAJARSHI MUNI

Yoga: The Ultimate Spiritual Path is a groundbreaking work for serious seekers and scholars about spontaneous yoga—the yoga of liberation. Instead of discussing the physical exercises or meditations usually understood to be yoga in the West, this book focuses on a proven process by which you can achieve liberation from the limitations of time and space, unlimited divine powers, and an immortal, physically perfect, divine body that is retained forever.

The sages who composed the ancient Indian scriptures achieved such a state—as have people of all religious traditions. How? Through the process of surrendering the body and mind to the spontaneous workings of the awakened life force: prana. Once prana is awakened, it works in its own amazing way to purify your physical and nonphysical body. Over time, all the bondage of karma is released, and you become fully liberated.

978-1-56718-441-3
208 pp., 7½ x 9⅛   **$14.95**